Lloyds Bank Annual Review

Lloyds Bank Annual Review
Volume 3

Changing Exchange Rate Systems

Edited by

Christopher Johnson

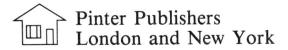
Pinter Publishers
London and New York

© Lloyds Bank Review, 1990

First published in Great Britain in 1990 by
Pinter Publishers Limited
25 Floral Street, London WC2E 9DS

British Library Cataloguing in Publication Data

A CIP catalogue record for this book is available from the
British Library
ISBN 0–86187–810–8
ISSN 9053–5004

Library of Congress Cataloging-in-Publication Data

LC card number 88–656283

Typeset by Mayhew Typesetting, Bristol, England
Printed in Great Britain by Biddles Ltd,

Contents

Introduction

Christopher Johnson

Exchange rates have always been a subject of intense controversy, both among academic economists and among practical policy-makers. Far from being resolved by strenuous research, disputes remain fiercer than ever. The sad state of exchange rate theory is demonstrated by the fact that any forecast that an exchange rate will rise based on one hypothesis can be countered by another forecast that it will fall based on a rival hypothesis. Alongside and linked with these disagreements about exchange rate theory are the conflicting claims of different exchange rate systems. In the real world, fair tests of either theories or systems are difficult to control for extraneous influences, such as oil shocks, recessions, and wider political factors. There has been a variety of exchange rate systems, some put into practice, others presented as blueprints, during the last two decades. The articles in this volume, many of them new, give insights into the varying attitudes to exchange rates and the balance of payments at various times up to and including 1989. The first part deals with different policy rules, and the interaction between internal and external objectives. The second part covers the history of the 1970s and 1980s as it looked at different moments during the period, ending with an assessment of the present situation and the outlook for the 1990s. Since the European Monetary System (EMS) was set up in March 1979, it has received special attention in the context of the long-standing debate about exchange rate systems. This is the subject of the third part of the volume.

Exchange rates have to be seen as one part of an economic model with many variables, of which some are also policy instruments or targets. At one extreme is the *benign neglect* model adopted during certain periods by the USA. Here the policy objectives are domestic — high growth and low inflation, for example — and the exchange rate is left to find its own level. The neglect remains benign, even from the practitioner's point of view, only as long as the exchange rate does not interfere with domestic objectives. In a large economy

---

The author is Chief Economic Adviser, Lloyds Bank.

such as the USA, with a relatively small external sector, it is easier than in most others to pursue benign neglect. Even in the USA, however, a falling exchange rate can jeopardize the inflation objective, and a rising one the economic growth objective, as Dornbusch points out.

A freely floating exchange rate can also prove to be incompatible with balance of payments objectives, as well as with strictly domestic objectives. The exchange rate is generally seen as an important policy instrument with which to achieve a desired balance of payments position. However, the evidence cannot sustain the simple view that a balance of payments deficit causes the exchange rate (of the domestic currency) to fall, and that this then eliminates the deficit. A balance of payments deficit on current account may cause the interest rate, and thus the exchange rate, to rise, so that the deficit gets worse, but may then be financed by capital inflows. In any case a fall in the exchange rate, were it to result from a payments deficit, does not necessarily improve it, particularly if it is a fall in the *nominal*, but not the *real* exchange rate, in other words, if its main effect is to raise prices rather than improving competitiveness. Similar reasoning can be applied to a rising exchange rate.

At the other extreme, the exchange rate can be regarded as a policy target. During the Bretton Woods era fixed but adjustable exchange rates became policy targets. More recently, *fixed real*, as opposed to *nominal exchange rates* have been proposed as policy targets for a new system, as indeed they already are in a number of countries. However, fixed exchange rates in themselves may carry only minor welfare benefits, and should be regarded as an intermediate target, or as an instrument designed to achieve the ultimate targets of policy.

There are three main policy targets for which exchange rates can be used as an instrument, whether they be fixed or adjustable. The first is to increase international trade and investment, which in its turn serves the economic growth objective. The evidence that they can do so is compelling, if not conclusive, and has been cited by advocates of the UK's entry into the EMS exchange rate mechanism (ERM). The second is to achieve equilibrium in the balance of payments. They are not guaranteed to do so, whether fixed or floating, and in any case, in this age of internationally mobile capital, balance of payments equilibrium, particularly in the accounts of the private sector, may no longer be an important objective, as Congdon argues, in a line of reasoning recently echoed by Nigel Lawson, when Chancellor of the Exchequer. The third policy target is price stability. Clearly fixed exchange rates in themselves cannot achieve price stability if all countries are inflating at similar rates. The hegemony of a low-inflation country is also required, such as the

USA under Bretton Woods, or West Germany under the EMS. However, structural differences between countries are such that there could be zero inflation everywhere with changing exchange rates, or different inflation rates in each country with fixed exchange rates. At least there is a correlation, if not a necessary connection, between fixed exchange rates and convergent price levels.

The hegemony of a low-inflation country has prevailed only intermittently. World financial leadership is increasingly being shared by the USA with Japan and West Germany, and the USA is for the time being not a low-inflation country. An alternative anchor has been provided in the past by the gold standard, and the US administration has recently revived the idea of a commodity standard. While it seems sensible to do as the US Federal Reserve does, and watch commodity prices as one indicator in setting monetary policy, the practical difficulties of a commodity standard seem insuperable. Commodity prices are an important source of changes in industrial country inflation, but they are volatile, sensitive to shocks, and difficult to combine into an acceptable index. The weights to be given to oil, and to gold, are both politically and statistically difficult to determine.

There are many possible positions between the two extremes of benign neglect and fixed exchange rates. Few countries do in fact neglect their exchange rates, but they may shy away from setting targets for them. Intervention, like floating rates, feeds back into domestic policy targets, but in the opposite direction. Intervening to keep a rate down increases the domestic money stock, and can cause inflation, just as letting the rate float upwards can reduce economic growth by its effects on the external trade sector. Intervention can be sterilized, in this case by raising interest rates, but even so the net effect on the domestic economy is unlikely to be totally neutral. Official reserves are now heavily outnumbered by private sector international financial assets, so that the effectiveness of intervention, as well as its desirability, is open to question.

Countries tend to use exchange rates as part of a package of other instruments in order to achieve their policy targets, which may mean raising, lowering, or keeping them stable according to circumstances. This has the advantage that exchange rate intermediate targets are both more likely to be achievable when backed up by monetary and fiscal policy, and more likely to yield the desired results. However, the exchange rate is unlike other instruments in that its use affects the exchange rates of other countries. In the absence of an international co-ordinating mechanism, too many countries may be trying to move their exchange rates in the same direction simultaneously. Competitive devaluation designed to increase exports leads only to inflation all round, while competitive appreciation aimed at reducing inflation leads only to unemployment all round.

The difficulties of international policy co-ordination using the exchange rate as an instrument, even when countries are all using the same policy rules, is well illustrated by Meade. His model illuminates the behaviour of both the USA and the UK at the present time, at least on his assumption that countries are trying to achieve both overall external payments balance and internal budget balance at the same time. In the USA, the right policy is to depreciate the exchange rate, then offset the external stimulus to the economy by raising taxes, so as to bring the budget deficit back into balance. In the UK, this would be the wrong policy from his point of view, because the budget surplus would be still further increased by the tax rise needed to offset the stimulus of lower exchange rates. So the right policy for the UK would be to raise interest rates so as to finance the current account deficit, then offset the dampening effect on the domestic economy by cutting taxes so as to bring the budget surplus back into balance. However, if budget balance is not an objective, then the UK would be right to follow the US example, in spite of its different budgetary position, and use the exchange rate to achieve external balance, while raising taxes and increasing the budget surplus. This would be a case of competitive devaluation, but as long as other countries in external surplus, such as Germany and Japan, allow their exchange rates to appreciate, international harmony prevails. If Germany and Japan are worried about their budget deficits, however, they will resist the tax cuts required to offset the dampening effects of currency appreciation, and therefore prefer to cut interest rates rather than letting their exchange rates rise, dealing with their surpluses by a financial outflow rather than a current account adjustment. The surplus and deficit countries would then be pursuing incompatible policies.

Against the background of this discussion, the various systems of the last two decades can be assessed. Bretton Woods was given a last, despairing kiss of life by the Smithsonian Agreement of 1971, so that in the following year Haberler could still put forward a hopeful prospectus for survival. The dollar had apparently solved the problem of being the one currency unable to devalue in response to a balance of payments deficit, by changing the price of gold, and thus explicitly moving from a dollar–gold to an outright dollar standard. Although the Smithsonian doubled the Bretton Woods bands to 2¼ per cent either side of parity, the dollar, being the pivot currency, could not use the full width of the bands, and there was an argument for removing this asymmetry by using the SDR as the pivot, in much the same way that the EMS was later to use the ECU. It was still hoped that the USA could keep inflation low enough to make the dollar an acceptable standard for other currencies.

Just as the Vietnam War, and its effects on the US twin deficits, had brought about the move from Bretton Woods to the Smithsonian, so the oil price shock of 1973 was the death blow to the Smithsonian. Inflation not only became unacceptably high in the USA, but impossibly divergent between it and other major countries, because of the differential impact of the oil price rises, and the varying policy responses to them. The Committee of Twenty had to admit defeat in 1974 in its final attempt to bring the corpse of Bretton Woods back to life.

Countries such as the UK had already welcomed floating rates, turning their back not only on Bretton Woods, but on the European currency snake inaugurated in 1971. Floating rates, it was thought, were a way of liberating domestic policy from external constraints. Unfortunately it soon turned out that they were a way of achieving a higher than average inflation rate, without a higher than average economic growth rate. The external disciplines of Bretton Woods had been too quickly forgotten. Floating rates would achieve external balance only if they were accompanied by monetary and fiscal policy packages of the kind recommended by the IMF, as the UK discovered in 1976. At first, floating rates did not bring about substantial real exchange rate changes, because inflation differentials moved in tandem with exchange rate movements, as Emminger points out. They therefore did not bring about balance of payments adjustment, but they did obviate the need for intervention and the accumulation of unwanted dollar balances. As time went on, however, real exchange rate changes did occur, so that adjustment was sometimes facilitated.

Floating became discredited, not because real exchange rate changes did not occur, but because they were sometimes in the wrong direction, or overshot by wide margins. As Lamfalussy points out, the liberalization of capital movements, and the international financial integration to which it led, was a new disturbing factor, causing prolonged exchange rate misalignments.

The pound needed to rise in the early 1980s, because of the North Sea oil surplus, but went so high that domestic recession was brought about, against the government's policy objectives. The rise in the dollar later in the 1980s was an even worse misalignment, because it coincided with a widening deficit in the balance of payments, which needed a falling exchange rate; only very belatedly, from February 1985, did the dollar begin to fall. By then, the USA had abandoned its policy of benign neglect, and was prepared at least to let other countries intervene, if not to intervene very much itself, to bring the dollar down.

Floating rates were followed by the Plaza and the Louvre agreements, and all the blueprints for new systems to which they gave rise. The Plaza agreement came in September 1985, some months after the dollar had begun to fall from its peak in February 1985. It was a collective and public reaffirmation of the intervention by the central banks which had already helped to bring the dollar down, and reflected the consensus that the dollar needed to fall some way further. It was a case of 'leaning into the wind', since the financial markets were already marking the dollar down in any case, and was therefore not a particularly remarkable achievement. Its main feature was the admission by the USA that the exchange value of the dollar was no longer a matter of concern just to countries other than the USA.

The Louvre agreement of February 1987 was more ambitious, in that it sought to keep the dollar stable, and thus to end the downward slide abetted by the Plaza agreement. It was never publicly stated what the central exchange rates were, nor how wide the bands were within which they were to be allowed to fluctuate; it was not even clear that all the central banks came away with the same precise understanding of what had been agreed. While this studied vagueness robbed the system of credibility, it made it easier for the central banks informally to change the parities and bands from time to time, if they had not been able to stick to those previously agreed. Credibility, as Loehnis argues, can also be destroyed through discordant statements made in public.

There was massive intervention to hold the dollar up during 1987, with an addition of some $125 billion to official dollar reserves. It was never clear whether the UK's intervention, amounting to $25 billion added to reserves, was designed mainly to keep the dollar up or the pound down. At least the two countries' exchange rate objectives were compatible and complementary. During 1988, as the dollar rose again, the Louvre agreement was shown to be asymmetrical, giving the dollar downwards but not upwards stability. The USA did not intervene, nor did it press other countries to do so, to prevent the dollar rising. An opportunity to build up the inadequate US reserves of non-dollar currencies was missed for the sake of a modest and short-term pre-electoral gain on the inflation front. By 1989, there was little left of the Louvre agreement, and countries again seemed to be giving priority to domestic economic targets, while letting exchange rates find their own level.

The main weakness of the Louvre agreement was that the accompanying commitments to co-ordinate domestic monetary and fiscal policies were not taken seriously enough. The USA made an attempt to reduce the Federal deficit in late 1987, as the dollar had fallen at the time of the October stock market crash, but the international pressure came off as soon as the dollar started rising again in 1988. Japan gave its economy a large fiscal stimulus, but the tax reflow was such that there was little increase in the Budget deficit, and little shrinkage in the current account surplus. The UK's policy of shadowing the Deutschemark at a fixed rate of about DM 3 lasted for about a year to February 1988, but was then abandoned in favour of a return to the old policy of letting the pound rise to curb inflation. Contrary to what has been said, it was not shadowing the Deutschemark which caused British interest rates to fall and money stock to increase. Interest rates were cut to 7½ per cent in May 1988, to moderate the rise in the pound and to offset its dampening effect on the economy, not to keep the exchange rate at DM 3, since this objective had been abandoned two months earlier. After that, interest rates were raised to 15 per cent, and the exchange rate ceased to be a target.

Among the many blueprints circulating as floating rates went out of favour was that of Williamson and Miller, which Williamson discusses in this volume. It incorporates fundamental equilibrium exchange rates, set at levels such as to achieve agreed balance of payments objectives, which would not necessarily be a precise balance on current account, and at the same time minimize domestic inflation. This could mean real exchange target bands with nominal bands being allowed to move in line with inflation differentials, but allowing for a good deal of flexibility within the bands. At the same time, in the absence of a US anchor for the system, countries would control domestic growth and inflation objectives by means of nominal domestic demand targets, to be achieved by a mix of monetary and fiscal policy. Williamson neatly sidesteps the need for any alternative anchor by means of the rule that, if world demand is growing too rapidly, weak-currency countries should raise interest rates, while, if it is growing too slowly, strong-currency countries should lower interest rates.

While fixed real exchange rates allow more flexibility than fixed nominal rates, they may in the end become no better than floating rates from which overshoots have been eliminated. High-inflation countries tend to accommodate inflation by depreciating their currencies in line with it. The IMF's advocacy of such a policy of constant real exchange rates for countries such as Brazil has in fact proved to be a mechanism for perpetuating inflation. Other countries, such as Chile and Mexico, have at various times used deliberate currency overvaluation as a way of reducing inflation. The implications of any system for developing countries need to be thought out, since it is here that the IMF still has its main influence.

The most successful example of a new post-Bretton Woods system is the EMS, whose exchange rate mechanism has operated successfully since March 1979. Currency unions, as Morgan points out, exist between regions of one country as well as between different countries. Just as there is a case for allowing regions with a 'balance of payments deficit' and relatively high unemployment to devalue against other regions, there is a case, he argues, for allowing one country in a monetary union to devalue against the others. Such realignments have in fact been able to take place in the ERM without damage to the system. In each case, the need for devaluation can be avoided by giving financial aid from the centre to the region in question, as has happened both within the UK currency union and now, thanks to the structural funds, within the EMS. The need for a growing redistributive federal budget can be avoided if private sector financial flows move from prosperous to poorer members of the union in response to higher-yielding investment opportunities; such flows often need to be prompted by pump-priming public subsidies.

The EMS has largely lived up to the sevenfold objectives set out for it by Jenkins in his classic 1977 Florence speech. Business cross-border investment has been encouraged by greater exchange rate stability, which is why the Confederation of British Industry wants the UK to join. The 1992 single European market reinforces the importance of this objective, since trade and investment are likely to flow more rapidly with greater exchange rate certainty. The ECU has made progress as an international currency, even though its future may be more as a substitute for than as a complement to national currencies. The EMS still needs to develop an international exchange rate policy towards other major currencies. Price stability has been served by the convergence of inflation rates among ERM members; while UK inflation appeared until 1984 to be converging without the need for ERM membership, it has diverged upwards markedly since then in the absence of the external discipline from which ERM members have benefited.

Until 1986, it was thought that the EMS had achieved lower inflation only at the expense of lower growth. Other members of the ERM had apparently come down towards the low German inflation rate by bringing economic growth down to the same low figure as Germany. Since then, as Pöhl argues, both Germany and the other members have shown that they can increase their growth rates and reduce unemployment while keeping inflation rates low. Germany has had the advantage of a falling real exchange rate, since the increasingly rare realignments have not fully compensated for the inflation differentials between Germany and the other members. Much of the German external surplus is with other ERM members, but its significance is diminishing, as private investment flows have largely compensated for current account deficits. The operation of the ERM has left countries a great deal of autonomy in fiscal matters, although their fiscal and monetary policies have been constrained by the need to meet exchange rate objectives.

Jenkins's final point, that European monetary union is seen by some as a vehicle for political integration, has proved the most controversial. After the first ten years of the EMS, the heads of member governments agreed at the Madrid summit in June 1989 that they wanted to go further towards economic and monetary union (EMU), along the lines suggested by the Delors Report. While some welcome EMU because it is a stage towards political union, others want to water it down because they argue, like Mrs Thatcher, that it is impossible without political union, which they do not accept. As a pragmatic compromise, it looks as if a monetary union can be set up by means of a European system of central banks, with co-ordination of national monetary and fiscal policies still leaving a degree of national autonomy for decisions on taxation and public expenditure.

Goodhart raises the important question whether there is a satisfactory half-way house between the present ERM of narrow and adjustable bands and the ultimate objective of irrevocably fixed exchange rates between national currencies with no variation at all. The more closely integrated the EMS economies become, the more disruptive even small and infrequent realignments might be. However, as long as national currencies continue to exist, even at fixed parities against each other, the possibility remains that one might change its parity, as the Irish pound did against sterling in 1978, and the Luxembourg franc has threatened to do against the Belgian franc in some EMS realignments. There is a further argument for moving to a common currency — which could be called the ECU — rather than continuing to keep national currencies in being. There are considerable once-for-all transactions costs, and lengthy logistic preparation, in a currency substitution operation, as the UK found in the case of decimalization. These are likely to be less than the continuing, and pointless, transactions costs of changing national currencies into each other at irrevocably fixed rates with conversion factors of up to six places of decimals.

The UK wasted the first ten years of the ERM first opposing membership, and then arguing that the time was not yet ripe to join. The arguments for and against set out by Dennis and Nellis have not fundamentally changed. The UK's desire to pursue an independent domestic monetary policy has been incompatible with the exchange rate objectives of ERM membership, even if over the years interest rates rather than monetary aggregates have become the preferred instrument of monetary policy. Yet the argument in favour of membership is that the exchange rate is a more satisfactory instrument of monetary policy than either monetary aggregates or interest rates. At the same time, advocates of membership must acknowledge that, with domestic monetary policy driven by the exchange rate in order to achieve price stability, fiscal policy must then be varied in order to achieve domestic economic growth objectives. Stable prices and exchange rates mean renouncing any objective of balance in either the external current account or the public sector accounts.

The Delors Report has aroused predictable opposition among UK monetarists unwilling to surrender control over domestic monetary policy. It has also been more widely opposed by those who regard its insistence on budgetary limits as an unnecessary infringement of fiscal sovereignty, to which the House of Commons as an institution is particularly attached. A compromise could be found on this point by allowing countries to set for themselves whatever fiscal targets were implied by the need to reconcile the monetary policy objectives of the ERM with domestic economic growth and employment objectives. In the case of the UK in 1989, this would have meant lower interest rates, higher taxes, and a bigger budget surplus, for example. The fiscal effects of EMU must be such as to limit the scope for tax harmonization in the interests of the 1992 single European market. While tax systems may be harmonized, countries will need to vary tax rates to make their fiscal policies compatible with fixed exchange rates.

The UK is committed to ERM membership by her acceptance of the first stage of EMU at the Madrid summit. The first condition is that France and Italy should lift their remaining exchange controls. They are pledged to this step by July 1990, so the UK is not committed to joining until after that. There is little chance that the ERM will be fatally disrupted by the abolition of these exchange controls, which would thus give the UK nothing to join. Another condition is that the UK inflation rate should be coming down. This is somewhat perverse, since one of the main arguments for joining is that it helps to reduce inflation. However, the closer the UK's inflation rate to the average, the less chance there will be of damaging speculation on a sterling devaluation soon after entry into the ERM. The final condition is that the 1992 single European market measures should be agreed. This could, but need not, mean waiting until the end of 1992 for every single directive to be agreed and ratified.

In view of the timetable, it seems unlikely that the UK will join before the next general election. The pound will be unstable during the run-up to an election if there is a strong chance of the Labour

Party taking over power from the Conservatives. It could be argued either that the instability would be mitigated if the UK joined the ERM first, with bipartisan support, or that it would be so hard to deal with, that it would be better not to put the ERM to such a test so soon after the UK joined. The UK might thus not decide to join until after a general election in 1991 or 1992. On present showing, it is as likely to be a Labour as a Conservative government which joins. The unexpected cannot be ruled out. Spain joined the ERM in June 1989, a full year before the date on which she had previously announced that she would join. Governments should have learned by now that the best way to outwit foreign exchange markets is to surprise them. Foreign exchange markets should have learned that the most likely source of surprises is unanticipated changes in government policies. Indeed, there is a possibility that the UK may join the EKM soon after July 1990. An unanticipated change would occur only if she joined even sooner.

Part 1 Exchange rates and the balance of payments: policy rules

1 International financial integration: policy implications

*Alexandre Lamfalussy**

This paper deals with some of the policy implications of the current trend towards international financial integration — a trend often described by the financial press (but, thankfully, not yet in academic literature) as the 'globalization' of financial markets. My own comparative advantage lies decidedly in the discussion of policy issues rather than in the areas of theoretical analysis and econometric verification. But the concept of international financial integration is not unambiguous; moreover, a great deal of academic work has been published concerning both the underlying notion of capital mobility and its statistical measurement. It therefore seems appropriate, by way of introduction, to consider briefly the concept of financial integration and the possibility of verifying it econometrically.

Financial integration and capital mobility

For most practitioners international financial integration is a fact of life so obvious that its existence hardly deserves to be questioned at all. They know from personal experience — and it can readily be confirmed by an analysis of international banking statistics — that since the 1960s the banking systems of practically all industrial countries have gradually become more open internationally. There has been a trend increase in several key ratios: the share of external claims and liabilities in balance sheet totals; the proportion of assets and liabilities denominated in foreign currencies; the importance of international transactions in off-balance-sheet items as well as in the financial services provided by the banks; and, naturally, the share in total income of profits derived from international transactions. At the same time banks have greatly increased their presence in other countries via branches or subsidiaries. International interbank

*The author is General Manager of the Bank for International Settlements.

Reprinted, with permission, from Alfred Steinherr and Daniel Weiserbs (eds), *Employment and Growth: Issues for the 1980s*, Kluwer Academic Publishers, Dordrecht, 1987.

business has grown just as much as, or even more than, cross-border lending to non-banks.

Practitioners are also aware of the very rapid growth of international financial transactions. Any foreign exchange dealer knows that foreign-trade-related (even remotely related) foreign exchange operations have become a tiny and diminishing proportion of total deals. The treasurer of any large industrial corporation, whether it is oriented towards the domestic market or operates internationally, has learned from experience that for both his financial investments and his funding operations he can look way beyond national borders. And if he did not yet know it, bankers knocking on his door would soon enlighten him about his widening choices. The same applies to sovereign borrowers or to central banks managing their countries' foreign exchange reserves. Institutional investors — the Japanese provide the most recent example — are in the process of shifting a growing proportion of their investments into assets denominated in foreign currency or at least into claims on foreign borrowers. Even in the retail securities market things are moving: the legendary Belgian dentist has found many companions.

A casual look at the statistics on international capital movements confirms these impressions. Ten years ago no one would have had the temerity to predict that between the end of 1978 and mid-1982 Latin America's external indebtedness *vis-à-vis* banks would more than double from $92 billion to 191 billion. Five years ago no one would have imagined that in the three-and-a-half years from 1983 to the first half of 1986 the United States could experience a net spontaneous capital inflow of about $330 billion. But beyond statistical evidence of this kind on net capital flows we also possess information on the spectacular expansion of gross capital movements — at least in the case of those few countries that collect information on such flows.

Professional economists are, however, right in believing that institutional, anecdotal or even statistical evidence of this nature does not permit firm conclusions to be drawn concerning the impact of financial integration in such areas as exchange rate formation, the international transmission of monetary impulses emanating from large countries, or the international allocation of real resources. The key question is whether the growing interconnection of financial markets, as illustrated by the examples just quoted, has in fact brought about a high degree of, or perhaps even perfect, capital mobility.

The concept of international capital mobility seems to be relatively simple, at least in the abstract: it means the responsiveness of capital flows across borders to expected yield differentials. The difficulties start with attempts at econometric verification, and they are all linked to the fact that financial assets are a heterogeneous brood. The major heterogeneity, of course, is the fact that crossing the border may mean in one very precise sense a change in the currency denomination of financial assets. Tests of the assumption of high international capital mobility have in most cases consisted of trying to measure the degree of equalization of interest rate levels between financial assets denominated in different currencies. This can be done via one of several interest parity assumptions.

The simplest is the 'covered' or 'closed' interest parity assumption, which states that capital mobility is perfect when an interest differential between financial assets of the same quality but denominated in different currencies is exactly offset by a forward exchange cover, in other words when the covered interest differential is zero. Many tests have demonstrated that this assumption holds when the measurement is applied to Euro-market interest rates — thus confirming the practitioner's intuitive knowledge that the Euro-market is indeed perfectly competitive. This is neither a very original nor a very significant discovery.

Things become less clear when it comes to testing the covered interest parity assumption for financial assets traded in domestic markets. There seems to be a fairly broad econometric confirmation of the common-sense view that capital mobility tends to improve when capital controls or other market imperfections, such as withholding taxes or compulsory reserve ratios, are removed. But even in such cases the tests rarely suggest that capital mobility has become perfect. On the basis of my own experience as a market participant I suspect that the reason for which the parity assumption does not hold lies not only in the existence of controls or government regulations but also in the great diversity of assets. Such diversity — in terms of quality of debtor and size, depth and segmentation of markets — makes it more difficult than in the case of the Euro-market to select truly comparable interest rates for the purpose of international comparisons. I might add, moreover, that even in the Euro-market the significance of comparisons based on either LIBOR or LIBID has diminished with the ability of the better-capitalized banks or banking systems to attract deposits at variously lower rates.

But the real difficulties start when the assumption of closed parity is abandoned, i.e. when interest parity has to incorporate expectations regarding exchange rate developments. As far as I understand the empirical evidence from econometric studies in this field, it does not permit an unequivocal verdict: it does not point to a general trend towards the equilization of expected yields converted into one numeraire. I must confess, however, that I am highly sceptical about the possibility of making meaningful guesses as to how exchange rate expectations are formed and, therefore, about the value of econometric measurements of this kind.

Now what can be said about *real* interest rate parity as a measure of capital mobility? Not much that is positive, I am afraid. It is obvious, to begin with, that the existence of real interest rate differentials, when nominal interest rates are deflated by observed changes in the rate of increase of domestic prices, does not mean that capital is not mobile. In any case, what would seem to be more important here is the expected rates of domestic inflation. But even this statement has to be carefully qualified. Suppose that real interest rates (based on expected domestic inflation) are 3 per cent in Belgium while they are 5 per cent in the United States. I see no reason whatsoever why an investor would wish to shift assets out of Belgium francs into dollars *merely* on the basis of this information. The only thing that matters to him is the maximization of the yield on his financial holdings measured in a common numeraire — and this is influenced exclusively by the *nominal* interest rate differential adjusted for the expected exchange rate movement between the dollar and the Belgian franc. The expected rate of inflation in respect of goods and services may influence his choice between holding financial assets and buying goods and services, the timing of his decision, as well as his choice of the country for the purchase of his goods; but as long as he can feel sure of being able to make a foreign exchange deal freely at any time in the future, the country in which he plans to buy goods need not be the one in whose currency he will hold his financial assets. For *this* choice, only nominal yields and future exchange rates matter.

What this means is that real interest rate differentials can only have an *indirect* impact on capital flows via their influence on exchange rate expectations. This could be the case, for instance, if the different inflation rate expectations in domestic markets are validated by an appropriate exchange rate adjustment — i.e. if the *ex-ante* version of purchasing power parity holds; or if market participants do not understand what I am saying and stubbornly believe that real exchange rate differentials *will* induce capital movements and thus will alter the exchange rate, in which case they themselves will be the first to move.

The practical conclusion would seem to be that it is a hopeless exercise to try to test the real interest rate parity assumption (properly redefined in its indirect version). I do not see how one could ever tell that a lack of parity reflects a lack of capital mobility or that it should be attributed either to the wrong way of guessing expectations regarding domestic inflation rates or to the fact that market participants establish no link between real interest rate differentials and expected exchange rate movements, or to a combination of both. If econometricians really want to make guesses about expectations I suggest that they try to guess exchange rate expectations directly; they will probably not be able to do that either, but at least they would avoid the kind of expectational muddle I have just referred to.

But where should we go from here? My suggestion is that until economists can come up with a convincing test of the perfect capital mobility assumption — and we may have to wait some time for this to happen — we should accept the practitioner's view that the observed institutional trend towards financial integration has in fact substantially increased the cross-border mobility of capital; and by this I mean specifically the responsiveness of capital flows, from one currency into another, to expected yield differentials expressed in a common numeraire. There are, of course, differences between countries: mobility into or out of France or Italy (i.e. into or out of assets denominated in francs or lire) is not the same as mobility into or out of the United States, the Federal Republic of Germany or the United Kingdom; and Japan is a case apart. But with the prevailing liberalization of capital movements and the deregulation of financial markets, the differences are narrowing. It would, therefore, seem in order to speculate a little about the policy implications, for the industrial world as a whole, of a situation in which capital mobility is in the process of approaching perfection.

One last and not unimportant warning, however. Growing international integration is not the only major structural change affecting our financial markets. The financial systems of most Western countries are caught up in several types of change; they all interact. One is financial innovation, i.e. the emergence of new products and new techniques. Some of these are localized in individual domestic markets (e.g. NOW accounts); others, while originating in one country, spread to other countries as well (the technique of floating rates, options and forward rate agreements); still others have emerged more specifically from international banking activity (NIFs, RUFs, currency and interest swaps). These last have without doubt become a vehicle for speedy international capital flows. At the same time domestic financial deregulation proceeds at a pace at least as fast as the removal of capital controls: the forthcoming 'Big Bang' in London illustrates this. The converging result of international financial integration, innovation and domestic deregulation is a threefold blurring of traditional demarcation lines between (a) financial assets and money, (b) banks and other financial institutions, and even (c) financial intermediation and securities markets. It is this third phenomenon that is nowadays called 'securitization'. In analysing the policy implications of international financial integration it is impossible not to take into account the other structural changes since they are hopelessly interwoven with the growing interconnection of domestic financial markets.

Now let me turn to three major policy concerns that I see arising out of these various developments: the implications for exchange rate developments; the problems created for the conduct of monetary policy; and the question of financial fragility.

Implications for exchange rate developments

The main implication, of course, is that in a world of high capital mobility capital movements may on occasion 'swamp' the influence of trade in goods and services on exchange rates. What I have in mind is not the phenomenon of 'overshooting' (when the exchange rate overreacts to an impetus coming from a current-account imbalance), but exchange rate movements induced by capital flows that could result in persistent real exchange rate 'misalignments', i.e. exchange rate levels that deviate drastically from purchasing power parity. Such deviations are likely to foster large, undesirable and unsustainable current-account imbalances, with potentially damaging consequences for the 'real' economy.

There have been several recent cases of major exchange rate misalignments — involving, for instance, the pound sterling and the yen — but the prime example was the clear overvaluation of the US dollar in 1983–5, which reached its peak in March 1985. The large rise in the real effective exchange rate of the dollar (of about 50 per cent between 1978 and the first quarter of 1985), which played a major role in the sharp deterioration of the US current account, was brought about by a spontaneous inflow of capital into the United States.

The disturbances caused by this overvaluation in the real economy are by now universally acknowledged. In the United States whole segments of industries producing internationally traded goods have been wiped out, with a heavy and regionally concentrated impact on employment. The protectionist pressures that have been building up gradually have up to a certain point been courageously resisted by the administration, but they have also led to measures with distorting effects on trade. The rest of the world has, of course, benefited from the combined influence of the large US current-account deficit and the overvaluation of the dollar. But it is arguable that for the world economy as a whole these benefits have been more than offset by disadvantages. One is precisely the long-run universal damage brought about by the growth of protectionism. Another is that, because of the uncertain sustainability of an exchange rate pattern including a manifestly overvalued dollar, the expansion led by exports to the United States has not included a corresponding investment boom. In one way this is perhaps fortunate, for had such an investment boom materialized the misallocation of real resources would have been even greater.

By now (May 1986) the real effective exchange rate of the dollar has declined by about 30 per cent from its March 1985 peak without, so far, any of the crash-landing elements that many of us feared a year ago. Whether a crash-landing could still occur is an open question; more generally, it is far too early to speculate about the outcome of the adjustment process or to try to assess the long-term damage to the world economy that was brought about by the development that culminated in 1985. It does seem to me, however, that some preliminary conclusions can be drawn from this recent experience — in particular as regards the willingness of governments, and the means at their disposal, to counter the undesirable exchange rate misalignments that may arise in a world of high capital mobility.

First, one cannot fail to note how difficult it seems to be to obtain a consensus among the governments concerned as to the desirability of trying to do something about the prevailing exchange rate. It took several years of almost uninterrupted dollar appreciation to force the US administration to recognize that something was wrong with the exchange rate — a recognition that formed gradually in the summer of 1985 and took concrete shape at the Plaza meeting in September. The plain lesson is that the misalignment has to be persistent and very large and must have directly damaging effects on the domestic economy before a government may be ready to consider policy action. It is possible that the US government was exceptionally slow to react. But it has to be admitted in all fairness that we lack the analytical tools that would enable governments to reach agreement at the early stages of an emerging 'misalignment' on whether it has already led, or will lead, to an 'unsustainable' or otherwise damaging imbalance in the international economy. With all the goodwill in the world, identifying a problem is a difficult task. And the goodwill is not necessarily there as long as there are no signs of obvious damage to the domestic economy.

Second, there is the question of how to try to correct an exchange rate deemed to be unacceptable. The first part of this question concerns the effectiveness of exchange market intervention in achieving this objective. Until the concerted intervention put into effect as a result of the Plaza meeting, many governments were deeply sceptical about the usefulness of exchange market intervention — a scepticism which echoed that of the academic world. It was argued that sterilized intervention was basically powerless to have any lasting effect on the exchange rate; and, to the extent that it did have some influence, it would be through its 'signal effect', i.e. by conveying a message to the market that government policies were about to be changed so as to validate the intervention. Since the Plaza meeting and the subsequent, and sustained, fall of the dollar, which, more-over, has taken the unexpected form of a 'soft landing', a much more sanguine view of the efficiency of exchange market intervention has come to prevail. This view seems to be shared by market partici-pants: witness the fact that more recently utterances by policy-makers have tended to produce almost instantaneous price adjustment in the market. This had not always been the case before the Plaza meeting.

My own views have always been somewhere in between. I never thought that 'leaning against the wind' could basically correct exchange rate movements prompted by a market perception that fundamentals (more about these shortly) were pushing the rate in a certain direction — although it may well be that central banks can make a substantial profit on such intervention (as some of them in fact did). But there are other circumstances in which intervention may influence the exchange rate, even lastingly, without necessarily signalling any shift in underlying policy mixes. Such a situation may arise when, as a result of a speculative 'bubble', the exchange rate has reached a level at which the market itself begins to have second thoughts. Intervention, preferably involving governments on both sides, can then bring about a decisive turn in market sentiment and induce a lasting correction. But this is a policy of leaning 'with' rather than 'against' the wind, which means that by definition it can be successful only after a prolonged period of manifest imbalance. It has no preventive powers.

This means that in order to prevent the emergence of major exchange rate misalignments policy action has to be directed towards the causes of capital movements or, more precisely, towards what market participants believe to be 'fundamentals'. My perception is that in 1982–5 the dollar's rise was caused by a textbook case of mismatch of policy mixes, i.e. by a combination of fiscal expansion and monetary restraint in the United States with fiscal retrenchment and a less restric-tive monetary stance in the rest of the OECD. The result was a persis-tent interest rate advantage for the US dollar *vis-à-vis* the Deutschmark and the yen. Other factors, such as the safe-haven aspect of confidence in President Reagan's policies, may have added to the attraction of the United States as an investment outlet, but they would not have been powerful enough to support a rising tide of capital inflows without the incentive provided by the mismatch of policy mixes.

This emphasis on the need to correct policies in order to prevent the development of an exchange rate misalignment raises a host of problems of which I would like to mention just two. One (close to the specific interests of central banks) is that the correction needs to be directed towards the policy *mixes*, not towards one of their components. The trouble is that, given the unavoidable rigidity of fiscal policies, the burden of the adjustment would tend to fall on monetary policy. This need not always be a bad thing but it could at times be more than awkward, as was seen precisely in the case of the overvaluation of the US dollar. With unchanged fiscal policy stances, the dollar's rise could have been halted only by substantially more expansionary US and more restrictive German and Japanese monetary policies. What would have been the consequences for long-term US inflation prospects? And what hope would there have been of economic recovery in Europe and Japan?

Another problem is that identifying what is wrong with the policy mixes is not necessarily easy. The overvaluation of the dollar seems to have proved the textbook argument that fiscal expansion combined with monetary restraint will induce a capital inflow. But is it so certain that this will always be the case? I can well imagine a situation in which a growing fiscal deficit, even if it was accompanied by a relatively restrictive monetary policy, would set in motion a chain reaction of current-account deficit, expected exchange rate depreciation, *ex-ante* capital outflows and therefore further pressure on the exchange rate. This is the kind of thing that happened in France in 1981, and the German experience of 1979–80 was not so very different. We know far too little about the mechanics of exchange rate expectations to accept unreservedly that the 1983–5 US experience is of universal validity.

This somewhat agnostic view of the chances of preventing real exchange rate misalignments from emerging among the major floating currencies seems to be contradicted by the experience of the European Monetary System. It is true that the EMS has been able to shield the currencies participating in the exchange rate mechanism (ERM) from disruptive real exchange rate misalignments, not to mention its success in controlling short-term volatility. But three facts have to be borne in mind when one considers the likelihood of the same being possible on a world scale. First, the EMS includes two large countries — Italy and France — that have lagged far behind the general trend of liberalizing capital movements and deregulating domestic financial markets. In short, they have so far not been part of a world of near-perfect capital mobility. The sizeable spreads that developed at times of stress between domestic and Euro-franc interest rates substantiate this point. Second, none of the currencies participating in the EMS exchange rate mechanism — not even the Deutschmark — has assumed the same importance as an international reserve currency, or as an international currency generally, as the US dollar. Third and most important, much of the success of the EMS must be attributed to the willingness of member governments to subordinate the totality of their domestic policies to the objective of preserving an acceptable exchange rate relationship with the rest of the group. This fact stood out quite clearly in the 1983 policy shift of the French government, which encompassed not only (not even principally) monetary policy but also fiscal and even incomes policy. The key question is precisely whether one can expect anything approaching this kind of policy subordination at the world level, as opposed to in a Community whose members have long had close trade, political and formal institutional ties going well beyond the ERM. My own conclusion is that the very desirable control of real exchange rate developments within the Western world at large will occur at best as a result of a long evolutionary process, of which the Plaza agreement was just a first essential but insufficient step.

Problems for the conduct of monetary policy

These problems are the direct consequence of the threefold blurring of traditional demarcation lines mentioned above (page 000). As banks become difficult to distinguish from other financial intermediaries, as money loses its distinctive characteristics *vis-à-vis* other financial assets and as securitization spreads, the conduct of monetary policy is becoming difficult in two major respects: the selection of an 'intermediate' target; and the use of operating techniques. I propose to concentrate on the first of these problem areas.

The targeting of various Ms has clearly run into trouble, in particular in those financial centres, namely the United States and the United Kingdom, where financial innovation appears to have been most active. How can transactions balances be identified when a growing proportion of sight deposits bear market-related interest rates? What is the impact of back-up and issuing facilities of all kinds on corporations' demand for 'money'? More generally, what is a corporation's demand-for-money function when its treasurer has become a banker? Does securitization reduce the general need for financial or non-financial market participants to hold liquid balances? What should be done about financial claims held outside the country or in a different currency? It should be noted that any attempt to answer questions such as these poses two interconnected problems. The first would appear at first sight to be merely one of statistical identification: which liabilities of which institutions should be included in the targeted M? But there is a second, more intricate, problem: what is the transmission mechanism that leads from the targeted M to nominal GNP? There can be no useful reply to the first question before the second has been answered.

It is the difficulties encountered when trying to solve this twofold problem that have led many to question the usefulness of any M as an intermediate target of monetary policy. The fact that the gradual process of disinflation has also shifted the demand-for-money function to an extent difficult to evaluate only adds to the temptation to reject money supply targeting altogether.

But what is the alternative? Targeting the interest rate level (as an intermediate rather than as an operational objective) would run into difficulties no less serious than those raised by the use of aggregates. What to do with the fiscal policy component of the policy mix, which clearly has a bearing on the level of interest rates? Should one forget the past failure of interest rate targeting, i.e. the inflationary bias that was so patently obvious in the late 1960s and early 1970s? And, in the context of financial innovation, notably the wide spread of floating rates or the availability of hedging devices against interest rate volatility, how can one assess the likely impact of any interest rate level on nominal GNP?

The fashionable alternative at present is to suggest that the exchange rate itself should become the intermediate target of monetary policy. This suggestion is based on the success of EMS countries in gearing their monetary policies to keeping the exchange rates within the fluctuation band. However, two features of this policy behaviour should be noted. First, as was already mentioned above, the task of meeting the exchange rate target has not been left exclusively to monetary policy. True, in the short run it was monetary policy (and naturally exchange market intervention) that had to ensure that the exchange rate remained within the band; but, whenever major pressure developed, other policy tools were used as well. Without the actual or at least potential use of other policy instruments interest rate fluctuations could have been intolerably sharp. Second, it has to be borne in mind that for obvious reasons not all countries can use the exchange rate as their sole intermediate monetary policy target at the same time. Indeed, not all EMS members did: German monetary policy continued to aim primarily at a money supply target. And since Germany has so far been doubly successful in implementing this policy — in reaching its target and in remaining a low-inflation country — the EMS practice has in fact made a lot of sense. Ironically, the relative paucity of domestic financial innovations in Germany, leaving the targeting procedure relatively undisturbed, has played a most useful role in the success of European monetary management. Is this going to last? Since the beginning of this year the targeted German M has run ahead of its target. Let us hope that this turns out to be only a short-term aberration.

The tentative conclusion that I would draw from the EMS experience is that in a world in which central banks were tempted to use the exchange rate more widely as an intermediate target we would still need a United States — the dominant economy of the world — that relies essentially on a domestic monetary policy target, that is willing to supplement this with a sensible fiscal policy, *and* that also succeeds in achieving the ultimate target of non-inflationary growth. This is not to say, of course, that the US authorities should pay no attention to the exchange rate. They *should*; but they cannot gear the whole of their policy to an exchange rate target. In other words, I find it difficult to imagine any kind of international, institutional or co-operative arrangements that could withstand the destructive impact of undesirable domestic macro-economic management on the part of the United States. To avoid this, the US authorities will have to rely on some sort of intermediate target for domestic monetary policy. Given the unhappy experience of interest rate targeting, I see no alternative to retaining the monetary aggregates for this purpose — tempered by pragmatic, discretionary but publicly justified deviations from the target.

If a solution were to be found to the US problem and, within the EMS, Germany were able to pursue its successful monetary policy, the way would be open for the use of explicit exchange rate targeting by the monetary authorities of other countries. This would not, however, eliminate problems connected with the use of operating techniques. Within the time and space allotted to me it would be impossible to do justice to a topic of such technical complexity. Let me simply state, without analysis, my own broad conclusions. The techniques and procedures to be used by central banks to meet their exchange rate objective (or their own domestic target) in the new deregulated, innovative and securitized financial environment will have to be based more and more on market intervention and flexible market-related instruments. In doing this, however, central banks will promote the swift transmission of the interest rate impact of their own operations to all segments of the market, including its long end. In all probability interest rates will become more volatile — a development that could be accentuated by gearing monetary policy to the pursuit of an exchange rate target. Hence the paramount importance for governments adopting such a target to be willing, and to appear to be willing, to use the whole range of macro-economic policies at their disposal for the realization of this objective.

The question of financial fragility

It has first of all to be recognized that international financial integration, coupled with financial innovations and the deregulation of domestic markets, is in the process of bringing about tough, institutionally and geographically generalized competition between financial market participants throughout the industrial world.

This increased competition can be expected to improve the efficiency of the financial markets in several meanings of the term. First, in the technical sense, it will make prices adjust instantaneously to all available information. Second, it may improve the market's allocative efficiency; and I use the word 'may' on purpose, for it is difficult to forget the accumulation of South American debt that took place in a highly competitive international banking market. Third, greater competition will put pressure on the profit margins of financial intermediation, transferring income to the non-financial sectors of the economy. Fourth, there is the insurance aspect of innovations: many of the new instruments provide risk-averse market participants with an opportunity to protect themselves against unforeseen changes in interest rates, exchange rates and the availability of funds. It is, of course, true that the system itself cannot obtain protection against such risks. Risks are simply redistributed to willing (and, it is to be hoped, stronger) risk-takers. While I have a nagging fear that something could go wrong in this process of redistribution, it nevertheless remains true that those market participants that make enlightened use of the new devices will still benefit from them.

The key question is whether increased competitive efficiency does not go hand in hand with increased financial fragility. Competition has to be regarded as a dynamic process which implies a continuous shake-up of structures and the emergence of new products, techniques and enterprises; the counterpart is the elimination of outdated products and techniques and also of enterprises or even whole industries if they prove unable to adapt to the changing pattern of an innovative market. We are accustomed to regarding this Schumpeterian process of creative destruction with equanimity in the 'real' economy. But is 'destruction' in the financial industry not something more dangerous? The traditional answer to this question has been that it is, and this is what has justified the existence of the lender of last resort, of banking supervision and of financial regulation more generally.

The major structural changes affecting financial markets — integration, deregulation, innovation, 'securitization' — may increase financial fragility in the following way. To begin with, there is the risk that financial intermediaries, particularly banks, may on occasion make large losses — as a result of the careless handling of innovations untested by experience, large interest rate swings or simply large cross-border lending. The use of innovations (in particular, of off-balance-sheet items) in many cases reduces the transparency of balance sheets, with the result that market participants find it harder to detect emerging problem situations gradually and at a relatively early stage. The probability of sudden financial shocks increases, in particular if the 'real' economic environment deteriorates. The growing interdependence of domestic markets speeds up the international transmission of such shocks. Finally, with the spread of securitization and the weakening of the ability of the banking sector to perform its liquidity buffer function, the handling of crisis situations is likely to become more difficult.

Are these concerns not exaggerated? Perhaps they are. Some may well prove to have been based on an understandable, but excessive, fear of the unknown. Most of the innovations, after all, have been conceived as a hedging device; and the fact that we do not know who the 'insurers' are is no proof that the mechanics of insurance will collapse. Incidentally, most of the recent losses made by banks have involved very conventional lending to domestic customers rather than cross-border loans or innovations. Finally, we should not underestimate the inertia of our domestic financial systems: retail banking is not changing at the same pace as wholesale banking.

Be that as it may, the broadening and deepening of the competitive process present not only market participants but also the public authorities with serious challenges. Domestic deregulation in itself raises the tricky question of how financial supervision should be integrated into the broader surveillance of financial intermediation and of the securities markets. The problem is multiplied tenfold when it comes to co-ordinating supervision effectively on the world scale. And this involves only crisis prevention. The crisis handling function will have to be performed, of necessity, through international co-operation — as it was, quite effectively, in 1982. But this is a far cry, at least in terms of intellectual neatness, from a system in which responsibilities are clearly assigned. Or perhaps this is inevitable in an area in which, even domestically, the lender-of-last-resort responsibility has remained ambiguous.

Concluding remarks

International financial integration, occurring alongside domestic deregulation and the tide of financial innovations, is leading the industrial world into uncharted waters. Freedom of capital movements had, of course, existed prior to the First World War; but at that time our financial techniques, products and systems were of great simplicity in comparison with what they are today, the sheer quantity of accumulated financial assets was lower in relation to GNP, and the technology of communications was relatively primitive. Most importantly, the role and responsibility of governments in the conduct of national economic affairs were more limited than at present. It is in this new setting that financial interdependence has now reappeared after a fairly long eclipse. Moreover, this has happened at a time when trade interdependence has already reached an advanced stage, after a gradual development that began in the 1950s.

This new environment, for which I see no historical precedent, throws up a great many intellectual challenges to the academic world. It does so also for governments in the conduct of their domestic policies. It is not easy, however, to identify these challenges. It would be nice to be able to believe that a high degree of capital mobility will create a welcome constraint for wrong domestic macro-economic policies. Admittedly, it has performed this function in the cases of some European countries — although even in these cases, international lending has, on the whole, been generously accommodating of large fiscal deficits. But what is one to think of the Latin American experience up to 1982? Or of that of the United States, where the external constraint has so far been totally absent, except through the indirect influence of an overvalued dollar?

Similarly difficult questions arise when one considers the international responsibility of governments. Admittedly, at a fairly high level of abstraction it is not difficult to make the general point that the advanced financial and trade interdependence between our countries needs to be matched by co-ordinated policy actions between governments taking due account of their interdependence. Failing this, we may be unable collectively to influence, let alone to control, exchange rate developments, the international flow of real resources or simply to ensure the smooth working of the financial markets. Lack of control of developments in these fields could lead to mounting political pressure in favour of retreating from trade or financial liberalization, or from both — as is demonstrated by the current revival of protectionism. To combat such a danger, policy co-ordination is essential. But it is not easy to devise this; and it may on occasion be even more difficult to enforce it.

2 The 'blueprint' proposals for international monetary reform

John Williamson

The world has come a long way from the laissez-faire in macro-economic policies of the early 1980s that permitted the emergence of the massive payments imbalances that still haunt us. It has nevertheless not established a new international monetary regime capable of banishing the unnecessary macro-economic crises of the past. That will require a greater consensus on the appropriate objectives, mechanisms and techniques of macro-economic policy than currently exists. If the new regime is indeed to avoid future crises, it will also require that the consensus be consistent with reality.

Work undertaken in recent years by Marcus Miller and me (see especially Williamson and Miller 1987) has been directed to the design of a regime intended to meet those needs. Exchange rate policy is a part — an important and indeed crucial part, but still only a part — of the regime we were led to propose. This paper starts by providing a summary of our proposals, which we named the 'blueprint' for policy co-ordination. It then proceeds to identify and discuss five crucial postulates that underlie the design of the blueprint. A concluding section suggests the conditions that would be needed to transform the blueprint into reality.

The blueprint

The blueprint assumes a conventional specification of the goals of macro-economic policy. Governments like a high level of activity (implying also a high rate of growth[1] and a high level of employment). They dislike inflation, with an intensity that grows progressively as inflation rises. And they have some objective, at least within a range, for their balance of payments on current account. This is not necessarily a zero balance, but at a minimum it must be a range within which any imbalance will not raise questions about the

The author is a Senior Fellow of the Institute for International Economics.

sustainability of financing. Of course, some governments may have well-defined ideas about the desirable level of lending to, or borrowing from, the rest of the world.

Governments cannot in general have everything they would like. Trade-offs must be faced. In particular, lowering inflation generally requires some temporary slack in the economy. Higher activity tends both to increase inflation and to worsen the current account. A more competitive exchange rate, designed to improve the current account at a given level of activity, tends to increase inflationary pressure.

The blueprint is based on using a medium-term framework to resolve these trade-offs. Each of the participating countries — say the members of the Group of seven (G7) — would be expected to have some notion of the natural rate of unemployment (NAIRU). Their choice should be continuously monitored for realism by whatever international secretariat (presumably the IMF) was charged with responsibility for servicing the policy co-ordination process. Each country would also select a current account target. Where a government had no precise view on what current account balance was appropriate, one could take the middle of the range that was judged to be sustainable as the provisional target. The secretariat would then have to appraise the mutual consistency of the various targets, taking account of what appears sustainable and acceptable to the rest of the world. If an inconsistency emerged, it would have to be bargained away; the less governments have precise views on current account targets, the less troublesome this should be. Finally one would need to check that the chosen NAIRUs were consistent with the current balance targets. (To the extent that a more favourable current balance implies a more competitive exchange rate and thus lower real wages, it would tend to raise the NAIRU if wage-earners have a target real wage: see Barrel and Wren-Lewis 1989.)

Each country would commit itself to a macro-economic strategy designed to lead to simultaneous 'internal balance' — defined as unemployment at the natural rate and minimal inflation — and 'external balance' — defined as achieving the target current account balance — in the medium term. Since exchange rates affect trade only with long lags, this implies a commitment to hold the exchange rate close to the level[2] needed to reconcile internal and external balance during the intervening adjustment period. This is the exchange rate that I have previously called the 'fundamental equilibrium exchange rate' (FEER), in recognition that it is the exchange rate that implies an absence of 'fundamental disequilibrium' in the old Bretton Woods sense (Williamson 1985). Policy should be directed to keeping exchange rates reasonably close to their FEERs. (Because of doubts as to whether the authorities of the major countries would be wise to give overwhelming priority to exchange rate targeting, the proposal allows for wide bands and, *in extremis*, soft margins.)

The other intermediate target, in addition to the exchange rate, is growth of nominal domestic demand. The idea of targeting this is a slight variation on the proposal to seek a constant growth rate of nominal income (see Brittan 1987; Meade, 1984; McCallum 1988). It has most of the advantages of a nominal income target, in terms both of providing a constraint on inflation (a 'nominal anchor') while allowing some elasticity to mitigate a supply shock, and of avoiding the shocks that come from a money supply rule when velocity changes.

Our proposal to endogenize the rule would allow rather more accommodation of an inflationary shock and rather more effort to combat a recession, for two reasons. One is the view that a limited softening of policy is capable of reducing the short-run costs of adverse shocks. The other is that if governments are asked to subscribe to excessively 'harsh' rules they are likely to abandon them just at the time when continued confidence demands that their resolve to stick to rules that will re-establish price stability in the medium run needs to be reinforced.

Our other innovation is to require governments to target the growth of *domestic demand* rather than *income*: the difference between the two is the change in the current account balance. Our rule calls on a country with an undesirably large current account deficit (surplus) to target a slower (faster) growth of domestic demand than its desired growth of nominal income, so as to promote correction of the trade imbalance.

The final step involves translating the implications of the two intermediate targets into 'rules' to guide monetary and fiscal policy. We suggested three such rules, subject to two constraints.

Rule 1 says that interest rate differentials among countries should be adjusted when necessary in order to reinforce intervention in the exchange markets in limiting the deviation of exchange rates from their FEERs to target zones.

This rule recognizes the elementary fact of life that the only effective instrument for managing exchange rates is monetary policy. It does not imply that monetary policy must be devoted exclusively to exchange rate management, because a wide target zone allows substantial scope for monetary policy to be directed to domestic objectives, but it does require that in extreme situations the authorities give priority to the exchange rate.

Rule 2 says that the average world interest rate should be adjusted upwards when the aggregate growth of nominal domestic demand is threatening to exceed its target value (the weighted average of the national targets), or downwards when demand growth is too low.

Rule 1 only deals with interest differentials and fails to pin down the average interest rate in the system. It raises the question as to which country should adjust if two currencies reach the limits of the target zone: the one with the weak or the one with the strong currency. The answer offered by Rule 2 is that if aggregate 'world' (in practice G7) demand is growing too rapidly the weak-currency country should raise its interest rate, while in the converse case of inadequate growth it should be the strong-currency country that should cut its rate. This provides a world rule for aggregate monetary policy to replace the 'dollar standard rule' that the nth country should seek domestic stability while the other n minus 1 countries follow Rule 1. It is the key to constructing a symmetrical monetary system of the form that will be appropriate for the multipolar world of the twenty-first century.

Rule 3 says that if the monetary policy called for by Rules 1 and 2 threatens to prevent nominal domestic demand growing at close to the target rate, fiscal policy should be adjusted to compensate.

This rule calls for the 'Keynesian' use of fiscal policy to ensure that an exchange-rate-oriented monetary policy does not destabilize domestic demand. Such overt use of fiscal policy became unfashionable in the 1980s, but for no good reason: on the contrary, experiences such as the post-1982 expansion in the United States and the post-1987 expansion in Japan demonstrated that fiscal policy had lost none of its power when the conditions assumed by Keynes (excess capacity and financial confidence) were present.

Constraint 1 says that if fiscal policy is threatening to lead to an unsustainable debt build up, Rule 3 should be overridden if it calls for an expansionary fiscal policy.

According to Constraint 2, if world real interest rates remain abnormally high (say, more than 4 per cent per year) for a sustained period, there should be a concerted global fiscal contraction.

On reflection, I am not sure that the combination of a short-run anticyclical 'rule' and two constraints motivated by medium-term concerns is necessarily the best way to have specified the conduct of fiscal policy. Perhaps one might instead have started off by asking each country to identify the medium-run fiscal stance compatible with its current-account target, a sustainable debt position, and a 'normal' real interest rate (say 3 per cent). It would then identify a medium-run (say five-year) path for adjusting its fiscal deficit towards the target position. Rule 3 might then be interpreted in terms of deviations from this target path. This reformulation would make clear the medium-term link between fiscal policy and the current account deficit that has been emphasized by Boughton (1989) — while differing from his policy assignment in retaining exchange rate management. This is still needed in order to avoid leaving exchange rates subject to all the whims of speculative fads with the resultant danger of eroding the link of real trade adjustment to exchange rates (Krugman 1988).

So much for the content of the blueprint. I proceed to outline and discuss five fundamental and controversial assumptions that underlie its design.

Macro-economic management

The first of these assumptions is that governments should manage their economies with a view to pursuing internal and external balance as defined above. The view that governments should do this was taken for granted during the heyday of Keynesianism. Friedman's initial monetarist attack on Keynesian thought largely accepted this framework; it argued that the two objectives could be better attained by policies of constant monetary growth and flexible exchange rates than by the demand management and generally fixed exchange rates that prevailed in the 1960s, not that those two objectives were misguided. While both Marcus Miller and I were trained in the Keynesian tradition and neither of us has ever felt moved to renounce his heritage, the proposals embodied in the blueprint incorporate important elements of thought introduced or advocated by monetarists. Thus nominal income targeting is a compromise between Keynesian targeting of real output and monetarist targeting of the money supply; the need for a nominal anchor is motivated by acceptance of the long-run vertical Phillips curve; and the blueprint allows for exchange rates to change in order to neutralize differential inflation, to achieve real adjustment, or to permit international differences in the anticyclical stance of monetary policy. Hence, the blueprint is better viewed as an eclectic synthesis of Keynesian and monetarist traditions than as old-fashioned Keynesianism. The major respect in which a traditional monetarist might dispute the blueprint's framework is the interpretation of external balance as a current-account target rather than a zero change in reserves, a target that can by definition be achieved by free floating.

The attack on macro-economic management has been taken to greater extremes by the two schools that have succeeded monetarism, namely the new classical macro-economics and supply-side economics, although the intellectual content of the attack goes little further. Both schools would concur with monetarists in challenging the propriety of governments formulating current-account targets. New classical macro-economists go further in proclaiming the futility of any policy of demand management beyond ensuring a steady rate of monetary growth. I have never found their arguments convincing (they seem to me to fail the most basic test of providing some sort of understanding of daily events), but I am in no position to provide an argument that will persuade its adherents. Supply-siders seem to think that any concern to improve supply incentives precludes the need (or the ability?) to manage demand, which strikes me as about as logical as arguing that a deficit should be met either by expenditure cuts or by tax increases but not by some combination of both.

Thus the significant issue is whether it is proper for governments to formulate current-account targets. I have in fact always regarded the choice of a set of current-account targets as by far the most problematic step in calculating FEERs, and I have considerable sympathy with the argument that it would be silly to invest any great effort in seeking precise control of current account outcomes since there is such ambiguity about what is desirable. One benefit of capital mobility is that it can allow current account fluctuations to be accepted with equanimity — within certain bounds. The question is to define those bounds before a policy predicated on their non-existence leads to the sort of catastrophe that has afflicted Latin America since 1982 — for it was precisely a policy of blithely ignoring potential limits to creditworthiness that led to the debt crisis. Recall that bankers were still competing to lend money to Mexico as late as 1981. Until someone provides a convincing reason for believing that no such limits apply to the United States or that any comparable collapse of creditworthiness would be an altogether more benign process, I shall continue to regard the dismissal of concerns about current-account outcomes as irresponsible.

Indeed, the wider the limits to creditworthiness, the more important it may be to try and analyse what current-account balance is in the long-run national interest rather than simply to accept passively whatever outcome is implied by the path of least political resistance to overcoming problems like inflation. To take the obvious example, Britain is today the world's third largest creditor. A debtor position of equal or greater magnitude might well be feasible before creditworthiness called a halt to the debtor's progress. But how many of us would feel that the government had fulfilled its duty to succeeding generations if it in fact pursued its current high-exchange-rate anti-inflation policy to the point where net British foreign assets were replaced by a debt of equal size? Anyone who would feel uncomfortable with such an outcome should be willing to agree that governments need to be in the business of targeting current-account balances as well as domestic stability.

International consistency of targets

A second basic assumption of the blueprint is that it is important that macro-economic management in pursuit of internal and external balance be directed toward targets that are internationally consistent. Most obviously, if countries are going to target exchange rates, those targets had better be the same, or there is a danger of excessive monetary expansion (contraction) as countries compete to drive their exchange rates down (up). Going one step back, if they are to have current account targets, those targets need to be mutually consistent or else countries may be unable to agree on exchange rate targets. Nor are international spillovers confined to obviously international variables like the exchange rate or current account. The faster is growth in the world as a whole, the easier it is for any individual country to expand its domestic demand (because the balance of payments constraint is eased), but the less desirable it is for demand to be expanded (because of the additional world-wide demand-pull inflationary pressure; see Beckerman 1985).

The contention that policy co-ordination is needed to ensure the international consistency of targets has been criticized at two quite different levels. One is from those who dispute the desirability of macro-economic management in pursuit of internal and external balance: their position was already examined in the previous section. The other criticism comes from authors like Oudiz and Sachs (1984), who accept the principle of macro-economic management but dispute the empirical importance of securing target consistency. A large academic literature, which is generally judged to be inconclusive at this stage, has subsequently grown up on this issue.

Let me sketch the two reasons why I find the Oudiz–Sachs conclusion unpersuasive. The first stems from their method of inferring a welfare function to evaluate alternative outcomes. They assumed that the actual outcome was what each country would have wanted given that countries were not co-ordinating their policies (technically, that they reached a Nash equilibrium). So the fact that the United States developed a vast payments deficit during the period they studied (the Reagan–Sprinkel years) was taken to imply that the United States placed little weight on a payments deficit. Hence, a co-operative solution that would have achieved a much lower deficit for little loss of output or increase in inflation would not have been identified as a significant welfare improvement. Such an approach assumes away the scope for policy co-ordination to improve matters, but it is valid only if governments both know what they are doing and choose to act in the public interest (two assumptions that strike some of us as singularly inappropriate for the Reagan–Sprinkel period).

My other reason for scepticism is that they adopt the modeller's customary frame of reference, which assumes that governments manipulate fiscal and monetary policy in the light of some model of their effects on ultimate targets (output, inflation, and the balance of payments) and no concern for their impact on intermediate variables like the exchange rate. In my view this is undesirable, partly because the linkages between intermediate and final targets are firmer than those from policy variables to final targets, and partly because it would preclude governments playing any role in stabilizing exchange markets against speculative fads. More important, it is also unrealistic; governments do concern themselves with exchange rates that depart too far from what they conceive the fundamentals justify, as post-Plaza experience has demonstrated. This fact creates a potential for conflict among countries that is again assumed away by the Oudiz–Sachs analysis.

Capital mobility

The next two controversial postulates underlying the blueprint are less philosophical. One is its assumption that capital mobility is here to stay and cannot be wished away by capital controls. It is because of this assumption that the blueprint devotes monetary policy, or at least international differences in monetary policy, in large part to exchange rate management.

Presumably no one believes in the feasibility of reverting to administrative controls on capital movements among the major industrial countries that have experienced a decade or more of unimpeded capital mobility. Recent discussion has tended to concentrate instead on the use of fiscal measures. Two possible approaches have been mentioned: one is the imposition of interest equalization taxes, which would involve a weak (strong) currency country taxing foreign lending (borrowing); the other is the imposition of a small tax on all foreign exchange transactions (the 'Tobin tax', first suggested by Tobin 1978).

Effective interest equalization taxes that could be altered promptly in order to counter undesired changes in exchange rates could unquestionably relieve monetary policy of the need to manage the exchange rate. Given the difficulty — admittedly often self-imposed — that many governments seem to have in making flexible use of fiscal policy, this would certainly be helpful. But there are, of course, two critical characteristics that an interest equalization tax would have to possess in order to fulfil this function: that it be effective; and that it be capable of prompt alteration in order to counter a change in conditions in the exchange markets. It is not obvious that the prospects for effective enforcement of an interest equalization tax would be markedly better than those for capital controls. Perhaps even more decisive, one could hardly alter tax rates part way through a fiscal year in order to counter a change in exchange market conditions, which would seem to rule out the possibility of making sufficiently prompt changes in tax rates to make this a useful instrument for exchange rate management.

The objections to the Tobin tax are different. True, there might be problems of preventing avoidance of the tax by relocation of exchange markets to jurisdictions that did not impose it, which would require fairly comprehensive participation in a treaty providing for imposition of the tax in order to reduce the problem of avoidance to an acceptable level. Moreover, the tax would presumably need to be imposed not just on spot transactions but also on trading in forwards, futures, swaps and any other ersatz instruments that might be created in order to avoid the tax. While these complications are not negligible, they might well be worth tackling if one could feel confident that a transactions tax would indeed be an effective instrument for reducing exchange rate misalignments.

The most compelling evidence for believing that it would be is provided by the finding of Frankel and Froot (1986) that for an extended period during the dollar's run-up in 1980–5 most exchange market operators expected the dollar to decline in the medium term even while they anticipated — and acted on the expectation of — further appreciation in the short term. By making short-term transactions less profitable, the Tobin tax should increase the relative weight given to medium-term expectations, which would in this case have helped reduce the dollar's overvaluation.

The critical question is whether one can rely on things always working out this way. This is not clear. For example, the speculative run-up of the dollar in the early summer of 1989 led one of the most prestigious groups of exchange rate forecasters to seek to rationalize the irrational and extrapolate further medium-term dollar appreciation (Morrison 1989). While even serious forecasters are capable of such errors, it is not clear that the Tobin tax would be much help.[3]

If the evidence should indicate that taxes would be capable of providing significant ability to manage exchange rates and thus relieve the burden on monetary policy, it would be silly to pass the opportunity by. But at the moment the evidence seems to indicate that it would be imprudent to count on such help. That is why the blueprint assumes continued high capital mobility.

Real versus nominal exchange rate pegging

The blueprint proposes that participating countries stabilize their real (inflation-adjusted)exchange rates. Since inflation differentials are negligible relative to potential exchange rate movements in the short-term, this is the same as pegging nominal exchange rates in the short-term. What a real peg implies is that the nominal band be altered regularly in the light of differential inflation in order to maintain the real band unchanged in the medium-term (*ceteris paribus*, of course).

Choice of a real rather than nominal peg means foregoing the opportunity of using an exchange rate peg to provide a 'nominal anchor', i.e. to import some centre country's monetary policy to stabilize (hopefully) the price level. The blueprint instead provides each country with its own nominal anchor in the form of a non-inflationary rule for the expansion of nominal domestic demand. This is surely appropriate for a global system encompassing the three major financial powers: one can hardly envisage the United States agreeing to import the monetary policy of West Germany or Japan, nor the latter reverting to a dollar standard where their monetary policies are subservient to those of the Federal Reserve Board.

Indeed, I have grave doubts as to whether it makes sense for medium-sized powers like the UK, France, Italy and Spain to tie themselves into a system of fixed nominal exchange rates where they rely on the Bundesbank to supply them with price stability, which is the popular image of what the EMS is all about. In fact, because of the many past realignments, the EMS has up to now acted as something of a hybrid between a system of fixed nominal and fixed real exchange rates. The ambition towards the former may have been of some help in reducing the cost of curbing inflation differentials, but the main reason for the success of the EMS is that it has accepted sufficient of the logic of a system of fixed real exchange rates to avoid creating intolerable tensions. Unfortunately the payments disequilibria that have been allowed to build up in recent years are so large as to raise doubts about the sustainability of the EMS, especially if an attempt is made to continue resisting needed realignments.

Nominal exchange rate stability is an inefficient way of securing price stability (even if the centre country does in fact remain inflation-free, which is never certain). As long as domestic inflationary pressures remain stronger than those abroad, the mechanism needed to secure price stability is a currency overvaluation large enough to create price arbitrage pressures that neutralize the excess domestic inflation pressure.[4] This means that the country will suffer either a payments deficit or output below potential. It would be much better for the country to face the need to resolve its inflationary pressures by appropriate domestic policies — labour market liberalization, an incomes policy, deindexation, deregulation, whatever may be the appropriate solution in the specific national context. Exchange rate pegging makes it too easy to avoid these hard policy choices.[5]

Fiscal policy

The final controversial assumption of the blueprint is that fiscal policy can and should be used to help manage demand.

I have already indicated my dismissal of most of the 'reasons' that have been invented for criticizing the use of fiscal policy for demand management. The evidence indicates that it does work (the Ricardo–Barro offset on savings is incomplete; see Masson and Knight 1986). There is no reason in the world why the structure and level of spending and taxes should not be managed with a proper concern to sharpen supply incentives at the same time as the full-employment budget deficit is altered with a proper concern for its impact on aggregate demand. What is needed is not fiscal 'fine-tuning', but a willingness to recognize that the impact of fiscal policy on demand matters.

Thus in the United States today the first priority should be to convince Americans that, given the savings rate, they are being undertaxed to the tune of $100 billion per year or more. The second should be to secure tax increases in a form that minimizes any supply-side disincentives and distributional inequities — or preferably that improves incentives by taxing the output of goods, like non-biodegrable packing materials and gasoline, with harmful environmental effects. The least important issue is the precise timing of the phasing-in of the increased taxes, though presumably everyone would prefer to see this accomplished in a way that avoided an unnecessary recession.

The obstacle to the stabilizing use of fiscal policy is not economic uncertainty, but political myopia.

Conclusion

Since not all G7 governments subscribe at present to all the assumptions that underlie the blueprint proposals for international monetary co-ordination, it is not surprising that the G7 has stopped short of endorsing such an approach to re-establishing a structured monetary system. If the blueprint is ever implemented, it will surely be because either intellectual debate or the force of events leads to a consensus on the issues identified above at a time when the G7 is dominated by two or three forceful and farsighted leaders who share the consensus and wish to establish it in a form that will to some extent bind their successors. The model is the way in which Schmidt and Giscard established the EMS in 1978–9; the successor who has so far been most successfully constrained, Francois Mitterrand, shows every sign of being grateful.[6]

Notes

1. At least, there is a one-to-one correspondence between the level of activity and the growth rate if the growth of supply-side potential is exogenous. This is a reasonable assumption for the short-run, but not for the long-run.
2. Or, strictly speaking, the trajectory.
3. It may be asked whether government forecasters are immune to similar errors. The answer is that they are much less prone to error because they would start off by asking the right question: is the exchange rate consistent with a satisfactory evolution of macro-economic outcomes in the medium term? (Morrison did not claim that a higher dollar would be consistent with a decline of the US trade deficit to a level that might be acceptable to the G7.)
4. The classic example is Chile, which by 1981 did secure price stability through a fixed exchange rate — at the cost of a 50 per cent overvaluation.
5. The extent of the inefficiency induced by relying on a strong currency to control inflation depends on two factors: the credibility of the commitment not to devalue, and the pervasiveness of arbitrage pressures. A common currency would establish complete credibility in a way that no commitment to a fixed exchange rate can ever hope to. A common internal market can be expected to enhance arbitrage pressures and thus limit the extent to which a European country suffering excess domestic inflationary pressures would end up overvalued after 1992. Hence a common European currency is not necessarily to be rejected on the grounds outlined in the text which emphasize real rather than nominal exchange rate stability as the goal among separate currencies. That conclusion applies rather to the EMS in the interim stages and, even more decisively, the G7.
6. Had Mr Callaghan signed on, perhaps Mrs Thatcher would today be equally grateful that the EMS had restrained her from allowing the excessive appreciation of the pound in the early 1980s.

References

Barrell, Ray, and Simon Wren-Lewis (1989), 'Fundamental Equilibrium Exchange Rates for the G7', National Institute of Economic and Social Research, mimeo.

Beckerman, Wilfred (1985), 'How the Battle against Inflation was Really Won', *Lloyds Bank Review*, January.

Brittan, Samuel (1987), 'The Case for Money GDP' in S. Brittan, *The Role and Limits of Government* (London: Wildwood House), revised edn.

Boughton, James M. (1989), 'Policy Assignment Strategies with Somewhat Flexible Exchange Rates' in B. Eichengreen, M. Miller and R. Portes, eds, *Blueprints for Exchange Rate Management* (London: Centre for Economic Policy Research).

Frankel, Jeffrey, and Kenneth Froot (1986), 'Understanding the US Dollar in the Eighties: The Expectations of Chartists and Fundamentalists', *Economic Record*, supplement.

Krugman, Paul (1988), *Exchange Rate Instability* (Cambridge, Mass: MIT Press).

McCallum, Bennett T. (1988), 'Robustness Properties of a Rule for Monetary Policy', *Carnegie-Rochester Conference Series on Public Policy*, Autumn.

Masson, Paul R. and Malcolm Knight (1986), 'International Transmission of Fiscal Policies in Major Industrial Countries', *IMF Staff Papers*, September.

Meade, James E. (1984), 'A New Keynesian Bretton Woods', *Three Banks Review*, June.

Morrison, David (1989), 'The Dollar's Cushion and Why It's Full of Air', *The International Economics Analyst*, June.

Oudiz, Gilles and Jeffrey Sachs (1984), 'Macroeconomic Policy Coordination Among the Industrial Economies', *Bookings Papers on Economic Activity*, 1.

Tobin, James (1978), 'A Proposal for International Monetary Reform', *Eastern Economic Journal*, July, reprinted in J. Tobin, *Essays in Economics* (Cambridge, Mass: MIT Press, 1982).

Williamson, John (1985), *The Exchange Rate System* (Washington, DC: Institute for International Economics).

Williamson, John, and Marcus Miller (1987), *Targets and Indicators: A Blueprint for the International Coordination of Economic Policy* (Washington, DC: Institute for International Economics).

3 Domestic stabilization and the balance of payments

James Meade

The purpose of this paper is to consider the general principles on which countries which are adopting national policies for the domestic stabilization of their economies should conduct their external financial relationships with other countries and, in particular, with each other.

Let me first explain what I mean by the adoption of national policies for domestic stabilization. By domestic stabilization I shall mean a state of affairs in which a high and stable level of economic activity — what I shall unrepentantly call full employment — is maintained and is combined, if not with exact stability of some stated price index, at least with only a moderate, steady, non-explosive rise in the general level of prices — what I shall call the control of inflation.

I shall confine my attention to those countries which are aiming at full employment and a control of inflation by means of two sets of policies, namely demand-management policies and incomes or wage-fixing policies. This clearly covers any countries which are adopting domestically what I will call Orthodox Keynesian policies. By this I mean fiscal and monetary policies designed to expand total money expenditures on goods and services so long as employment is below some high predetermined full-employment level, combined, if necessary, with a centralized incomes policy which controls money rates of pay so as to prevent the high level of demand from leading to a runaway inflation of money costs and prices. But my analysis will also cover those countries which are adopting what I shall call New Keynesian policies. Let me explain what I mean by this distinction between Orthodox Keynesians and New Keynesians.

Recent experience in all of our countries and in particular in the United Kingdom has thrown doubt on the wisdom of expanding total

The author is Emeritus Professor of Political Economy, University of Cambridge. This paper is based on a lecture given in Hamburg in October 1980 and published by HWWA-Institut für Wirtschaftsforschung, Hamburg. It first appeared in *Lloyds Bank Review*, January 1982.

money expenditures so long as employment is below some high pre-determined full-employment level. This policy has been found in fact to imply a threat of runaway price-cost inflation. The problems and implications of meeting this threat by an effective centralized incomes policy are so acute that I for one have come to the conclusion that one must stand Orthodox Keynesianism on its head. In other words, demand-management policies should be used to maintain a steady but restrained rate of growth of the total flow of money expenditure on the products of labour and so on the services of labour itself and thus to control inflation; and, against this background of a steady but moderate rate of growth in the total money earnings of labour, employment should be maintained by introducing into each sector of the economy methods of wage-fixing suitably devised to promote the level of employment in that sector rather than to obtain the highest possible monopolistic reward for a limited number of persons in that sector. This is what I mean by New Keynesianism.

This view does not imply acceptance of strict monetarism. Indeed my own position differs from that of strict monetarism in three important respects. First, it seems to me that the direct objective of financial policy should be to control the flow of money expenditures rather than the stock of money, since the relevant stock of liquid assets is Protean in its ability to change its form and in any case is to be regarded only as an indirect means of controlling the level of total expenditures. Second, for reasons which I will mention later, I believe that fiscal and not only monetary measures are needed to achieve the desired stabilization. Third, I do not believe that stabilization through financial policy is enough and that wage-fixing arrangements can be left to look after themselves. At any rate in the United Kingdom a radical reform of wage-fixing arrangements is, I believe, a necessary feature for the achievement of full employment against the background of a steady, controlled, moderate rate of growth in the total level of money demand for labour.

My analysis will be conducted on one other basic assumption. In the present state of development of national and international economic and financial institutions it seems clear to me that the primary responsibility for stabilization policies of the kind which I have outlined must remain in the hands of the national authorities. I shall accordingly assume in this paper that each national government is devising its own national financial policies and its own wage-fixing institutions in such a way as to promote its own employment and to control its own inflation.

It is not my purpose to argue the choice between what I have called Orthodox Keynesianism and New Keynesianism. I shall, however, assume that by one or other combination of wage-fixing arrangements and of demand-management policies, a country has succeeded in controlling inflation, while maintaining a high and stable level of employment.

A closed economy

Before I turn to the international aspects of the problem I must analyse in a little more detail the implications which would arise in a closed economy. Demand-management policies, whether they be used by Orthodox Keynesians for the maintenance of full employment or by New Keynesians for the control of inflation, can be implemented either by monetary policy (which I will call interest rate policy) or by fiscal policy (which I will call tax rate policy). Which of these two, or what combination of the two, should one use for the management of demand?

I personally believe in fine-tuning the demand-management policies as far as possible. In this case there is much to be said for placing the first emphasis on the tax rate. Changes in the rate of interest resulting from tighter or more relaxed monetary policies are likely to have a rather delayed action. It is true that rates of interest can probably be more promptly changed than can rates of tax; but their effect on money expenditures, by causing people to revise their plans and programmes for capital investment in new plant, machinery, houses, and so on, is likely to be much delayed. If short-run reasonably fine-tuned control is desired, it is probably essential to search for suitable fiscal reforms which will enable certain rates of tax to be varied reasonably frequently and promptly. Changes in national insurance contributions and in VAT might be suitable instruments to influence consumers' expenditures.

If the rate of tax is to be used as the primary weapon to stabilize money expenditures, what, if any, is the role to be played by the rate of interest? At this point another domestic character enters the stage to play the role of the third target — namely, the budget balance. The analysis can best be made by considering one possible illustrative situation. Suppose that at a given ruling rate of interest it is found necessary to slash the rate of tax to a very low level in order to prevent money expenditures from falling below the desired level. There results an excessively large budget deficit. The government is having to mop up by borrowing part of the private sector's savings at the full-employment level of real incomes to spend on governmental current consumption, because the borrowing of funds for private investment is insufficient. The cure for this situation is an expansionary monetary policy with a reduced rate of interest gradually leading to increased private investment. As this happens, in order to prevent an inflation of money expenditures above the desired level, the rate of tax must be raised so as to restrain private consumption, with the result that the budget deficit will be reduced.

In what follows I shall accordingly speak of the budget balance as a third target for macro-economic policy. But I do not mean to imply that the target should necessarily be a zero deficit or surplus. A budget surplus is a form of public saving which supplements private saving; and in conditions of full employment it may be judged desirable that there should be such a supplement to private saving, because insufficient weight is being given privately to the needs of future generations — or alternatively that a budget deficit of a certain size is desirable because the level of private savings is considered to impose an excessive burden on the current generation. The budget balance target would be a zero deficit or surplus only if the authorities had no desire in conditions of full employment to be adding to, or subtracting from, private saving. For shorthand I shall talk of a country having a budget surplus problem if in the interests of short-term demand management the authorities are having to run a budget surplus at a higher level, or a budget deficit at a lower level than they would otherwise desire; and conversely for a budget deficit problem.

One may summarize this strategy for the short-run stabilization and control of the closed economy as follows: (1) use the rate of tax and the rate of wages in combination to maintain full employment and to control inflation; and (2) if the rate of tax needed to maintain the desired level of money expenditures is so low as to result in a persistent budget -deficit problem, lower the rate of interest in order gradually to stimulate private investment which will alleviate the need for such excessively low rates of tax; and vice versa to avoid a persistent budget surplus problem.

If one were not concerned with the relative speeds with which the rate of interest and the rate of tax are likely to effect money expenditures, what I have just said would amount to no more than the familiar proposition that in devising demand-management policies one should use tax policy if one wants primarily to influence private consumption expenditures and interest rate policy if one wants primarily to influence private investment expenditures. All that I have added is the view that in the short run it is more important to prevent undesirable booms or slumps in total money expenditures than it is to keep investment and consumption in any optimal relationship to each other, and that as an instrument for control of money expenditures, tax rate changes can probably be made more prompt in their effects than can changes in interest rates.

It is time, however, to turn to an examination of the international implications of these proposals; and this, it will be found, greatly reinforces the desirability of relying on tax rate changes rather than on interest rate changes for the control of a country's money expenditures.

A single open economy

I will start the analysis of an open economy by considering a small country in relationship with a large rest of the world, this rest of the world having a set of tax rates, wage rates, price levels, incomes, and so on, which will not be to any appreciable degree influenced by what goes on in the small open economy under examination.

The rules given for the closed economy can be summarised as: use (1) the tax rate and the wage rate to control employment and inflation; and (2) the interest rate to control the budget balance. When we turn to the open economy, we can add one 'target', namely equilibrium in the balance of payments, and one 'weapon', namely the rate of foreign exchange. At first glance it may appear reasonable to assume that the rules just given for a closed economy should remain unchanged and that the exchange rate should be used as the instrument for maintaining equilibrium in the balance of payments, being depreciated in order to expand exports and to contract imports in the case of a balance of payments deficit and being appreciated to cope with a balance of payments surplus.

But can the effect of changes in the rate of interest on the balance of payments be neglected in this way?

Before I discuss this basic question let me define some of the terms which I shall be using. For shorthand I shall use the term 'balance of trade' for a country's balance of payments on current account, that is, an excess of the value of a country's exports of goods and services over its imports of goods and services. A surplus on the balance of trade so defined is the same as the country's foreign investment, since it measures the net amount of the country's real resources which are being used to increase the country's net hold of foreign assets; and it measures also one element of expenditure on the country's goods and services, the total of which it is the object of short-run domestic financial policy, and in particular of tax policy, to keep on a moderate, stabilized growth path or to control in the interest of full employment.

By a surplus on the country's balance of payments I shall mean an inflow of foreign exchange reserves or transactions in official inter-governmental or inter-central-bank financing with similar effect. This will occur when there is an excess of the country's balance of trade over any outflow of capital funds on autonomous or private account. A country's balance of trade will be determined by such factors as the country's level of money incomes, money prices, and money costs relative to foreign money incomes, money prices and money costs, adjusted for the foreign exchange rate. The international flow of capital funds will be determined by other factors such as the expected yields on different forms of assets at home and abroad, the yields being determined, among other things, by the rates of interest at home and abroad and by expected changes in the foreign exchange rate as it will affect the value in home currency of assets denominated in terms of foreign currency. The problem of maintaining equilibrium in a country's balance of payments is the problem of matching a country's balance of trade (which is determined by one set of factors) with the international flow of capital funds (which is determined by another set of factors).

A rise in a country's domestic interest rate may be expected to cause a large but temporary inflow of funds as fundholders at home and abroad adjust their existing portfolio holdings in favour of the higher-interest-rate country. Once the portfolio adjustment had taken place this large shift of funds would cease; but it would, however, be succeeded by a permanent but smaller improved flow as the continued new savings of fundholders at home and abroad were attracted in the newly adjusted proportions to the higher-interest-rate country. From this one may conclude that if a country's domestic rate is gradually raised the gradual change in existing portfolios will cause a continuing flow of funds to the country concerned, and that when the rise ceases to take place and a higher rate has been established there will result a continuing increased flow out of current savings.

In view of these considerations it is impossible to neglect the effect of a country's interest rates upon its balance of payments. This is an important reason why, for the purpose of the domestic demand management of the total money expenditures on the country's products, stress must be laid on the use of fiscal policy (or what I have called tax rate policy) rather than on the use of monetary policy (or what I have called interest rate policy). Both rate of tax and rate of interest will, of course, affect the balance of trade by affecting the level of total money expenditures on goods and services. But we are not concerned with that effect except in so far as there may be some difference in the import contents of tax-controlled and of interest-controlled expenditures, since we are assuming that, whatever policy weapon be used, it will be used to the extent necessary to maintain the total money demand for the country's products on the desired target level. But the rate of interest will have the additional direct and immediate effect on the balance of payments of affecting the international flow of capital funds. The rate of tax will have no such similar additional marked effect.

If, then, wage rate policy and tax rate policy are to be used domestically on Orthodox Keynesian or New Keynesian lines to maintain full employment and to control inflation, we are left with two weapons, interest rate policy and exchange rate policy, to achieve two targets, budget balance and equilibrium in the balance of payments. The purpose of this paper is to consider the appropriate use of these two weapons to achieve these two objectives against the background of a successful use of wage rate policy and tax rate policy to avoid unemployment and inflation.

A country may be facing a budget-deficit problem or a budget-surplus problem as a result of the use of tax rate policy to prevent the level of money demand for its products from falling below or rising above the desired level. At the same time it may be facing a balance of payments deficit or surplus, as a result of its balance of trade falling below or rising above the outflow of capital funds. It may be facing any combination of these two sets of problems, which gives four possible cases.

Two of these cases present no analytical difficulty. Consider a country with a budget surplus problem. The closed-economy rule was to raise the rate of interest so as to reduce domestic investment so as to make it desirable to cut the rate of tax in order to promote an offsetting increase in consumption. If the country has at the same time a deficit on its balance of payments, the rise in the rate of interest which was effected in order to relieve the budget surplus problem will attract funds from abroad and thus relieve the balance of payments deficit. So long as the country has a surplus problem on the budget and a deficit problem on the balance of payments, the closed economy rule to use the rate of interest to deal with the budget surplus problem need not be modified.

Conversely, so long as a country is faced with a deficit problem on the budget and a surplus problem on its balance of payments, a lowering of the rate of interest to relieve its budget deficit problem will cause an outflow of funds which will relieve its balance of payments surplus.

Problems, however, arise in the two remaining cases where the country has either a deficit problem or a surplus problem simultaneously on both budget account and balance of payments account. If the country has a deficit problem on both counts, the closed-economy rule which calls for a reduction of the rate of interest to relieve the budget deficit problem would encourage the outflow of capital funds and intensify the balance of payments deficit. I shall talk of a country's budget deficit problem as being intractable if it has not at the same time a surplus on its balance of payments, that is to say so long as a reduction in the rate of interest needed to relieve its budget deficit problem would create a new, or intensify an existing, balance of payments problem. Conversely a country's budget surplus problem will be said to be intractable so long as it is not combined with a deficit on its balance of payments.

Let me consider at some length the case of a country with a deficit problem on both its budget balance and its balance of payments. An obvious possibility would be to depreciate the exchange rate. If the immediate effect of the depreciation was to shift demands at home and abroad from foreign goods to the country's goods on such a scale that the balance of trade improved, all would be well. The balance of trade represents the country's real investment of current resources abroad. This increase in the net demand for the country's goods for investment abroad would enable the rate of tax to be raised to induce an offsetting reduction in the country's consumption expenditures. The increased foreign investment would relieve the country's budget deficit problem as well as its balance of payments problem.

If the exchange rate variations worked promptly in this fashion the rules of the game would be simple. A country which has a deficit or a surplus problem on both the budget and the balance of payments simultaneously should make use of the exchange rate so as to relieve its balance of payments problem, and this will work in the right direction to relieve its budget problem. On the other hand, a country which has a surplus problem on one count and a deficit problem on the other count should make use of the rate of interest so as to relieve its budget balance problem, and this will work in the right direction to relieve its balance of payments problem.

But let us return to the country with what I have called an intractable budget deficit problem. Suppose that it does reduce its interest rate in order to promote domestic investment so as to relieve its budget deficit problem in spite of the fact that it will create or intensify a deficit on its balance of payments. Suppose that it frees the exchange rate to find its own level as a means of dealing with this intensified balance of payments problem. What will happen?

In fact the resulting depreciation of the currency which reduces the country's money prices and costs relatively to those in the rest of the world, while it will almost certainly in the long run have the desired effect of improving the country's balance of trade, is likely to do so only with considerable delay as trade is gradually diverted into the more profitable channels. Indeed, the immediate effect may be perverse and the well-known J-curve may display itself. Before the channels of trade are diverted in consequence of the changes in relative prices, the rise in the price of imports may cause a temporary deterioration in the balance of trade.

If this happens the exchange rate depreciation will be intensified as the temporary worsening of the balance of trade is added to the adverse effect of low domestic interest rates on the international flow of capital funds. In fact the depreciation will have to go so far as to cause fundholders at home and abroad to consider: (1) that the exchange rate has become grossly undervalued; (2) that the exceedingly favourable rate of exchange will gradually improve the balance of trade; (3) that the improvement in the balance of trade will cause an appreciation of the exchange rate from its present grossly undervalued level; (4) that the appreciation of the exchange rate is about to start; and (5) that the rate of appreciation will be sufficiently rapid. The expected rate of appreciation is, of course, crucial. In comparing yields on assets at home and abroad it is the rate of interest at home plus the rate at which the home currency will appreciate in terms of foreign currency which must be compared with the rate of interest on foreign funds.

It is possible that a solution of the problem can be found in this way. I am not sure whether such a solution will necessarily always exist, if the channels of trade do not respond much and/or respond very slowly to changes in relative prices. In such a case the initial worsening of the balance of trade might be very great so that the inflow of funds to be attracted by expected exchange rate appreciation might have to be very large; and the rate of expected appreciation of the exchange rate might not be sufficiently rapid to cause a sufficient expected gain on the exchange rate to offset the interest rate differential sufficiently to attract the large flow of funds needed until the balance of trade was sufficiently improved.

I am afraid that the problem needs formal dynamic analysis which I have not given it. But what is quite certain is that violent swings in the exchange rate may well take place if the solution of freely floating exchange rates is adopted. This would lead to marked temporary changes in relative prices which will need subsequent reversal. In my example it could lead to marked increases in the cost of living due to temporary excessive rises in the cost of imports and to misleadingly high temporary boosts to the country's tradable products. Appropriate wage-fixing and informed business planning might be much easier if the temporary collapse of the exchange rate were avoided.

This might be done to some extent by the use of the country's official foreign-exchange reserves. But if the problem were on a large scale and such reserves were inadequate, it would be inevitable that during the temporary strain on the balance of payments the interest rate would have to be raised to attract foreign funds in spite of any adverse effect on the budget deficit problem. The exchange rate adjustment will itself ultimately relieve the budget deficit problem by increasing the country's foreign investment. The aim should, therefore, be to postpone the adjustment of the interest rate as much as possible, if necessary by the use of foreign exchange reserves, and to make any adjustments of the interest rate which may be needed on budget balance grounds later, as and when the exchange rate adjustment develops its favourable effect on foreign investment. The ultimate need on budget balance grounds may in fact turn out to be no fall or conceivably even some rise in interest rates as foreign investment grows.

This suggests that the basic principles for the open economy should be on the following lines. Let the rate of interest always be adjusted so as to help maintain equilibrium in the balance of payments so long as the change is also in the direction needed to relieve any budget deficit or surplus problem. If, however, there is what I have called an intractable budget deficit or surplus problem, seek ultimate adjustment of the exchange rate, and ease this process of adjustment by relying as much as possible on the use of foreign-exchange reserves rather than on interest rate changes as the means for dealing with the immediate balance of payments problems.

The final result of using the interest rate to cope with tractable and the exchange rate to cope with intractable budget balance problems on the principles just outlined would be that the country, preserving full employment and controlling inflation by means of its domestic fiscal and wage policies, would also be in balance of payments equilibrium. At the same time total savings, private and public, will be at the desired level and will be being used to finance domestic and foreign investment in proportions determined by relative yields at home and abroad as capital funds flow in the search for such yields.

This strategy involves using the exchange rate as the leading element for setting in motion an otherwise intractable structural change of the level of a country's total investment, domestic and foreign. But this does not imply that there is no day-to-day exchange rate problem of short-run balance of payments equilibrium. The money price level of the country's products will be the outcome of the rate of change in the country's output per head and in the money wage rate set by incomes policy or resulting from the rate of growth which has been set for the total money demand for labour, according as one has adopted an Orthodox Keynesian or New Keynesian policy. There is no prior reason to believe that the country's money price and cost levels will be moving exactly in line with those in the rest of the world. The structural adjustment which may be needed to control the country's balance of trade and so its foreign investment is not in fact an adjustment of the exchange rate itself. What is needed is an adjustment of the country's domestic price and cost levels relatively to those of the outside world after conversion at the current rate of exchange or, in other words, an adjustment of the real terms of trade between the country's own products and the competing products of the rest of the world.

This suggests that exchange rate policy should be considered at two levels. First, the day-to-day adjustment of the exchange rate through an exchange equalization fund should be conducted in such a way as to keep constant a competitiveness index of the country's products *vis-à-vis* the competing products of the rest of the world. Second, there should be from time to time structural adjustments of the level at which the competitiveness index should be stabilized, competitiveness being increased if greater domestic and foreign investment was needed in order to relieve an otherwise intractable budget deficit problem, and vice versa. I shall refer to exchange rate adjustments of this kind which are needed to alter the competitiveness of the country's products in overseas markets as 'structural exchange rate adjustments'.

Manna from Heaven

I will illustrate the application of the principles which I have just outlined by means of a parable which I will call the story of Manna from Heaven rather than the story of Oil from the North Sea. I choose this title because I want to emphasize a certain element of the miraculous in my parable, namely that the country enjoying this bounty of nature is successfully applying the domestic policies which I have advocated; that is to say, it is suffering neither from inflation nor from unemployment since it has a set of appropriate domestic fiscal and wage policies.

Imagine, then, that the bounty of Heaven starts to pour into the coffers of the country's Treasury an annual supply of Manna, a primary product for which there is an insatiable overseas market. Taken by surprise the Treasury simply sells the Manna abroad. The impact effect is thus straightforward. There is an added annual budget surplus and an added positive balance of payments taking the form of an annual addition to the country's foreign-exchange reserves equal to the value of the annual supply of Manna from Heaven.

In my parable the labour and capital needed to gather up the Manna is negligible and those who do find it have to pay all but a negligible part of it in tribute to the government. Thus the authorities are faced with no immediate need to change their demand-management or wage-fixing policies in order to maintain full employment and to control inflation. All that has happened is the increase in the budget surplus matched by an increase in the authorities' holdings of foreign exchange reserves as the Manna is sold abroad. In the rest of the economy money expenditures, prices, wages and incomes continue unchanged.

So far the effect would be that the citizens of the fortunate country were saving and investing abroad the whole of the community's income from Manna. The anomaly of this situation might even be intensified if the monetary authorities felt compelled on balance of payments grounds to ease monetary conditions and reduce interest rates to help to restore equilibrium to the balance of payments by encouraging an outflow of capital funds to match the export of Manna. Any such reduction in the interest rate might have some effect in stimulating domestic investment; and in order to prevent this from causing an unwanted inflation of total money expenditures on the products of the country's labour, the rate of tax might have to be raised and the budget surplus further increased in order to encourage some offsetting reduction in consumption.

This would indeed be an anomalous outcome. Even if the flow of Manna were not expected to be permanent, it would be anomalous that the citizens as consumers should enjoy no benefit from the bounty, much more anomalous that they should actually be asked to tighten their belts. If the flow were expected to be temporary, it would be reasonable to save some part of it. One possible target would be to use the temporary flow of Manna to finance a permanent rise in consumption levels. This would involve saving enough so that, when the flow of Manna ceased, the yield on the additional capital wealth of the community would be sufficient to maintain in perpetuity the initial higher level of consumption.

It would thus be natural for the authorities to decide that the supplement to the country's saving which was represented by the uncorrected budget surplus was excessive. The country is thus faced with what I have called an intractable budget surplus problem. It would be desirable to raise the rate of interest to discourage investment at home in order that taxes might be reduced so that citizens spent more on consumption out of their post-tax incomes and devoted less resources to domestic investment since their foreign investment had grown so greatly. But any rise in the rate of interest would worsen the balance of payments problem and would add to the large surplus in the balance of trade (inclusive of Manna) an additional inflow of capital funds.

According to the rule book this intractable budget surplus problem should be remedied by a structural appreciation of the country's currency so as to reduce the competitiveness of the country's products other than Manna, thus reducing the country's balance of trade in products other than Manna. This reduction in foreign investment of such products would have to go far enough to cause a net reduction in the total of domestic and foreign investment of such products. This would make room for a reduction in taxation to stimulate an offsetting rise in the consumption of such products. The balance of payments problem would be relieved as foreign disinvestment in products other than Manna offset the foreign investment of Manna; and the budget surplus problem would be relieved as tax rates were reduced to stimulate consumption to offset the net reduction in domestic and foreign investment of products other than Manna.

Such are the basic features of the story which I have related simply to illustrate the operation of the rules which I am advocating. Any such domestic structural change as that which would result from a rich stream of Manna from Heaven would, of course, bring with it many other important economic problems. In particular the necessary shift of resources from the production of exports and import-competing goods other than Manna to the production of the additional goods and services which the citizens would purchase when their tax burdens were reduced, would involve changes in relative prices and incomes and problems of structural unemployment, all of which important disturbances would somewhat impair the benefits of the gift from Heaven. On the other hand, another set of changes would increase the benefit to the country concerned at the expense of the rest of the world; the country's terms of trade, so far as tradable products other than Manna were concerned, would be improved as a result of the appreciation of the exchange rate and the reduction in the required competitiveness of its tradable products. The country would obtain more imports per unit of its remaining exports other than Manna. But the scale and precise nature of all these disturbing and beneficial price and structural adjustments would depend essentially upon the particular economic structure and conditions of the particular country which Heaven had chosen for its bounty; but that is not the subject matter of this paper.

An international order

So far I have been dealing with the rules appropriate for a single relatively small country in a large world in which the other countries are operating a miscellany of other policies with their price levels, rates of interest, total levels of demand, and so on, all given as exogenous variables to the decision-makers in the single country under examination. But the question must be raised whether the system could be successfully generalized. If every country in the free-enterprise world operated the set of policies which I have proposed for the single small country, would the system work without appropriate modification of existing international institutions?

The answer is, I think, that principles of international co-operation in the setting of exchange rates and interest rates can be devised which would make the generalization of the system effective and in the interest of all participants. In this paper I cannot attempt more than a sketch of these principles with a very broad brush. For this purpose I shall talk in terms of a two-country world made up of countries Delta and Sigma, Delta being a country with a deficit on its balance of payments and Sigma, therefore, having an equal and opposite balance of payments surplus. The principles deduced from this two-country world could, I think, be readily applied with suitable modifications to a many-country world, and one can think of Delta as standing for a group of countries with balance of payments deficits and Sigma as standing for the corresponding countries with balance of payments surpluses. Each of the two countries Delta and Sigma may have a budget surplus problem (which I will denote S) or a budget deficit problem (which I will denote D). Thus by way of example ΔS stands for a country with a balance of payments deficit problem and a budget surplus problem. There are then four possible states of the world economy which are expressed in the following taxonomic schema:

	Country Delta	County Sigma
State 1	ΔS	ΣD
State 2	ΔD	ΣS
State 3	ΔS	ΣS
State 4	ΔD	ΣD

By consideration of these various states of the world economy one can, I think, deduce the general outlines of the principles for international monetary and financial co-operation in a world in which all countries are using domestic fiscal and wage policies to maintain full employment and to avoid inflation.

State 1 is a case in which if both countries adjust their interest rates, upwards in Delta and downwards in Sigma, so as to relieve their budget balance problem, then this will also relieve their balance of payments problems. Both are faced with what I have called tractable budget balance problems. This is a clear case for both countries using interest rate policies to look after their own domestic and international positions.

State 2 is the case where both countries are faced with intractable budget balance problems and is thus the reverse of State 1. In State 1 the country with the balance of payments deficit was having to fight a domestic inflation of money expenditures by undesirably high tax rates, while the country with a balance of payments surplus was having to slash taxes to fight domestic deflation. Tighter money in Delta and easier money in Sigma was the obvious answer. But in State 2 easier money in Delta would be needed to fight deflation but would make the balance of payments worse; and the tighter money which would be needed in Sigma to help to fight inflation would make the balance of payments surplus still worse.

In this case the rule book previously devised for the single country instructs Delta to depreciate and Sigma to appreciate its currency, Delta relying as little as possible on a rise, and Sigma as little as possible on a fall, in interest rates as a means of looking after the balance of payments. In due course the change in the exchange rate should move the balance of trade in Delta's favour; the increase in Delta's and decrease in Sigma's foreign investment would then relieve both countries' domestic demand-management problems as well as the problem of the balance of payments between them.

The rules devised for a single country are thus appropriate in this case also and, indeed, would by obvious international co-operation be made even more effective than in the single-country case. During the process of adjustment of the channels of trade resulting from the exchange rate adjustment the balance of payments problem will, as we have seen, continue and may indeed be intensified. To avoid the temporary use on balance of payments grounds of interest rate adjustments which are undesirable on budget balance grounds, Delta will need, and Sigma will have the means, to finance the temporary disequilibrium in the balance of payments. This is the case where official arrangements for the finance of international balances of payments is most desirable and also in the interest of both parties.

Whereas in State 1 both countries have tractable and in State 2 both have intractable budget balance problems, States 3 and 4 are cases where one country has a tractable and the other an intractable budget balance problem. I suggest that in such cases the international rule book should put the onus of responsibility in the first place on the country with the tractable budget problem to initiate action by the adjustment of its interest rate. Let me illustrate by considering State 3, leaving the reader to apply the corresponding analyses to State 4.

In State 3 both countries have to fight undesirable domestic inflationary pressures by excessively high tax rates, but Delta has a deficit on its balance of payments with Sigma. Suppose that Delta raises its interest rate sufficiently to restore equilibrium to its balance of payments by attracting capital funds from Sigma. Sigma will continue presumably to have a budget surplus problem since neither its domestic nor its foreign investment is yet affected.

When the rise in interest rates in Delta has worked out its effect on domestic investment in Delta, Delta's initial budget surplus problem may have been converted into a budget deficit problem. We are then in essence back in State 2, where both countries have intractable budget balance problems, since Delta cannot lower its interest rate nor Sigma raise its interest rate without provoking a re-emergence of the balance of payments disequilibrium between them.

An alternative possibility is that the initial rise in Delta's interest rate, undertaken to establish equilibrium in the balance of payments, will leave Delta still in a budget surplus position. In this case what is needed is a further rise in interest rates in both Delta and Sigma, preserving the interest rate differential needed to maintain equilibrium in the balance of payments between them, but raising the whole structure of interest rates so as to reduce the budget surplus problems in both countries.

Such interest rate adjustment might to all intents and purposes solve both domestic and international problems. But at some point, with interest rate differentials maintained to keep equilibrium in the balance of payments, one of the countries may solve its budget surplus problem long before the other. With interest rate differentials which preserve equilibrium in the balance of payments, there may be no absolute level of the whole structure of interest rates which will at once satisfy budget balance in both countries, so that one will have a budget deficit problem and the other a budget surplus problem.

Once more the world will be back essentially in State 2, where both countries have intractable budget–balance problems. An adjustment of the exchange rate is needed to increase the balance of trade and foreign investment of the country with the budget deficit problem and to decrease the foreign investment of the country with the budget surplus problem. But it should be noted that one cannot deduce from the original State 3 position that, as the rule book for the single country would suggest, Sigma should be the country to appreciate its currency. We do not in fact know from the original State 3 position that, as the rule book for the single country would suggest, Sigma should be the country to appreciate its currency. We do not in fact know from the original State 3 position which country will ultimately be left with the intractable budget deficit problem and which with an intractable budget surplus problem when the appropriate adjustments of interest rate differentials and structures have been made.

This analysis suggests that, for a world order in which countries are making successful use of fiscal and wage-fixing policies to maintain full employment and to control inflation, the following five guidelines for international co-operation in monetary and foreign-exchange policies would be appropriate.

1. All countries with tractable budget balance problems should use domestic monetary and interest rate policies so as to maintain equilibrium in their balance of international payments. If this rule is effectively observed, any remaining balance of payments problems will be associated with intractable budget balance problems and the world economy will be in State 2 in my schema.

2. Guideline 1 might, however, solve all balance of payments problems but leave all countries with only budget deficit problems. A second guideline should, therefore, be that when the world economy is suffering, not so much from balance of payments problems, but from a general need to use fiscal policies to fight the threat of inflation of money expenditures, there should be co-operation to tighten national monetary policies so as to raise the whole structure of interest rates without affecting the differentials needed to preserve balance of payments equilibrium. And conversely, if the world-wide problem is a fight against deflation of money expenditures.

3. This concerns exchange rate policy and states that there should be international co-operation for normal, continuous, gradual exchange rate adjustment to maintain international trade competitiveness unchanged as domestic policies for the control of inflation lead to some moderate divergences in the developments of national money price and cost levels.

4. If the first three guidelines are observed, the remaining problems will be those of individual countries facing intractable budget balance problems. Structural exchange rate adjustments should be made to increase the competitiveness of the products of countries with intractable budget deficit problems and/or to decrease the competitiveness of countries with intractable budget surplus problems, and should be confined to such cases.

5. Where structural exchange rate adjustments are made under guideline 4, co-operative arrangements should be made for the official financing of the balances of payments of such deficit or surplus countries, while the exchange rate adjustment is working out its effect on the balances of trade.

4 A new approach to the balance of payments

Tim Congdon

The balance of payments remains in the forefront of policy-makers' attention in many countries, particularly in the Third World. Discussion has been given new urgency by the prospect of default by sovereign borrowers, unable to repay substantial bank debts incurred in the 1960s and 1970s. As these practical problems have been subjected to considerable theoretical analysis, it may seem surprising that there is anything novel to say. However, the argument of this paper is that valuable insights can be gained by a new method of formulating the balance of payments. The critical point of departure from previous work is to divide the economy into the public and private sectors, and to assess their contribution to a nation's overall balance of payments separately. By suggesting that a deficit incurred by the private sector results from freely taken decisions by individuals and is not a problem for policy-makers, the spotlight is turned onto the deficit incurred by the public sector. A government's payments difficulties are interrelated with fiscal and debt management problems. Indeed, we shall claim that the central misunderstanding of traditional theories has been to regard the balance of payments problem as distinct from the problems of the budget deficit and government debt sales. The provocative conclusion reached here is that these supposedly independent problems are, in fact, one and the same.

This has drastic implications. The most important is that restrictions on international trade and financial flows are of little value in curing payments imbalance. They help only in so far as they improve tax revenues or increase domestic acquisition of public sector debt or, in other words, only because they affect fiscal and monetary variables. It would be more honest, and also less prone to cause distortions, to operate on these variables directly. There is an obvious

---

The author is Economic Advisor to Gerrard and National and is the author of 'Monetary Control in Britain' (Macmillan, 1982). This paper first appeared in *Lloyds Bank Review*, 1 October 1982.

message for the many Third World nations which, in response to balance of payments weakness, are now busy erecting tariff and non-tariff barriers to trade. But the point is equally relevant for advanced industrial countries. In the UK, the Cambridge Economic Policy Group has warned that the balance of payments is damned beyond redemption by adverse long-term import trends and that the only reliable method of countering these trends is import control. Although its prognosis has not so far proved correct, the Group's work has attracted much comment and seems to have encouraged the Labour Party to favour import restrictions. The ideas developed in this paper suggest that, on the contrary, import restrictions would be almost useless as an antidote to international payments imbalance.

To help organize the argument we start with the familiar flow-of-funds identity. This states that the foreign sector's financial position is the counterpart to that of the public and private sectors combined.

Overseas sector's net acquisition of financial assets (NAFA)
= public sector's NAFA + private sector's NAFA

When the overseas sector's net acquisition of financial assets is positive, a country is running a current-account deficit. The conventional view is that a 'problem' exists if the deficit is unsustainably large and must be corrected by policy action. We may break down the total current-account deficit into two parts.

Current-account deficit = public sector deficit + private sector deficit

This is not strictly accurate because either the public or private sector might have a positive NAFA outweighed by a negative NAFA by the other, but it simplifies the discussion to assume that both sectors contribute — at least, in an arithmetical sense — to the current account deficit.

The private sector position

Let us suppose initially that the current-account deficit is attributable to the private sector. The private sector is running into debt with the rest of the world.

Why does this matter? Within an economy it is an everyday event for companies and individuals to borrow from one another. They do so with advantage because they have different time preferences, different production opportunities or different cash flow patterns.

Equally, it is possible for the set of private companies and individuals which comprise one economy to incur debt to the set of private companies and individuals which comprise another economy. Although every agent is acting independently, in the aggregate the private sector agents in one country have a current account deficit. Since the numerous borrowing decisions responsible for the deficit are taken freely, it is unclear why the government should be concerned or why policy needs to be amended. Perhaps, as Corden has remarked, 'One should . . . just assume for the purposes of discussing balance-of-payments issues that the private sector knows what it is doing, and what is good for it, as far as its spending and savings decisions are concerned.'[1]

The objection might be raised that private sector agents may not be properly informed about the eventual results of particular financial transactions across frontiers. But the domestic and foreign agents concerned have to make their own judgement about the credit-worthiness of the debt incurred. The task of ensuring that it can be serviced and repaid falls on them, not on the government.

In the past, many countries have registered persistent private sector current-account deficits with no detriment to their economies. The characteristic explanation is that they have been able to cover the deficits by capital inflows, normally attracted by a better rate of return than in the source country. The consequent higher level of capital accumulation has accelerated the growth of output, including exports, and enabled the debts to be repaid without difficulty. A classic illustration is provided by the USA in the nineteenth century. In the decade to 1878 its trade deficit averaged 0.8 per cent of net national product and the current-account deficit, boosted by interest and dividend payments to foreign investors, was even larger. But in the early twentieth century it began to earn substantial trade surpluses and became a capital exporter.[2]

Another possibility is that the domestic private sector may experience a temporary dip in income due, for example, to an adverse terms of trade shift. If consumption is related to 'permanent income', private individuals may wish to borrow from abroad in the expectation of better times ahead. If their expectations prove correct, and no one should be able to make forecasts better than themselves, they will be able to repay when the improvement materializes. ('Permanent income' is a concept advanced by Friedman in his 1957 study on *A Theory of the Consumption Function*. It abstracts from 'accidental' or 'chance' influences on income.)

But some economists might protest that these arguments are based on too sharp a differentiation between public and private sector decision-taking. What happens if a private sector current-account deficit emerges because companies and individuals misinterpret macro-economic signals given by unsound official policy? When these signals are shown to have been wrong and the private sector cannot repay, should not the blame be placed on the government? And does not this carry the implication that policy-makers should be worried about a private sector current-account deficit and take remedial measures if they think it excessive?

These questions raise some potentially awkward issues. The most troublesome example is where a central bank keeps interest rates 'too low', promoting heavy borrowing by the private sector and hence leading to a current-account deficit. But it is necessary to remember that, unless they are prevented by official restrictions, private sector agents have discretion about the currency in which debts are denominated. Suppose that interest rates in, say, Brazil are 'too low', that bank credit and so the money supply are expanding quickly, and that the cruzeiro is under pressure. The probability of depreciation is known to private agents at home and abroad. Foreign lenders and Brazilian borrowers can intermediate in cruzeiros or, if they so wish, in dollars or another recognized convertible currency. The foreigners — aware that depreciation of claims expressed in cruzeiro terms is likely — will take this into account when drawing up debt contracts. If they have little trust in the Brazilian bank because it is setting 'too low' interest rates, Brazilian individuals will be unable to borrow in cruzeiros from foreigners. It is a mistake to imagine that central banks can saddle residents of their country with huge foreign debts by tampering with interest rates in home currency terms. Of course, if Brazilians borrow in dollars they will have to pay a more appropriate interest rate and any exchange rate loss due to cruzeiro depreciation.[3]

The plain fact is that risk attaches — and, in a market economy, is understood to attach — to every credit transaction between private agents. Part of this risk stems from the difficulty of forecasting macro-economic trends. This element in risk is found in borrowing and lending between residents of the same country. The main new dimension in borrowing and lending between residents of different countries is exchange rate variation. But, just as a central bank is not responsible for compensating agents in its own country when they have been upset by an unexpected interest rate change, so it should not be responsible for compensating agents at home or abroad because of an unexpected exchange rate change. The Federal Reserve need be no more involved if a company in Brazil defaults on a dollar loan than if a company in Massachusetts does so. By extension, why should a current-account deficit between the private sectors of the USA and Brazil be of any more interest to it than a current-account deficit between the private individuals of Massachusetts and California?

It is quite possible that, after international financial flows, private sector agents in both debtor and creditor countries find they have made mistakes. But, when one party to a credit transaction undertaken between nationals of one country defaults, there is no presumption that the government will automatically help the other party. It is therefore unclear why the government of one country should intervene if its citizens fail to honour their foreign debts. Apart from providing law courts to arbitrate on disputes, the state has no particular duty or obligation. To put the argument at its most polemical, there is no such thing as a balance of payments 'problem' between consenting adults.

The government's position

The matter is quite different when we consider a current-account deficit attributable to the government's behaviour. The deficit can be covered either by drawing down foreign currency reserves or by increasing external indebtedness. Reserve depletion is a finite process and must, at some stage, be reversed. There must also be some upper limit to the external indebtedness a government can tolerate, although the scope for debate about what that limit may be is considerable. Since both reserve depletion and foreign borrowing cannot continue for ever, a public sector current-account deficit poses a genuine problem for policy-makers. They must sooner or later take action to solve it. But what action is needed?

The answer is contained in the identity:

Public sector current-account deficit = Public sector financial deficit − sales of public sector debt to the domestic private sector (including money creation)

This makes the obvious statement that the public sector's contribution to a current account deficit is equal to the total increase in its financial liabilities minus that part of the total increase taken up by domestic savings. It is clear that the external deficit can be reduced in two ways — by reducing the public sector financial deficit (which, from now on, we shall call 'the budget deficit' for brevity) or by increasing domestic sales of public sector debt. Any policy measure which does not affect the budget deficit or the domestic demands for government debt is futile as a response to balance of payments difficulties; any measure which does affect these two variables also changes the public sector's current-account deficit. As we have already argued that the private sector's current account is not a relevant concern for policy-makers, it follows that the solution to payments imbalance is to be sought only in fiscal or debt management policy. This is a strong assertion. If it is accepted, much previous analysis of the balance of payments is superseded.

There is no doubt that economists have not in the past seen balance of payments problems exclusively in fiscal terms. In the next two sections we shall, therefore, consider the characteristic symptoms of payments imbalance in two recent periods, the fixed exchange rate regime before 1971 and the floating exchange rate regime subsequently, and relate these symptoms to fiscal and debt management policies.

A typical balance of payments crisis in the 1950s and 1960s

In the Bretton Woods system of fixed exchange rates one key pressure-gauge for assessing balance of payments difficulties was the movement in foreign currency reserves. Central banks were expected to sell foreign currency and buy their own if the exchange rate was in trouble. By using their ammunition of accumulated dollars they could fight back against speculative attacks on their currency; if the ammunition was exhausted they had to admit defeat and accept the ultimate disgrace of devaluation. According to Johnson, the balance of payments concept relevant to 'policy properly defined and to the corresponding instruments of macroeconomic policy is the net inflow or outflow of international reserves'.[4] The theme can be dated back to his celebrated 1958 paper, 'Towards a general theory of the balance of payments', in which he stated that the 'balance of payments relevant to economic analysis' was the difference between residents' receipts from and payments to foreigners, with a deficit being 'financed by sales of domestic currency by residents or foreigners to the exchange authority in exchange for foreign currency'.[5] Johnson clearly assumed the presence of an exchange authority, in the form of a central bank, acting as the principal intermediary between the citizens of one country and those of another. The pivotal role of such an authority was emphasized by the 'official settlements' definition of the balance of payments, which for several years in the late 1960s and early 1970s was deemed the best indicator of the need for policy adjustment. It corresponded roughly to the change in reserves, although it also included items which would alter the monetary authorities' international creditor/debtor position without affecting the reserves.

The need was to derive a theory which accounted for changes in the reserves. The monetary approach to the balance of payments was developed, notably by Johnson, in response to this need. It explained how the official settlements balance of payments was determined by the difference between the increase in the demand for money and domestic credit expansion. As such, it was 'a monetary phenomenon, representing a disequilibrium in the demand for money', Johnson made strong claims for the monetary approach — for example, that it debunked much Keynesian analysis which had paid excessive attention to aggregate expenditure decisions as an influence on international payments.

But our formulation contains an alternative explanation of the official settlements balance. We make the assumption that the central bank has only two assets — claims on the domestic government and foreign-currency reserves. In the 1950s and 1960s this would have been a realistic assumption in the overwhelming majority of countries. We also assume that the central bank is reluctant to expand its liabilities because additions to high-powered money may become the raw material for excessive growth of bank credit. In this case, if the government fails to borrow from the domestic private sector to cover its budget deficit, it must appeal to the central bank. The central bank can meet the demand only by selling foreign exchange — and any sales represent a deficit on official settlements. We seem to have turned Johnson's argument on its head. Far from being a monetary phenomenon, the official settlements balance of payments can be interpreted in fiscal terms. The solution to unfavourable official settlements is to be sought in reductions in the budget deficit or more aggressive attempts to sell government debt to domestic entities other than the central bank.

In fact, our conceptual somersault is only apparent. It is largely a semantic artefact and should not be taken too seriously. The budget deficit itself constitutes part of domestic credit expansion and may therefore be regarded as a monetary variable, while the demand for public sector debt is susceptible to monetary policy shifts, particularly changes in interest rates. There is no abrupt cleavage between monetary and fiscal instruments.

However, by stating the problem in fiscal terms some fresh insights have been generated. We have identified the government as the most likely culprit for an unsustainable imbalance on official settlements. The sequence of sterling crises in the UK illustrated the point clearly. Following recommendations from its Keynesian advisers, the government from time to time embarked on fiscal reflation which involved a deliberate increase in the budget deficit. After a relatively short period, often no more than a year or eighteen months, there was a run on the reserves. The official reply was typically a 'package' of public expenditure cuts, taxation increases and higher interest rates. The balance of payments then convalesced and the reserve position improved. A rise in unemployment followed, prompting another bout of fiscal reflation, another sterling crisis and another 'package'. In Brittan's words, 'Chancellors behaved like simple Pavlovian dogs responding to two main stimuli: one was "a run on the reserves" and the other was "500 000 unemployed" — a figure which was later increased to above 600 000.'[6] The stop-go cycle may be interpreted as reflecting the imcompatibility of increased budget deficits with the maintenance of a fixed exchange rate against the dollar. This incompatibility was signalled by a fall in reserves.

A typical balance of payments crisis in the 1970s and early 1980s

The Bretton Woods regime of fixed exchange rates was effectively terminated by the USA's decision to suspend the convertibility of the dollar into gold in August 1971. Since then the major currencies have for most of the time been floating against each other. This has changed the form of the typical balance of payments crisis. In the 1950s and 1960s, when the reserves were both the first and last line of defence, a run on the reserves necessitated early action on the budget deficit or interest rates. Today the option of devaluation is also available. The environment for deficit countries has become more permissive in another respect. Large international capital markets with the capacity to lend to governments for balance of payments financing have developed, with OPEC members being an important source of funds after the oil price rise of 1973–4. Instead of having to appeal to the International Monetary Fund, which imposed conditions to ensure a return to payments balance within a set timetable, deficit countries have been able to borrow from private commercial banks. As long as the banks have been persuaded that their loans will be repaid eventually, they have not been as rigorous as the IMF in expecting responsible macro-economic policies.

The two new choices — devaluation and borrowing — have changed governments' perceptions about how they should meet payments difficulties. Particularly in the Third World, but also among many industrial countries attitudes have become more lax. Budget deficits represent a much higher proportion of national income in nearly all countries. Are the frequency of devaluation and the scale of borrowing for balance of payments purposes related to these large budget deficits and, if so, in what ways?

We stated earlier that the public sector current-account deficit was equal to the budget deficit minus domestic debt sales. At first sight, devaluation is not much help in curing the deficit because it has no obvious repercussions on either the budgetary position or debt sales. However, this is too superficial a view. There are indirect relationships, working through the balance sheets of the central bank and the domestic commercial banks, between devaluation and a government's ability to finance its deficit internally.

Devaluation is usually followed by a rise in the price level. The higher price level is accompanied by an increased demand for both the monetary base and money (that is, an increased willingness to hold the liabilities of the central bank and the commercial banks). As a result the banking system can expand its assets without disturbing monetary equilibrium. The central bank, as banker to the government, is always under an obligation to take on more public sector debt. In an economy free from official regulations, the commercial banks might refuse to lend to government if they thought the loans would be unprofitable. But in most Third World countries the banks are either nationalized or subject to some degree of official arm-twisting. They have to accept new public sector debt in their balance sheets.

In other words, devaluation enables a government to increase its domestic debt sales. The higher price level associated with it causes the private sector to wish to hold more notes and coin, and more bank deposits. By holding more monetary assets economic agents are — through a slightly circuitous route — purchasing more government debt. Notes and coin are claims on the central bank, but the central bank matches them by claims on government; and deposits are liabilities of banks, but banks match them by investing in government paper.

Indeed, it is an open question whether devaluation should be regarded as a method of promoting domestic debt sales or as a way of levying the inflation tax. An econometric analysis of Italy's exchange rate movements in the 1970s concluded that, 'the monetary financing of over one-third of the government's deficit effectively implied that . . . nine-tenths of the increase in the total monetary base was accounted for by the Treasury, causing an expansion in high-powered money well in excess of that which would have been consistent with a reasonable stability in the value of the lira'. Its author judged that 'the sharp increase in the monetary base plus inflation meant that the public paid a growing part of taxes in the form of the inflation tax on money balances. Indeed, according to some rough estimates I have made in the three years 1972–5 the yield from this tax turned out to be almost equal to that from income tax.'[7]

But Italy is only a mild example of the problems which can arise. In many Third World countries, particularly in Latin America, devaluation is almost synonymous with inflation. Consequently, it may seem preferable for a government with a large budget deficit to borrow abroad. No hard-and-fast criteria for deciding whether a government's external debt is excessive have been agreed. Clearly, one requirement for the sustainability of a foreign borrowing programme is that the citizens are willing to pay sufficient taxes to cover interest charges and maturing capital payments. But the question of the government's ability to repay principal is more awkward and problematic. There is no obvious rule which says whether a particular ratio of public sector foreign debt to taxable capacity (usually proxied by national income) is too high. Sovereign risk is a very controversial subject among bankers. In principle, a government could be running a continuous current account deficit as long as the resulting growth of its foreign debt and servicing costs is no faster than the growth of its national income. The situation becomes unsustainable only when this condition is violated. In that case the government must sooner or later take measures to reduce its foreign borrowing. If no measures are taken, the government will finally be unable to pay interest and will have to seek rescheduling of its debt.

Balance of payments crises since 1971 have, therefore, been rather different dramas from those in the 1950s and 1960s. Whereas the main actors in the play used to be the government and the IMF, and the most absorbing item of stage scenery a change in the reserves, today international bankers have been added to the cast, and devaluation and debt service ratios to the props. But the responsibility for balance of payment problems still rests with governments and their budget deficits.

The futility of direct restrictions

Direct restrictions imposed for balance of payments reasons are of two main kinds — import controls and exchange controls. Are either of any value in solving a public sector current-account deficit?

Import controls on private sector transactions are by themselves of little use. A public sector current-account deficit is equal to the difference between two numbers — the public sector financial deficit and sales of public sector debt to the domestic private sector. Import controls can reduce it only in so far as they affect these variables. Tariffs yield revenue to the government and therefore lower the budget deficit. But, otherwise there are no obvious linkages at work.[8] Some favourite Third World responses to payments imbalance, such as quotas or placing luxuries on a list or prohibited imports, are futile, as public sector finances are unaffected. Aside from the boost to revenue from tariffs, import controls are pointless as an instrument for reducing the public sector's current-account deficit. Nothing more needs to be said.

Exchange controls are more interesting. The most characteristic exchange control is a requirement that the private citizens of a country keep no foreign exchange in their own names and transfer any holdings to the central bank in return for domestic currency. Two observations may be made here.

First, exchange control may be viewed as serving the same function as devaluation. It increases the private sector's demand for government debt. When private sector agents are legally obliged to surrender foreign exchange to the central bank, they receive central bank liabilities in return (i.e. that is, high-powered money in the form of notes or balances at the central bank). More frankly, they are forced to invest in the central bank. The central bank, as banker to the government, in turn invests in public sector debt. The private sector has indirectly financed the public sector deficit and may, to that extent, have reduced the public current-account imbalance. However, this arrangement, which in any case is rather distasteful since it rests on compulsion, is unstable. If the private sector's holdings of high-powered money are above desired levels because of exchange controls, it attempts to reduce them. It can do so most obviously by using the excess high-powered money as the base for inflationary credit expansion. The monetary authorities may hinder this by introducing credit restrictions on private banks. This reaction is extremely common and helps explain why so many central banks throughout the world are to be seen enforcing exchange controls and administrative credit restrictions simultaneously. The panoply of controls may be interpreted as the result of competition between the government and private sector for foreign exchange and, at a deeper level, for resources of any kind.

Second, exchange control resembles inflation in that it is a form of taxation. Without exchange control private sector agents would not convert their foreign currency into domestic. It follows that, after compulsory conversion, there is excess supply of the domestic currency and its market clearing price (in terms of foreign currency) is beneath the official price. The difference between the market clearing and official exchange rates is an incentive for the creation of black markets. It is also a measure of the government's exchange control tax. As an instrument of taxation, exchange control enables governments to finance their foreign purchases at a lower price in domestic-currency terms than would otherwise be the case. In this sense, it reduces the public sector financial deficit. The success of exchange control as a tax is, however, hazardous to estimate in advance, since the government cannot know what proportion of the private sector's foreign exchange may seep out through the black market. The existence of black markets is another symptom of competition between government and the private sector for resources; it is the result of government failure to pay for its expenditure by more visible and honest forms of taxation.

We have to concede that exchange controls, if they are effective, may cut the public sector's current-account deficit. But they do so through means — taxation and increasing domestic demand for public sector debt — which have always been available to governments in more transparent forms. Exchange controls have no merits compared to the conventional techniques and they suffer from several obvious disadvantages. Not least among these disadvantages is the contempt for government aroused by the arbitrary character of the exchange control tax.

The need for responsible budgetary policies

In summary, the message of the new approach to the balance of payments is that only foreign debts incurred by the public sector constitute a balance of payments problem and that the only solution is the pursuit of more appropriate fiscal and debt management policies. A further implication is that a country whose government has adopted responsible budgetary policies cannot have external payments difficulties. The new approach provides reinforcement for the 'old-time religion' of sound finance and balanced budgets.

But the contrast between the white of private sector deficits and the black of public sector deficits should not be exaggerated. There are grey areas. Two deserve particular mention, as they are of some topical interest. The first is where public sector agencies borrow abroad to finance capital projects. If these are expected to generate a rate of return above the cost of funds, no extra burden is imposed on the taxpayer and no strong case for differentiating this form of public foreign borrowing from private can be argued. The second arises when heavy overseas borrowing is conducted by private banks, which on-lend to companies and individuals. This should be distinguished from credit flowing directly from foreign entities to the domestic private sector because bank deposits are in most countries guaranteed by the central bank, which is a public sector body. If the companies and individuals who ultimately receive the funds are unable to repay the banks, the central bank has to interfere to protect depositors' interests. Central bank interference is necessarily a matter of public policy. This unintentional involvement of government in private sector financial transactions has occurred in some Latin American countries. A notable example is Chile which, in 1980 and 1981, simultaneously had a budget surplus and a big current-account deficit stemming from heavy private sector borrowing abroad. In 1982, many of the private sector loans went wrong and central bank refinancing of the bad debts contributed to a sizable budget deficit. Despite cautious fiscal policies, excessive borrowing by the private sector eventually undermined the country's credit rating.

These two special cases are only minor qualifications to the central theme. They in no sense invalidate the emphasis on fiscal policy as the key to the balance of payments 'problem'. Indeed, if bankers want to avoid some of the sovereign debt difficulties they are now facing, they should in future focus on fiscal variables to assess a government's ability to repay. The abundance of a country's natural resources is of limited value unless they can be translated into tax revenue. Assertions such as 'Mexico has oil' and 'Argentina's agricultural potential is so great that its finances can always be turned round' have been heard to justify the large loans extended to these two nations over the last decade. But Mexico's oil and Argentina's agricultural potential are not by themselves any help to foreign bankers holding claims on their governments. Bankers need dollars, not oil or beef. The only way, apart from borrowing, that the Mexican or Argentinian governments can obtain dollars is by purchasing them with local currency; and the only way, apart from printing, that these governments can acquire surplus local currency is by having an excess of tax receipts over expenditure. If there is no prospect of a Third World government reorganizing its public sector finances after a foreign borrowing programme, it is unwise for banks to participate in that programme while it is under way.

Although reschedulings of Third World debt are the most topical application of the new approach to the balance of payments, it is also relevant to recent policy debates in the developed countries. It shows, for example, that the Cambridge Economic Policy Group's advocacy of import controls as an answer to future payments imbalance in the UK is misguided and unsound. There is a balance of payments problem only if the government has a financial deficit which it cannot cover by domestic debt sales. A reliable method of creating such a problem would be fiscal reflation of the kind proposed in the 'alternative economic strategy' and supported by the CEPG. There is a further irony. Our approach to the balance of payments resembles the New Cambridge School theory of the mid-1970s. The gravamen of this theory, also developed by the CEPG, was that the government's budget deficit — and only the government's budget deficit — was responsible for payments imbalance. Cambridge economists seem not to have recognized that this conclusion is inconsistent with their subsequent enthusiasm for import controls. Tariffs on finished manufactures would mitigate the problem to the extent that they boosted tax revenue, but otherwise they would be quite pointless.

If the government wants to avoid external constraints on economic policy, it should ensure that budgetary policy remains responsible. As long as the public sector borrowing requirement is a low and declining proportion of national income, the UK will not suffer from a balance of payments problem.

Notes

1. W.M. Corden, *Inflation, Exchange Rates and the World Economy*, Oxford, 1977, p. 45. The aim of the present paper can be regarded as giving Corden's insight further elaboration.
2. G.E. Wood and D.R. Mudd, 'The recent US trade deficit', *Federal Reserve Bank of St Louis Review*, April 1978, p. 3.
3. I have clarified my thinking on this point after correspondence with Professor W.M. Corden. There is a special difficulty if the central bank, a public sector entity, is borrowing abroad at high interest rates and then extending cheap credit to the domestic private sector.
4. See H.G. Johnson, 'The monetary theory of imbalance-of-payments policies' in J.A. Frenkel and H.G. Johnson (eds), *The Monetary Approach to the Balance of Payments*, London, 1976, p. 262.
5. H.G. Johnson, 'Towards a general theory of the balance of payments' in *International Trade and Economic Growth*, 1958, pp. 153–68; reprinted in R.N. Cooper (ed.), *International Finance*, Harmondsworth, 1969, pp. 237–55. The quotations are from Cooper's collection, p. 239.
6. Brittan, *Steering the Economy*, Harmondsworth, 1971, p. 455.
7. R. Masera, 'The interaction between money, the exchange rate and prices: the Italian experience in the 1970s' in A.S. Courakis (ed.), *Inflation, Depression and Economic Policy in the West*, London, 1981, p. 244.
8. In countries where collection costs of domestic taxes are high, 'tariffs and export taxes may form part of a first-best tax package' (W.M. Corden, *Trade Policy and Economic Welfare*, Oxford, 1974, p. 66). In fact, there are many developing countries where tariffs are introduced or raised explicitly for revenue-raising rather than protectionist purposes.

Part 2 The development of exchange rates from the 1970s to the 1990s

5 Prospects for the dollar standard

Gottfried Haberler

After more than half a year of turmoil in the exchange markets and extensive floating, the international monetary system again came to rest on 18 December 1971 — at least for the time being. It took President Nixon's bombshell of 15 August 1971, the imposition of an import surcharge, official declaration of the inconvertibility of the dollar into gold, innumerable high-level conferences and several summit meetings to bring about a large realignment of currency values and an optional wider 'band' (around par values or 'central rates of exchange') which has been accepted by most countries.

The questions I shall discuss are: In what respect is the present system different from what we had before 15 August 1971, apart from the realignment and wider band? Is it at all viable and how long will it last? Where do we go from here? What are some options for international monetary reform and the chance of their realization? A central question will be the convertibility of the dollar.

What has changed?

Contrary to what has been widely predicted and confidently diagnosed — 'the Bretton Woods system is finished', 'the dollar standard is now history' – the international monetary system is pretty much what it was before August 1971. It is not surprising that the IMF, as a bureaucratic institution, survives. (International agencies never die. The best example is the Bank for International Settlements. It was officially declared dead and ordered to be interred in the Bretton Woods agreement; but there it is, alive and active). Actually, the Fund functions as it did before. Exchange rates have been drastically realigned, the dollar sharply devalued[1] and most countries, the largest trading nations among them, have adopted a wider band.

The author was formerly Resident Scholar at the American Enterprise Institute for Public Policy Research and Galen L. Stone Professor of International Trade, Harvard University. This paper first appeared in *Lloyds Bank Review*, 1 July 1972.

The dollar is still by far the most important international reserve, official intervention and private transaction currency. It has lost some of its lustre, there is much talk about reducing its role in the international monetary system, and it has been demonstrated that, contrary to what was widely assumed, the dollar can be devalued, although with great difficulties and under heavy pressure applied by the USA. In fact, the gold-dollar standard has for the time being been replaced by a pure dollar standard, as the Deutsche Bundesbank pointed out in its annual report for 1971.[2] Countries in surplus again buy dollars, adding to their reserves, to prevent their currencies from rising above the upper intervention point. Countries in deficit sell dollars from their reserves to keep their currencies from falling below the intervention point. And the USA again follows a passive policy, a policy of benign neglect with regard to the balance of payments, after the very active, if not aggressive, policy, adopted on 15 August 1971 had achieved its proximate goal: devaluation of the dollar and realignment of exchange rates.

Passive policy means, briefly, two things: first, that domestic monetary, fiscal and other general economic policies are guided by domestic policy objectives — price stability, employment, growth — and not by balance of payments considerations; second, that intervention in the exchange market and initiatives to change exchange rates are left to other countries. It does *not* mean lack of interest in the organization of the international monetary system, neglect of the interests of other countries, or indifference to the dangers of inflation.

How long will the calm last?

Ever since the Smithsonian accord of 18 December 1971, doubts about its viability have been widespread. Advocates of exchange flexibility have freely predicted that new crises are inevitable. In our present world, a fixed-rate system cannot work smoothly, they think, and the wider band can stave off only minor disturbances. Advocates of a truly international currency system, too, are sceptical of the present arrangement; the dollar standard is no longer acceptable, they believe. And the framers of the December accord themselves regard it as an interim solution; part of the agreement was, indeed, that 'discussion should be promptly undertaken — to consider reform of the international monetary system'.

Difficulties arose, in fact, soon after the Smithsonian agreement. At first, the dollar was near the upper end of the new band, presumably in anticipation of the widely expected repatriation of funds to the USA. When the back-flow did not materialize, the dollar fell later in January close to the lower intervention point and some foreign central banks had to buy dollars to prevent their currencies from rising above the permitted margin. In March, the dollar strengthened and there seems to have been a considerable back-flow of funds, partly the result of the shrinking interest differential, but probably largely attracted by the rising stock market, which, in turn, reflects the quickening pace of recovery.

US monetary policy had been sharply criticized both at home and abroad for letting short-term interest rates fall to low levels and thereby discouraging the back-flow of dollars. To my mind, this criticism was not justified and its full implications are rarely spelled out. To be sure, the Federal Reserve could make money sufficiently tight to induce a return flow of funds. But that surely would slow up recovery of output and employment. The critics should make it clear whether they wish to suggest that the USA should accept slower recovery and more unemployment for the sake of the balance of payments or that there is a possibility of raising interest rates sufficiently without adversely affecting recovery and employment.

The first suggestion, which may indeed be entertained by some foreign critics, is simply unacceptable and unrealistic. No US government — nor that of any other country — will consciously tolerate or create significantly more unemployment than may be needed anyway to curb inflation, solely for the purpose of improving the balance of payments. That it should be possible, on the other hand, to push up short-term interest rates sufficiently without adversely influencing recovery and employment is highly improbable. Some critics may have in mind what used to be called 'operation twist': that is to say, that short-term interest rates should be pushed up and long-term rates pushed down. The idea was that lower long-term rates would favourably affect the internal situation, while higher short-term rates would improve international capital flows. But this theory is defective for two reasons: First, it is very difficult, if not impossible, to twist significantly the structure of interest rates, and second, even if it could be done, the differential effect of a twist on internal and external equilibrium is more than doubtful.

Alternatively, the critics may think of 'operation mix': that is, to use fiscal policy for influencing the internal situation and monetary policy for improving the balance of payments. But quite apart from serious theoretical objections that could be raised about the effectiveness of 'operation mix', the argument overlooks the fact that fiscal policy is already extremely expansionary, with an estimated record deficit for 1971–2 of over $30 billion. A still larger budget deficit would hardly strengthen confidence in the dollar.

What should we conclude from this? Since the members of the Group of Ten wanted to return to fixed exchange rates and refused to accept a larger devaluation of the dollar in terms of their currencies, they should get used to sailing in a boat with an elephant — if I may use Mr Trudeau's colourful expression which Dr Emminger has very aptly applied to the dollar. Under fixed exchanges, minor heaves of the giant American economy can produce large flows of dollars across the border.

But is the present arrangement, the dollar standard, at all tolerable? My own opinion is that, abstracting from political and prestige considerations and assuming for the moment that the USA is able to keep inflation under control, the dollar standard could work quite well without imposing hardships on other countries.[3] It is worth elaborating briefly, first, because the dollar standard is likely to remain with us for some time until alternative arrangements can be worked out; and second, because many of its features would not be essentially changed after an SDR standard or something like it had been set up. Of course, the USA, as well as other countries, especially the members of the Group of Ten, would have to observe the rules of the game. These rules are not hard to formulate, or difficult or onerous to observe. Countries other than the USA, when in persistent deficit which they can no longer finance by depleting reserves, or by *ad hoc* borrowing, should promptly depreciate their currencies or, better, let them float. Countries in persistent surplus, if they do not wish to add to their reserves or to let prices go up, should promptly appreciate their currencies or, better, let them float up.

The greatest, nay indispensable, American contribution to the working of the system is to curb inflation. But, even if the price rise in America is reduced to internally acceptable proportions, we cannot be sure that dollar balances abroad will not continue to grow. So long as the dollar remains the most important international reserve currency and SDR creation is not sufficiently stepped up, there will be an upward trend in official, as well as private, dollar balances held abroad. Even if normal increases in reserve needs are satisfied by increasing SDR allocations, the USA could again develop a deficit. Moreover, without anything wrong with the US balance of payments, if any major currency, the Deutschmark or the yen, seems to become ripe for revaluation, dollar balances, official and private, from all over the world will converge on the countries concerned. Thus, a Deutschmark or yen crisis can easily take on the appearance of a dollar crisis.

I suggest that the USA should take a tolerant view if other countries accumulate dollars. Anyone who prefers to take dollars rather than real goods in exchange for part of his exports should be regarded as a benefactor and not as an evildoer. The opposite view, which is prevalent in the USA and elsewhere, reflects a mercantilistic fallacy. But mercantilism often has a grain of truth. Let us try to separate truth from fallacy.

Pressure on surplus countries

It will be recalled that an important feature of the Keynes plan for monetary reform was that surplus countries should be subjected to pressures to do their share in the balance of payments adjustment. The ruling system, in Keynes's view, put the whole burden of adjustment upon the deficit countries. What Keynes was afraid of, with experience of the 1930s in mind, was deflation in the deficit countries. Ever since, with or without reference to Keynes, plans for international monetary reform have invariably contained proposals to apply pressure, or even sanctions, against surplus countries, as well as against deficit countries.

The great concern with surpluses seems to me largely anachronistic, for the simple reason that practically no country, certainly not the USA is willing anymore to permit deflation and unemployment for the sake of the balance of payments. Needless to add, unemployment is still a very serious problem in the USA and elsewhere. But the reason is domestic dilemmas posed by the coexistence of balance of payment deficits and unemployment do, of course, occur but they are no longer solved by deflation, but by currency devaluation or by imposition of controls. The question of controls will be taken up presently. But the problem of persistent surplus countries requires further discussion from the American standpoint. It is, after all, the dollar that is subject to large accumulation. As yet, no other currency qualifies for that role, although recently there have been complaints that some countries have switched reserves from the dollar to Swiss francs and Deutschmarks.[4]

Why should the USA object to the accumulation of liquid dollar balances abroad? Surplus countries have several options. They can let prices rise or upvalue their currencies or let them float or they can reduce trade barriers and remove capital export restrictions. Clearly, there are no American objections to any of these measures. They can impose controls or engage in 'dirty floating'; to that I come presently. Or they can accumulate dollar balances. This option is supposed to have adverse effects and to present dangerous hazards to the US economy which cannot be tolerated.

A direct deflationary impact, through conversion of dollars into gold or other US reserve assets, of which Keynes was so afraid, is no longer possible. An indirect deflationary effect of dollar accumulation abroad is, however, conceivable if it reflects a trade or current-account deficit.

There exists, in fact, a vague and inarticulate but strong current of apprehension in American government circles which attributes the sub-optimal performance of the American economy at least in part to the deterioration of the trade balance. I find this theory unconvincing, because a $3 billion deficit of the current balance can hardly be regarded as the dominant factor in a trillion-dollar economy. At any rate, if it is true, as I think it is, that US general economic policies are determined by domestic policy objectives (growth, employment) and domestic policy constraints (inflation), the deflationary effect of a $3 billion shortfall of effective demand can and will be offset by monetary and fiscal measures, except for a possible temporary slippage. A $30–40 billion budget deficit supported by appropriate monetary measures should be ample for that purpose.

It has been argued that letting liquid dollars accumulate abroad is risky, because foreign countries sooner or later will get tired of holding dollars and will start to unload, thereby creating harmful instability. To be sure, other countries will not allow dollars to accumulate *ad infinitum*. But they have no way to stop further accumulation or to reduce existing balances other than the options mentioned: inflate, appreciate or impose controls.

The most powerful argument against allowing accumulation of dollars is that it hurts particular American industries. An undervalued yen permits the Japanese to export more cars, textiles, TV sets, and so on, than they would otherwise and this plays into the hands of American protectionists. There obviously is a tiny grain of truth in this argument: in fact, exactly as much — or as little — as in objections to free trade, capital imports or gifts from abroad on the ground that any of these may hurt particular industries and foster protectionism. I have argued elsewhere at greater length that only a small part of the damage done to particular American industries by imports can be attributed to the accumulation of dollars abroad or, expressed differently, to the temporary undervaluation of certain currencies.[5] Here I confine myself to saying that, for the US economy as a whole, since imports are a small fraction of GNP, the small part of imports attributable to dollar accumulations abroad can be only a tiny element.

Instead of inflating, appreciating or accumulating dollars, surplus countries may use controls, including 'dirty floating'. So far as commodity trade is concerned, since the ordinary import-restricting controls would aggravate the imbalance, the controls would have to be negative, so to speak; that is to say, import-stimulating and export-restricting, which can be described as 'dirty-appreciation' of the currency. But the policy is just as unpopular as 'clean appreciation'. Therefore, there is little danger that surplus countries will use 'negative' controls on trade.

Dirty floating — by splitting the exchange market into a 'free' (or loosely controlled) market for capital transactions and a pegged market for current transactions — as it is being practised by Belgium and France, is clearly an inefficient and wasteful method of disguised appreciation of the currency. It leads to evasion, progressive bureaucratization of trade and hurts the countries that engage in these practices as much as, or more than, others. For the USA, it is no more than pinpricks and the proper reaction, to mix a metaphor or two, is to let the dirty floaters stew in their own juice.

I conclude that, from the economic standpoint, the post-Smithsonian dollar standard is manageable and viable. In my opinion, it does not impose a burden on other countries, provided the USA keeps inflation under control. True, even under this assumption some countries, probably only a few, may find themselves with unwanted surpluses, either because their inflation control is better than in the USA or because international demand for their exports happens to be exceptionally favourable. Such countries then have the choice of floating (or appreciating) their currency or inflating their economy a little bit. I say 'little' because under modern conditions with numerous actual and potential export and import commodities the balance of payments is quite elastic in the medium and long run with respect to differential inflation and exchange rate changes.

However, many will say that this is an idealized picture. The fact is that the dollar standard has become rather unpopular both in the USA and abroad. Many Americans see it as a burden and a source of international embarrassment and dispute. And abroad it is widely regarded as an 'exorbitant privilege' of the US (de Gaulle's words). In my opinion, both views greatly exaggerate. It is neither a heavy burden nor an exorbitant privilege, but it has been a great boon for world trade at large. Be that as it may, let me turn to the problem of reform of the system, aimed at reducing the special role of the dollar, making it more equal to other currencies.

There is no lack of more or less ambitious plans of replacing the dollar by SDRs, of pooling and consolidating international reserves in the IMF which would issue SDRs or some composite reserve units ('CRUs') or of confronting the dollar with a new currency — 'Europa', 'Eurofranc' or 'Eurosterling' — of an integrated Europe. Only some general aspects of the problem can be taken up in a short paper. To put the problem in perspective, I first discuss the issue of dollar convertibility.

Dollar convertibility

On 15 August 1971, the dollar was formally declared inconvertible into US reserve assets. *De facto*, it had been inconvertible for quite some time for large drawings, although there had been some nibbling at the US gold stock by small conversion.

Ever since the Smithsonian accord, it has become popular in Europe, though less so in Japan, to demand that steps be taken to make the dollar again convertible. It is fairly generally agreed that convertibility into gold is out and that some bilateral or multilateral funding or consolidation of outstanding official dollar balances (overhang) would have to be achieved before convertibility of the dollar into some ultimate reserve asset could be considered. Even if this were done, the large volume of liquid or semi-liquid dollar liabilities in private hands which could easily find their way into official balances would constitute a potential threat, at least so long as the current (or basic) balance of the USA is in deficit.

The popular proposal that convertibility be restricted to dollar balances currently acquired through a US current (or basic) deficit is not a feasible solution. Surplus countries would ask for gold or SDRs, while deficit countries could not well be denied the right to finance their deficits by drawing down their existing dollar balances. Thus, US reserves could be depleted, even if the overall balance of payments were in equilibrium. Elaborate machinery, involving, *inter alia*, statistical determination of overall and bilateral balances of payments, would be required to cope with this problem.

Enough has been said to confirm the widely-held view that convertibility of the dollar into US reserve assets presupposes a major reconstruction of the international monetary system. To negotiate and carry out such a reform will inevitably take much time, probably years. It is of the utmost importance that, in the meantime, the international payments mechanism continues to function.

Asset versus market convertibility

Until now, world trade has suffered surprisingly little from the numerous currency crises of the last few years, including the dollar crisis of 1971. A factor contributing importantly to that happy result is that, in a deeper sense, the dollar has remained fully convertible all along. We must sharply distinguish between *asset* convertibility and *market* convertibility. In recent discussions, what people have in mind when they exhort the USA to take steps to make the dollar again convertible or, what comes to the same thing, to intervene actively in the exchange market in order to strengthen confidence in the dollar, is *asset* convertibility, convertibility into US reserve assets. But it is *market* convertibility that is important for world trade.

Market convertibility means that anyone can use his dollars not only to buy, invest and disinvest in the USA, but also to convert his dollars into any other currency in the market at the prevailing rate. Foreigners, including foreign central banks, enjoy full market convertibility of their dollars; for Americans, there exist certain restrictions, so far as investments abroad are concerned.

It will be recalled that, in the late 1940s and 1950s, currency convertibility was the topic of a lively international debate. It was market convertibility that was at issue, in other words, the elimination of the numerous stringent controls inherited from the war which inhibited the expansion of the world economy. The present inconvertibility of the dollar 'is not comparable to the inconvertibility of the currencies of other industrial countries in the 1950s', as a recent IMF document put it. At that time, the American government pressed for early restoration of convertibility, while the British government, stunned by the disastrous failure of the premature dash for convertibility in 1947, resisted. The currency realignment of 1949 paved the way for convertibility. In the later 1950s, more and more countries abolished controls and made their currencies convertible under Article VIII of the IMF charter. It was market convertibility that was indispensable for the subsequent rapid growth of world trade. Two things should be stressed. First, it is substantially full and unrestricted convertibility at uniform exchange rates that counts. In some more or less restricted sense, almost every currency is convertible, but some only via narrow black markets. Second, not only is market convertibility entirely compatible with changes in exchange rates and floating rates — thus, the floating Canadian dollar has been fully convertible all along — but market convertibility presupposes realistic exchange rates which in many cases only flexible rates can provide. On the other hand, split exchange markets, dual and multiple exchange rates and other devices of control are the very negation of true convertibility.

To repeat, the dollar is fully convertible in the market sense. For world trade, it is of the utmost importance to keep it convertible, until the dollar is replaced by SDRs or something else in a reconstructed international monetary system. However, it takes more than one country to keep a currency convertible. The USA should

continue its policy of not restricting the market convertibility of the
dollar. But other countries should refrain from reducing convertibility, and thereby damaging world trade, by splitting exchange
markets, introducing dual rates and other types of exchange control,
instead of devaluing or floating their currency when in deficit, or
appreciating or floating their currency if they do not wish to inflate
when in surplus. A few words will be said later about the desirability
of depreciating the dollar in terms of gold and SDRs, if it became
overvalued with respect to many other currencies.

Reconstruction of the system: to reduce the special role of the dollar

If the dollar is to be made convertible — in this section, convertibility
means *asset* convertibility, unless otherwise stated — the dollar
overhang must be eliminated or sharply reduced by multilateral consolidation or pooling. On this, almost everybody seems to agree. But
there are many important and complex questions of implementation
on which expert opinion diverges widely and official consensus is
nowhere in sight.

Should a pooling of reserves be compulsory or optional? If
compulsory, provision must be made for working balances; how are
these to be defined? How comprehensive is the scheme to be? Some
plans — for example, Edward Bernstein's famous Reserve Settlement
proposal — comprehend all types of reserves, including gold and
SDRs; others envisage that gold and dollar reserves be pooled and
exchanged for specially-issued SDRs. In these schemes, the USA
would become the debtor of the Fund for the dollars surrendered by
other countries, a gold guarantee would apply and presumably a
lower interest rate would be charged. A highly controversial question
that surely will be raised with much urgency is the 'link' between
SDRs and development assistance to poor countries.

The USA, before accepting a reform involving asset convertibility
of the dollar, would certainly require assurance or safeguards concerning the many billion more or less liquid dollar balances held
abroad in private hands. Furthermore, the removal of the alleged
'special privilege' of the inconvertible dollar would be conditional
upon elimination of the corresponding 'special handicaps' with
respect to exchange rate changes. There are two of these. First, under
present arrangements with a band of 2¼ per cent on each side of
parity, the exchange rate between any two currencies other than the
dollar can change, under certain circumstances, by as much as 9 per
cent, while the exchange value of the dollar *vis-à-vis* any other
currency can change by no more than 4½ per cent.[6] Second, under

present circumstances it is for the USA extremely difficult, until last year many people thought impossible, to change the par value of the dollar. The second is the more important and less tractable handicap.

The first handicap or 'asymmetry' stems from the fact that the dollar is used by all countries as the intervention currency to keep the exchange value of their currency inside the range of permitted fluctuations. Under this arrangement, any currency can change by 4½ per cent *vis-à-vis* the dollar if it moves from one end of the band to the other. Suppose now that for any reason — differential inflation or a change in international demand — currency A rises from the floor of the band to the ceiling and currency B falls from the ceiling to the floor; then they move by 9 per cent *vis-à-vis* each other, while the dollar has moved by 4½ per cent *vis-à-vis* each. For a country in deficit, a potential 9 per cent devaluation *vis-à-vis* many currencies could be a great help. For the USA, the maximum possible help provided by the present band would be a depreciation of the dollar of only 4½ per cent.

This could surely become a handicap for the USA if asset convertibility of the dollar were restored. But, so long as the dollar is inconvertible, it can be regarded as only a potential handicap, if one accepts the popular view that accumulation of dollar balances by other countries is a burden on the USA. I criticized this theory above as a mercantilistic fallacy, and I need not go through all that again.

This first asymmetry or handicap could be removed by making SDRs and gold (which now are rigidly linked) the 'pivot' and intervention currency, instead of the dollar. All national currencies, including the dollar, would then stand in symmetrical relationship to the international unit, as was the case under the old gold standard. The dollar would be allowed to fluctuate *vis-à-vis* SDRs within a band of the same width of 4½ per cent as all the other currencies. As a consequence, the maximum variability of the dollar *vis-à-vis* other currencies would then be the same as that of all other currencies: 9 per cent with a band of 4½ per cent.

The straightforward method of achieving that result and thus removing the first asymmetry would be to make SDRs negotiable instruments suitable for official intervention, as well as for private holding and trading. But that would require a change of the Fund's Articles of Agreement, basically not complicated but actually very difficult to negotiate.

Theoretically, the same result could be achieved, without a national or supranational intervention medium (dollar, SDRs or gold), by what has come to be known as 'symmetric' or 'multi-currency intervention'. In that case, too, it would be necessary to give the dollar a band in which to fluctuate around the SDRs as the numeraire. The existing (asymmetric) dollar-based intervention system or a hypothetical SDR- (or gold-)based system is largely automatic, market-orientated and makes use of the existing efficient, highly competitive exchange markets to maintain consistent cross-rates through private arbitrage with a minimum of public intervention. In contrast, the symmetric multi-currency intervention system would have to rely on elaborate rules and detailed guidance and supervision by the Fund to achieve the same result: namely, to make the dollar equal to other currencies in one respect: to give it the same maximum variability *vis-à-vis* other currencies, 9 per cent with the present band of 4½ per cent. It is not, however, worth persuing this subject any further. For the great complexity of the multi-currency intervention system, in contrast to its very limited objective, makes it highly improbable that it will be tried in practice.[7]

The second asymmetry — the difficulty, or alleged impossibility, of changing the par value of the dollar — is altogether different in nature and a much more important matter than the first-mentioned asymmetry. This, too, would be a handicap for the USA were asset convertibility of the dollar to be restored. So long as the dollar is inconvertible, it can be regarded as a handicap only if the fallacious view is accepted that accumulation of dollar balances abroad is a burden for the USA.

This asymmetry is more deeply rooted than the first and cannot be removed by mechanical changes of the intervention system. Nor can substitution of SDRs for dollar reserves in an international consolidation scheme give the USA complete freedom to devalue the dollar or to let it float without fear that the move will be frustrated by widespread imitation, although it may perhaps make it a little easier.

Why did other countries not accept as large a devaluation of the dollar as the USA wanted, even in the form of a depreciation of the dollar in terms of gold? The major reason surely was that they were afraid of impairing the competitiveness of their industries *vis-à-vis* those of the USA or, what comes pretty much to the same, that they were reluctant to give up or reduce their trade surplus. (That it is inconsistent to complain about imported inflation and, at the same time, to cling to a trade surplus, as many did, is another matter). The difficulty of devaluing the dollar is rooted in a basic asymmetry: namely, the large size of the American economy. If a small or medium-sized country devalues its currency, the rest of the world (apart from a few other small or medium-sized countries) can absorb the impact on its trade. If a large country devalues, there are bound to be repercussions on, and reactions by, many other countries. This asymmetry cannot be removed by monetary reform.

Exchange flexibility

Many of these problems could be solved, or at least reduced to small proportions, by greater exchange flexibility. If most countries that are dissatisfied with the working of the dollar standard followed the Canadian example and let their currency float *vis-à-vis* the dollar, the dollar itself would in effect become flexible and the asymmetry, privilege of handicap would disappear, in substance if not in form. But there is no use elaborating on this because no such solution seems to be negotiable at this point.

I am afraid the same holds of the less ambitious and, to my mind, quite feasible scheme proposed by Professor John Williamson.[8] Williamson links, in a highly ingenious way, SDR creation and a 'crawling peg' arrangement. It is true there is almost general agreement that there should be more frequent changes of exchange rates. But any generalized crawling peg or 'gliding parity' arrangement, either of formula or individual decision type, binding or presumptive, would seem to be out of the question at the present time.

Nowadays, almost every official document and speech on monetary reform stresses the importance of prompt diagnosis of emerging payments disequilibria and speedy adjustment of exchange rates. This is a great advance over the state of the debate a few years ago, when mention of frequent changes in exchange rates was taboo in official utterances. But the discussion rarely faces up to the basic difficulty of the adjustable peg (par value) system: that more frequent but still discrete and fairly large changes of exchange rates may make things worse rather than better. Concretely, if the international value of a currency is changed, say, every ten years, there is probably enough time after each change for confidence to be restored. If the change comes on the average after, say, every two years, the interval is too short for 'stability illusion' (analogous to money illusion) to be revived. Hence, destabilizing speculative capital flows may become larger rather than smaller. Full flexibility or gliding (or crawling) parities avoid this difficulty. The crucial problem is to determine how fast the glide or crawl has to be to avoid destabilizing effects.

The dollar standard once more

Our discussion comes to the somewhat negative conclusion that it will be very difficult and take a long time to reform the international monetary system so as to make the dollar equal to other currencies and to eliminate the special privileges and handicaps allegedly inherent in the present arrangement. In the meantime, the world is on the dollar standard. To repeat, in my opinion, the dollar standard is not a bad or highly inequitable system, provided US inflation does not get out of hand. But, whether this proposition is accepted or not, there should be agreement that it is of the utmost importance for the continuing growth of world trade and for world welfare that the free market convertibility of the dollar is preserved until something else can be put in its place. The market-convertible dollar is the indispensable lubricant of the wheels of world trade.

But what if US inflation gets worse? Or what if my judgement — that, if US inflation remains moderate (by present world standards), not much inflation abroad would be required to maintain payments equilibrium — turns out to be too optimistic? One thing is certain: there would then be plenty of trouble, recrimination, more or less justified criticism of the USA and a tendency to form rival currency blocs in Europe and possibly elsewhere. But in some basic respects the situation would not be changed by excessive inflation in the USA. Thus, the only rational choice of surplus countries which do not want to accumulate more dollars and refuse to participate in US inflation is (and would continue to be) to let their currency float up. But will they act rationally? Dirty appreciation or dirty floating is not a rational reaction. It would hurt the dirty floaters and everybody else more than the USA. To restrict imports and trade would be even more irrational; it would be tantamount to cutting off one's nose to spite one's face. These remarks result from straightforward economic analysis and are not intended to excuse or justify US inflation or to play down the dangers of inflation.

If, as a consequence of excessive US inflation, the dollar were to become overvalued with respect to many or most currencies, a depreciation of the dollar (in terms of gold and SDRs) might facilitate, politically, a realignment of parities, although it would not obviate other parity changes, because other currencies would not be uniformly undervalued. Basically, depreciation of the dollar is not a matter of great importance because, contrary to what is often assumed, it makes no difference, except from a political or national prestige standpoint, whether the dollar is depreciated or other currencies appreciated. According to Dr Rinaldo Ossola, 'It is incorrect to equate a devaluation of the dollar [in terms of gold] with the contribution of the US to the burden of adjustment'.[9] But, so long as the dollar is the world's foremost reserve, transaction and intervention currency and gold plays a role in the minds and expectations of many people, it is in the interest of world trade (no specific US interests are involved) not to tamper with the dollar price of gold for political and prestige reasons unless absolutely necessary.

There is one step that the USA could take which would make the dollar standard more acceptable and equitable, even in the case of excessive American inflation: to offer some sort of purchasing power guarantee to foreign official dollar holders. This proposal has been made by Professor Fellner.[10] The USA would offer to foreign official dollar holders the option to exchange their dollars for special bonds carrying a purchasing power guarantee and a correspondingly lower yield. These guaranteed bonds would be for official use only and could at any time be converted at par into ordinary bonds. The form of guarantee and the yield would have to be agreed upon. The most sensible type of guarantee would be in terms of a broadly-based price index of internationally traded goods. The US wholesale price index would be a good proxy. A gold guarantee inevitably would become more and more artificial as gold's monetary role diminished. An alternative might be to restrict the guarantee to recently acquired dollar balances.

The first reaction of the official mind to a purchasing power guarantee, as in most other cases of new ideas, will be to shrink back and think of all sorts of reasons why it could and should not be done. One argument might be that giving a purchasing power guarantee to foreign central banks would be a dangerous precedent and would be difficult politically without giving domestic savers the same privilege. But the precedent may not be bad at all. In an age of inflation there is much to be said, and there is indeed increasing demand, for giving at least the small saver a means to protect himself from inflation.

A guarantee for official dollar holdings surely is no panacea, but it would help to strengthen the present system until something better has been put in its place.

Outlook and concluding remarks

I believe the chances are good that in the future, as in the past, the USA will succeed better than most countries in curbing inflation. Consumer prices have risen less in the USA than in the great majority of other countries over somewhat longish periods. But this in itself is not a sufficient proof, for so long as the world is on the dollar standard, US inflation sets the pace for inflation in all the many countries that maintain fixed exchange rates and keep their currencies convertible. This follows from the fact that US monetary policy is determined by domestic policy objectives and that the feedback via the balance of payments is negligible, because of the small size of the foreign trade sector in the US economy.

The price dominance of the USA is not generally understood,

either in that country or abroad, notwithstanding the frequent complaints about US 'exporting inflation'. At any rate, most complainers do not understand that the only effective protection against imported inflation is a floating exchange rate and they are, inconsistently, very reluctant to accept a deterioration of their trade balance.

That most countries had more inflation than the USA could have been a case of induced (imported) inflation. But if, in any country, prices rise persistently much faster than in the USA, one would suspect a stronger propensity to inflate. The suspicion is confirmed if a country, to maintain equilibrium, is forced to depreciate its currency from time to time against the dollar and, in between depreciations, to use controls on capital and similar devices. It is not difficult to find examples, even among the loudest complainers about the US export of inflation.

Suppose now that the USA does in fact curb inflation (and makes its policy more attractive by offering some kind of guarantee to foreign official dollar holders). There will then be enough time for the community of nations to negotiate a reform of the international monetary system. If many countries really wish to replace the dollar by SDRs, it could be done gradually, on a voluntary and experimental basis. A fraction of the outstanding official balances could be turned over to the Fund in exchange for SDRs. It would not be necessary at once to set up a rigid schedule with a firm terminal date for complete conversion of all dollar holdings (apart from working balances) into SDRs. That could be left for later negotiations.

It would go beyond the scope of the present paper to suggest alternative solutions for the final reform of the system. Let me add one last observation. At an international gathering early in 1972 I was struck by the remark of a prominent German economist. He said that from the point of view of guarding against world inflation he preferred the dollar standard to the SDR standard. For the internal resistance to inflation in the USA was still strong, while an international body administering the SDRs might not be able to resist the strong inflationary pressures to which it would undoubtedly be subjected. This seems to me a refreshingly realistic evaluation of the inflationary dangers, especially if, as now seems likely, a link between SDR creation and development assistance will be forged. The framers of the reform of the international monetary system will be well advised to keep this danger in mind.

Notes

1. The magnitude of the effective overall devaluation of the dollar varies according to the method of calculation. At the end of 1971 the trade-weighted average effective devaluation since early May 1971 against *all* currencies, including those which were devalued against the dollar, was about 7 per cent. In some official statements a figure of 12 per cent was mentioned. That was *vis-à-vis* eight countries of the Group of Ten (excluding Canada). Because of the wider band the effective devaluation is apt to change a little from time to time. However, to speak of a roughly 8 per cent devaluation cannot be far off the mark.

2. Dr Edwin Stopper, the president of the Swiss National Bank, has expressed it as follows: 'According to a widely held view, on 15 August 1971 the dollar-gold exchange standard was put to rest. Actually it was not the existing monetary system that broke down, but the notion that it was based on the dollar-gold exchange standard. In reality it functioned, practically from the beginning, as a dollar standard' (speech, 28 April 1972).

3. The annual report of the *Deutsche Bundesbank* has this to say: 'There is a good chance that the position of the dollar as the key currency (*Leitwährung*) will again become stronger, if the US succeeds in regaining sufficient internal stability'.

4. A diversification of reserves resulting in the widespread adoption of multi-currency reserves would lead to a pyramiding of international liquidity which could become an inflationary factor in the world economy.

5. See Gottfried Haberler, 'US Balance of Payments Policy and the International Monetary System' in Wolfgang Schmitz (ed.), *Convertibility, Multilateralism and Freedom, Essays in Honor of R. Kamitz*, Vienna and New York, 1972; and Gottfried Haberler and Tom Willett, *A Strategy for US Balance of Payments Policy*, American Enterprise Institute, Washington, DC, 1971. For a quantitative appraisal, it must be kept in mind that only that part of dollar accumulation abroad that corresponds to the trade balance should be counted, not the huge speculative and interest-sensitive funds held abroad.

6. Since 24 April the six EC countries (later joined by the UK, Denmark and Norway) have given up some of their flexibility by restricting movements in their exchange rates among themselves so that the maximum deviation is 4½ per cent.

7. For an excellent analysis of the efficiency of the present dollar-based system, as compared with a multi-currency system, see Richard N Cooper, 'Notes on Eurodollars, Reserve Dollars, and Asymmetrics in the International Monetary System', *Journal of International Economics*, 1972. Another danger of multi-currency intervention is that it would probably lead to the widespread adoption of multi-currency reserves. As mentioned earlier, this development would constitute an inflationary threat through the pyramiding of international liquidity.

8. John Williamson, *The Choice of a Pivot for Parities*, Essays in International Finance, no 90, November 1971, International Finance Section, Princeton University, Princeton, NJ.

9. Rinaldo Ossola, 'Reflections on New Currency Solutions', remarks made in London, 15 February 1972.

10. William Fellner 'The Dollar's Place in the International System: Criteria for the Appraisal of Emerging Views', *The Journal of Economic Literature*, American Economic Association, Menasha, Wis., September 1972.

6 The exchange rate as an instrument of policy

Otmar Emminger

Since 1973, exchange rate policy has largely centred on the use of flexible exchange rates or 'floating'. It should not be forgotten, however, that only a minority of countries in the Western world have floating currencies — 38 of the 133 member countries of the IMF (of which, in June 1978, six maintained common margins in the 'snake' arrangement and five adjusted exchange rates according to a set of indicators) plus Switzerland as a non-member of the IMF. In the middle of 1978, 95 members pegged their currencies either to a single other currency — predominantly the US dollar — or to a basket of currencies, like the special drawing right (SDR). But currencies which are pegged are in reality also floating, against all the currencies which float against their own key currency. In fact, less than one-fifth of all international trade moves across pegged exchange rates.

Pegging one's currency to another currency (or to a currency basket) at a fixed rate indicates, of course, a particular choice in the use of exchange rates as an instrument of economic policy. It can be assumed that the reasons for pegging one's currency are not dissimilar to those prevailing in the Bretton Woods system of fixed but adjustable parities. For obvious reasons, pegging is practised mainly by developing countries and smaller industrial countries.

Pegging inside a regional bloc which floats jointly against all other currencies, as in the European Monetary System (EMS), raises particular problems. It is obvious that the close regional and institutional interconnection of the member countries provides an incentive for maintaining mutual exchange rates as stable as possible. On the other hand, it is clear that fixed parities in relation to the dollar and other 'external' currencies are practically impossible. Thus, such a regional currency bloc is beset with the problems of fixed but

---

The author was formerly President of the Deutsche Bundesbank. The paper is a revised and expanded version of the LSE Society Special Lecture given by the late Dr Emminger at the London School of Economics on 7 December 1978. It first appeared in *Lloyds Bank Review*, July 1979.

adjustable rates in its internal relations, and with those of floating in its external relations.

Why did the system of fixed parities break down?

The transition to widespread 'floating' among the major currencies in early 1973 was a reaction to the rgidities of the Bretton Woods system of fixed parities. Under this system the fixed but adjustable exchange rate has essentially been viewed as a means of providing a stable basis for external economic and monetary relations. In circumstances of 'fundamental disequilibrium' alterations of the exchange rate could — and should — be used as an instrument for balance of payments adjustment. In its first twenty years or so the Bretton Woods system had worked reasonably well. But over time it turned out that countries were not sufficiently prepared to adjust their domestic demand and price level to their exchange rate nor were they, as a rule, willing to adjust their exchange rate speedily enough to their domestic situation or to their fundamental payments position. Thus it was rightly called a system of 'reluctant adjustment' (by the late Professor Harry Johnson). In its final stage of degeneration this system had contributed to a distorted pattern of over- and under-valued exchange rates; to a consequent dislocation of productive resources; to an inflation of currency reserves and of the money supply in Europe due to excessive obligatory dollar purchases; and, last but not least, to a never-ending succession of exchange rate crises.

Up to this day the experts have been unable to agree on the causes of the breakdown of the Bretton Woods system. Nor have they been able to agree on the role to be attributed to 'floating' or even on its actual performance up to the present.

On the European side of the Atlantic many critics put the blame for the breakdown mainly on the fact that under the dollar exchange standard the United States was in a position to settle its payments deficits *vis-à-vis* the outside world by issuing its own currency, and that through this 'exorbitant privilege' (to quote General de Gaulle) they could run a 'deficit without tears' and thus escape the discipline of the balance of payments. According to this view the United States, by falling victim to inflation and by creating too many dollars in the world, had not lived up to its responsibilities as the leader of the system and as the provider of its key currency. Americans retorted that the others had not played the rules of the game properly. Rightly or wrongly, the Americans considered that the dollar, as the key intervention and reserve currency and as the link between the system and gold, was unable to adjust its gold parity. Thus the dollar was increasingly pushed into an overvalued position, partly through the fault of the Americans (Vietnam inflation), partly because of the inappropriate behaviour of other currencies. This culminated in the dollar crises of 1971 and 1973 — despite the rearguard battle of belated realignments of the dollar parity at the end of 1971 (Smithsonian Agreement) and in February 1973.

Other critics tried to find a scapegoat in the inadequacy of the international reserve system. Some — particularly in the UK — complained about an alleged insufficiency of international liquidity. This looks, however, somewhat odd in view of growing world-wide inflation in the last few years of the fixed rate system. Still others, following the lead of Professor Triffin, held that the reserve role of the dollar would lead inexorably to a breakdown of the system; they believed that the growing need for reserves of other countries would 'force payments deficits on the United States' until its external overindebtedness in relation to its own (gold) reserves would become untenable (at least under continuing gold convertibility of the dollar).

There is certainly a kernel of truth in this view. However, from 1970 to 1973 the creation of new dollar reserves was excessive and was certainly not forced upon the United States by a legitimate need for new reserves. Moreover, European countries did not go over to floating against the dollar because the dollar had become inconvertible into gold. On the contrary, since the suspension of the dollar's convertibility into gold in August 1971, they have multiplied their dollar holdings to an amazing extent. The absence of gold convertibility has not diminished the reserve role of the dollar.

In reality, the reasons for the breakdown of the fixed rate system were more complex. The growing external weakness of the dollar — in part due to the Vietnam inflation in the United States, in part to other causes — certainly played an important role. A dollar-based system cannot be stronger than its base. But there were additional reasons: since the beginning of the 1970s, *high and widely divergent inflation rates* among a number of major countries made a fixed rate system increasingly vulnerable; they would have necessitated a continuing series of exchange rate adjustments which would have kept the whole system constantly embroiled in speculative expectations and turmoil. Furthermore, *confidence-induced money flows* from one country to another often assumed enormous proportions with the growing internationalization of banking and of money markets, in particular the Euro-dollar market. 'The adjustable peg opened the floodgate for disruptive speculation', as Professor Haberler put it.

To this was added a fundamental *monetary asymmetry* of the system: in the surplus countries the central banks were obliged to intervene to support the fixed dollar rate, and thus had (often involuntarily) to expand their monetary base ('imported inflation'), whereas in the deficit countries, owing to their accommodating monetary policy, foreign exchange outflows usually did not lead to a slowing down of monetary expansion. This produced a ratchet effect, an international escalation of inflation, whenever even temporary imbalances or crises of confidence occurred with consequent large foreign exchange flows. It is no accident that in the final years of the par value system the inflation of the money supply in Europe reached record levels: in the three-and-a-quarter years from the beginning of 1970 to March 1973 the European money stock (in the wider definition) increased by no less than 54 per cent, while in the main deficit country, the United States, the money supply, far from slowing down, also experienced a record expansion. Thus, the system of fixed par values had become a 'perfect inflation machine', as it was called in 1971 by Karl Blessing, a former Governor the Bundesbank.

As one who participated in (and was partly responsible for) the decision of West Germany to go over to floating in March 1973, I can testify that the main reason for this decision was the effort to shield the German monetary system from further inflationary foreign exchange inflows, after the central bank had to absorb a dollar inflow worth more than DM 20 billion within five weeks, equivalent to more than double the amount of new central bank money required for a whole year.

If I had to name the single most important cause of the breakdown of the Bretton Woods system of fixed parities, I would put my finger on the huge dollar flows which — as a consequence of the US payments deficits, enlarged by confidence movements and by the Euro-dollar market — swamped the world monetary system at the beginning of the 1970s, and which in February and March 1973 became intolerably destabilizing for a number of countries.

Lessons from the breakdown of the fixed parities system

From these historical experiences a number of lessons for exchange rate policy can be drawn. *First*, a combination of a weak dollar and enormous volatile dollar holdings in the world would wreck, sooner or later, any attempt at a fixed parity or even a mere target zone for the dollar. For the foreseeable future we can, therefore, rule out any such arrangements in relation to the dollar.

Second, as long as there are wide divergences of cost and price movements in different countries, fixed parities between them are clearly not maintainable. 'It is virtually impossible to operate a system of fixed parities in a world of chronic inflation' (Edward M Bernstein, in a statement to the US Congress, March 1973). And this, in particular, because in an inflationary world wide divergences in inflation rates are unavoidable. The sensitivity to inflation differs widely from country to country.

Third, the transition to widespread floating in 1973 was not a deliberate act in search of a better international monetary system; rather it was forced on the major countries by the inflationary threat inherent in disruptive international money flows.

Fourth, the primary aim of floating in 1973 was definitely not to facilitate the adjustment of relative exchange rate levels, but to put up a defence against confidence-induced destabilizing flows of funds. It would therefore be wrong to judge the system of floating primarily according to its performance in the adjustment process.

Some of these points call for further comment. That there was *no free choice* between fixed and flexible exchange rates has been demonstrated by subsequent developments. Indeed, had the main countries not gone over to floating in the spring of 1973, they would quite certainly have been compelled to do so when at the end of 1973 the oil price explosion subjected the payments pattern of the world to enormous strains. As Mr Witteveen, the then Managing Director of the IMF, said in an address in London in January 1974, immediately after the oil shock: 'In the present situation, a large measure of floating is unavoidable and indeed desirable.'

That the transition to floating was primarily a defence against destabilizing money flows[1] and not necessarily a means of payments adjustment, is well illustrated by the West German and US experiences in the initial years of floating. In West Germany, the inflationary inflow of foreign exchange ceased entirely from the middle of 1973 to the end of 1975;[2] in 1976 there was again an inflow but this was entirely due to West Germany's obligation to intervene in the regional fixed rate system of the European common float (the 'snake'), while there was no net inflow from outside the 'snake' system. It was only from the autumn of 1977 onwards, with the increasing weakness of the US balance of payments, that floating against the dollar no longer provided a sufficient shield against foreign exchange inflows through involuntary intervention in the dollar market.

The use of floating for payments adjustment

As concerns payments adjustment through flexible exchange rates, this can be expected to a significant extent only in so far as floating leads to a change in the '*real*' exchange rate, that is to say a change in the average ('effective') exchange rate which exceeds a mere offsetting of cost and price differentials between various countries.

Now both for the dollar and the Deutschmark there was little net change in the 'real' rate of exchange in the four years from March 1973 to March 1977. There were relatively wide fluctuations up and down. But the net outcome over this period was for the dollar a 'real' (that is, price-adjusted) depreciation of only about 4 per cent, for the Deutschmark a 'real' appreciation of 2 per cent (measured by using trade-weighted variations in the respective exchange rates and adjusting them by relative consumer prices[3]).

In fact, the historical process correcting the long-standing overvaluation of the dollar had already been largely brought about under the previous fixed rate system; the 'real' (price adjusted) devaluation of the dollar between 1969 and March 1973 — approximately 17 per cent — was several times larger than anything achieved under the floating rate system between March 1973 and the middle of 1977. The same is true of the 'real' appreciation of the Deutschmark which was also several times larger from 1969 to 1973 than in the subsequent years of floating.

More generally, it can be said that at least in the initial period after 1973 floating did not lead to large shifts in the relative levels of major currencies. As the IMF summed up this experience in its Annual Report for 1976: 'Trends of most countries' exchange rates over the floating period as a whole have been broadly commensurate with major differences in rates of domestic inflation.'[4] And a year later it had to confirm:

The greater exchange rate flexibility . . . has been helpful to the adjustment process insofar as exchange rate movements have prevented certain current account imbalances from developing or widening owing to divergent inflation rates. . . . Exchange rate changes do not seem, however, to have played much of a role in recent years in reducing existing external imbalances among industrial countries.[5]

This raises the question: Was this failure to use floating as a means of payments adjustment — on the part of the major industrial countries — in the years up to the end of 1975 a deliberate policy decision?

There was indeed only a short period after March 1973, that is, after the transition to widespread floating, when major currencies were left to 'clean' floating, wholly determined by market forces. From July 1973 onward there was some occasional concerted intervention in the dollar/Deutschmark market by both the Bundesbank and the Federal Reserve (the latter mainly with Deutschmark borrowed from the Bundesbank). This ushered in the period of *managed floating*. However, in the first few years this was no more than a smoothing operation against erratic movements in the exchange markets in order to avoid disorderly conditions (which were sometimes defined as meaning a jump in the exchange rate by more than 1 per cent per day).

But there was no intervention in the Deutschmark/dollar exchange markets against underlying basic tendencies. The American current account began to move into surplus from the end of 1973 to the autumn of 1976, with the current account surplus reaching its all-time peak in 1975. During this surplus period the dollar did not need any particular (net) support through intervention in the foreign exchange market. On the opposite side, the German overall balance of payments was in deficit in both 1974 and 1975, the large current account surpluses of those years being more than offset by autonomous capital exports. Thus the absence of any further 'real' appreciation of the Deutschmark from the middle of 1973 through 1976 corresponded to basic market forces.

As concerns other major currencies, a completely new element entered the scene with the oil price explosion at the end of 1973 and the effects of the world recession of 1974–5. In early 1974 an international consensus came about among the IMF members countries that, at least for a certain period of time, payments imbalances due to the oil price explosion should not be absorbed by the exchange rate but should be 'accepted', that is, financed out of reserves or foreign borrowing. This led not only to heavy foreign borrowing by many countries (the total amount of current-account deficits which had to be financed out of reserves or net borrowing abroad jumped from $22 billion in 1973 to $77 billion in 1974) but implied a deliberate 'strong management of floating'.

A few years later, in 1976, both the IMF (through its Managing Director) and the OECD made out the case to member countries that now the time had come to shift from mere financing towards correcting payments disequilibria. Actually, 1976 was the year when — although for quite different reasons — several major currencies, in particular those of Italy, the UK and France, were under strong downward pressure, leading to an adjustment of the external value to the internal value of their currencies. In these cases it was the foreign exchange market, and in particular confidence-induced capital movements, that forced this 'real' depreciation on the currencies concerned.

As concerns the US dollar, the Deutschmark, the yen and the Swiss franc, it was the re-emergence of a huge basic payments deficit of the United States since 1977 which led to a significant 'real' depreciation of the dollar and a 'real' appreciation of the strong currencies. This — in my view inevitable — adjustment was again forced on rather unwilling participants.

To sum up my answer to the question whether floating has been an instrument of balance of payments adjustment: the exchange rate was in many countries deliberately exempted from such a role after the oil price explosion and during the world-wide recession, when financing, and not correcting, the imbalances was the order of the day. The exchange rate was used only grudgingly as a means of payments adjustment, often only when so-called destabilizing capital movements forced 'overshooting', and thus 'real' adjustment, of the exchange rate on both deficit and surplus countries — Italy, Britain, France, the United States on the one side, Japan, Switzerland, Germany and others on the other side. This often-criticized 'overshooting' has in several cases played a useful role.

A more general assessment of floating

Floating was legalized in the Jamaica Agreement of January 1976 and in the amended Articles of the IMF. Shortly after the Jamaica Conference of 1976, the then Secretary of the US Treasury, Mr William Simon, hailed the introduction of the floating rate system as 'one of the most significant and beneficial international developments of the decade'. But this was at a time when the US balance on current account was in surplus and the dollar was floating in relatively calm waters. More recently, and particularly since the end of 1977, there has emerged a *growing disenchantment and discontent* with the results of the floating rate regime. This has led, on the one hand, to a move towards a wider area of stable exchange rates in Western Europe (EMS); and on the other hand, to a greater degree of control and management of floating, including the management of the dollar rate. As the floating rate system seems to have entered a critical phase, it is perhaps worth reviewing briefly recent experiences with floating. This is a field where prejudice and preconceived ideas abound. I would put this review under five headings:

First, its effect on adjustment of external disequilibria. There can be no doubt that many high-flown expectations — entertained by uncritical believers in floating — have been disappointed. Some advocates had expected that in such a system the balance of payments would look after itself, giving the national authorities more freedom to pursue domestic goals. To quote Edward M Bernstein, the well-known economic adviser to the IMF in the 1950s: 'The reason for preferring a system of fluctuating exchange rates in a period of inflation and unsettled economic conditions is that it will facilitate adjustment to an appropriate balance of payments on both current and capital account' (in *EMB Report* No 75/15 of August 1975). And looking at the large current-account surplus which the USA had achieved in 1975 he wrote: 'There can be no doubt that it [the depreciation of the dollar from 1970 to 1975] has been effective in improving the US trade balance. In this respect, the system of fluctuating exchange rates has worked well — perhaps too well in a world that has massive oil deficits' [*sic*]. The factual basis for this last judgement proved to be short-lived, however, since a few years later a combination of cyclical and structural factors, as well as bad relative price performance, had converted the 1975 surplus into the largest American payments deficit ever recorded.

But it is still true that changes in exchange rates have performed reasonably well as a means for correcting external imbalances, provided they have led to 'real' changes in exchange rates, and provided they were supported by appropriate domestic policies. Samuel Brittan, one of the early advocates of floating, had expected 'that a floating exchange rate . . . in contrast to all alternatives, is almost too good at keeping overseas payments in balance'. But he expressly warned that 'it is no magic wand and will only work satisfactorily if backed by sensible internal policies'.[6]

Even with such support, trade flows often respond only slowly to changes in exchange rates, for a number of reasons which I need not enumerate in detail here. And when the volume of exports and imports has begun to change in the right direction, this is usually accompanied by a relative change in import and export prices (that is, the terms of trade) which can produce a perverse result in value terms for a considerable time (the J-curve effect). Thus, in Japan as well as in West Germany imports increased in 1978 much more than exports in volume terms; but in dollar terms their respective surpluses even increased for a while.

There can, however, be no doubt that, although changes in exchange rates by themselves are no panacea, they do work if they are accompanied by the right supporting measures. Econometric studies at the Federal Reserve Board in Washington for instance, have shown that the American trade deficit will narrow by between $750 million and $1 billion over a period of two years with every percentage point of 'real' dollar depreciation, that is, after allowing for inflation. As the IMF stated in its 1978 Annual Report:

There is considerable empirical evidence that relative price changes have a strong influence on the volume of imports and exports. Time is needed, however — so that only some fraction, say one fourth to one half, of the ultimate volume effects will be observed over a period as short as a year . . . In contrast to these volumes effects, exchange rate changes can affect a country's terms of trade rather rapidly. As a result of this asymmetry of timing, the trade balance generally degenerates before it begins to move steadily in the expected direction.[7]

And this perverse initial effect may, of course, sometimes lead to misdirected speculative movements (e.g. in leads and lags of payments).

To mention a few well-known cases where 'real' changes in exchange rates have produced equilibrating results: the improvement of the current account of the USA in the years 1974–6 as a consequence of the 'real' depreciation of the dollar from 1969 to 1973, the surprising reversal of the external balance of Italy, the UK and France from very large current account deficits in 1974 to equilibrium or surplus in 1978; and finally, the considerable volume effect on the Japanese trade balance in 1978, followed by a corresponding value effect in early 1979.

Second, because floating has turned out not to be a fast-acting panacea by itself for payments imbalances, it has not liberated domestic economic policy from all external constraint. It has given monetary policy more freedom to pursue national monetary targets, as both West Germany and Switzerland have experienced after their transition to floating in early 1973. But very often the dilemma between external and internal monetary considerations has cropped up again. It must have been a great disappointment to some US politicians that a floating dollar has not spared the Federal Reserve System the need repeatedly to increase increase rates in support of the external value of the dollar since January 1978; but in retrospect it has turned out that this would have been at least as necessary in order to preserve a better *domestic* equilibrium and to fight inflation.

Third, floating has not, by itself, ended 'the long agony of the dollar' (to use an expression of Henry Wallich, a member of the Federal Reserve Board). While the dollar's former overvaluation is now definitely eliminated, downward floating may, at least temporarily, have strengthened the pressures on the dollar arising from portfolio shifts. Floating has not given the US authorities full autonomy over the dollar's exchange rate.

Fourth, floating seems to have made some 'strong' currencies stronger by a virtuous circle of appreciation leading to a more domestic stability, and some 'weak' currencies weaker by a vicious circle of depreciation, increased inflation and more depreciation. But here again, the considered judgement of the IMF may be quoted: 'A needed exchange rate adjustment will become associated with a vicious circle only if demand management policy is sufficiently expansionary to permit it.'[8]

Fifth, flexible rates have sometimes moved in an abrupt and erratic manner, difficult to relate to variations in underlying economic conditions. The expected equilibrating effect of foreign-exchange speculation as well as of short-term money flows induced by interest rate differentials has often been badly lacking.

On the other hand, the worst fears of the critics and opponents have not materialized either. World trade has not been crippled. On the contrary: in the past six years of widespread floating, from the beginning of 1973 to 1978, the volume of foreign trade has continued to expand faster than total production (according to OECD estimates, the volume of international trade of the industrial countries rose from 1972 to 1978 by 37 per cent, while real GNP increased by 20 per cent). Contrary to fears that flexible rates would throttle international capital movements, such movements have in recent years risen to enormous — some might even say, excessive — levels.

Even more important, the floating rate system has demonstrated a high degree of shock absorption capacity. It has weathered several severe shocks and disturbances to the world economy — the oil price increases, the sudden and deep recession in the United States, inflationary crises in some countries, and the phasing out of sterling as a reserve currency — in a tolerable way.

The floating system, although it has often been criticized as fuelling inflation, has in fact not prevented the world economy from gradually overcoming the worst features of the inflation of the years 1972 to 1974. In my view it has even greatly helped this movement — on the one hand, by supporting monetary stabilization policies in low-inflation countries through shielding them against imported inflation; on the other hand, by depreciating exchange rates putting strong pressures on high-inflation countries to set up domestic stabilization programmes. In this connection, an overreaction of the exchange markets (or 'overshooting') may occasionally have quite a positive function.

The fear that floating rates would be widely abused for competitive depreciation and would end in economic warfare has turned out to be groundless. On the contrary, when after the sudden appearance of a huge oil deficit in 1974 it was agreed that for an interim period this supposedly 'irrepressible' deficit should be 'accepted' — bridged over by borrowing — there developed a tendency toward higher rather than lower exchange rates in order to ward off the inflationary impact of high world prices.

Finally, contrary to the fears of the opponents of floating, it has not led to a breakdown in international co-operation in the financial field. Thus, while the advocates of floating had to digest a certain amount of disillusionment, its opponents had to swallow a spoonful of realism.

Looking back over the last six years, and taking a broad general view, I would say that floating worked reasonably well up to 1977 — considering the prevailing circumstances, and considering also the available alternatives. Floating has, in particular, spared the world a series of exchange rate crises which would have been inevitable under a fixed rate system. This view is supported by the evaluation of the International Monetary Fund, which in its sedate language reads as follows:

On the whole, exchange rate flexibility appears to have enabled the world economy to surmount a succession of disturbing events, and to accommodate divergent trends in costs and prices in national economies with less disruption of trade and payments than a system of par values would have been able to do.[9]

This was like a sigh of relief after the worst of the oil crisis and the US recession had been overcome without a breakdown of the international system. In subsequent years, however, scepticism and frustration with pure floating have increased. This appears, for instance, in the more sceptical views about floating in the reports of the Bank for International Settlements, the central bankers' bank, and particularly of the Chairman of its Council of Administration, the Dutch central bank governor, Mr Zijlstra. He wrote in an Annual Report of his central bank a few years ago: 'Floating exchange rates for the major currencies have no alternative at present; but it is too early to make a lasting virtue out of necessity.' This sceptical view could also be expressed by adapting Churchill's famous dictum on democracy: floating may have been the worst system, except for all the other available ones.

Indeed, in its 1978 *Annual Report*, the IMF Board was unable to express a unanimous (positive) view on the performance of flexible exchange rates. It also had to take account of the more sceptical feelings of some of its members. But no practicable alternative has been put forward. So Churchill's dictum is still valid for floating — as it is valid for democracy.

The dollar as a special burden on the floating rate system

Fluctuating exchange rates have not always behaved according to textbook expectations. They did not always reflect relative price movements or changes in relative purchasing power, at least in the short run (but who really had good reasons to expect that the 'purchasing power theory' would work in the short run?). In other words, there was a considerable degree of over- and undershooting of the assumed 'normal' or 'ideal' exchange rates. The movement of some major currencies was occasionally completely insensitive to relative money supply movements or interest rate differentials. For instance, while up to 1976 the dollar/Deutschmark rate pretty well responded to variations in nominal interest rate differentials, this was no longer true in 1977 and 1978; even a widening of the interest rate differential up to 7 per cent (between dollar and Deutschmark assets of three or six months' maturity) in the middle of 1978 did not swing the dollar rate around immediately (although it certainly gave it some support). On the other hand, high interest rates in Denmark have very often made the Danish krone, one of the weaker European currencies, the strongest currency in the 'snake'; and also in the UK high interest rates have sometimes strengthened the pound to an amazing, and occasionally unwelcome, degree.

It is not my task in this paper to explain all these phenomena. But it might not be a bad thing for an academic investigation to try to analyse, on the basis of the experience of the 1970s, what really made the various major exchange rates 'run', or behave. I will, however, briefly describe one particular case which is important for international monetary policy: the forces working on the dollar exchange rate. It is often believed in high quarters, especially in the United States and the UK, that in recent years the main pressure on the dollar rate has arisen from the huge amount of so-called 'footloose' dollars created and held by the international banking system. In my view, however, by far the most important influence has been the sudden turnround in the American balance on current account, to which neither the US capital balance nor the official financing measures of the authorities were adjusted in time ('benign neglect').

Most people have already forgotten how abrupt a deterioration this was. In 1975 the United States had a surplus on current account of nearly $18 billion — its largest ever — and the dollar belonged at that time to the group of 'strong currencies' (some prominent bankers even suggested in 1976 that the four 'strong' currencies — dollar, yen, Swiss franc and Deutschmark — should form a stability bloc with target rates between themselves!). In 1976 the current account was in equilibrium. In 1977, all of a sudden, it plunged into a deficit of $15 billion, a shift of $33 billion in two years! This dramatic shift was due to a number of factors — structural reasons, such as the growing dependence on foreign oil or the inroads of Japan and a group of advanced developing countries into the US market; cyclical factors, namely the faster growth of demand in the United States compared with the rest of the industrial world; and, finally, an increasing inflation differential to the disadvantage of the United States. The floating rate system has been severely put to the test by this abrupt change. No other exchange rate system would have been able to cope with such a sudden shift in the external fortunes of the major economic power of the world.

There is no doubt that additional pressure on the dollar has emerged, particularly in the course of 1978, from a portfolio shift out of dollar-denominated assets, that is, the 'diversification' of internationally (and nationally) held liquid funds. Contrary to a widespread belief, the net volume of such diversification has up to now not been nearly as big as the deficit in the US basic balance of payments (that is, the balance on current account and 'autonomous' net capital exports of the USA). Diversification of dollar reserves of central banks has up to now been within manageable proportions. Here, certainly, the interest rate differential in favour of dollar assets and the ready availability of such assets have played an important role.

But it cannot be denied that the dual task of the United States to provide the key currency and to be banker to the world became too onerous when it could no longer rely on a reasonably good current account, a stable dollar and on general confidence in the dollar. The talk about 'lessening the burden on the dollar' by other currencies (or artificial reserve units) taking over part of the reserve currency role is rather pointless. For there are no sufficiently strong candidates for this role available. And even if there were, the process of shifting out of the dollar into other currencies or assets would not lessen but instead increase the pressure on the dollar (except if the shift out of the dollar into other assets were done outside the exchange markets, for example by depositing dollar holdings in a substitution account in the IMF). The only lasting solution to this problem is, of course, a decisive improvement in the 'fundamental' conditions, especially as concerns the inflation rate and the basic balance of payments of the United States. Only such an improvement can restore the confidence of foreign holders of dollar assets. Until such an improvement has been convincingly demonstrated — initial signs are already visible in the balance of payments field — the exchange rate system of the world will remain vulnerable.

A particular weakness of the US position has been — until recently — the absence of a reasonable and sustainable financing policy for the payments deficit. In 1977 the whole US payments deficit of about $35 billion was financed through the purchase of dollars by foreign central banks (with the Bank of England accounting for about half, and the Bundesbank for a modest share of about $4 billions). This potentially inflationary method of financing could not continue for very long. It is important that since November 1978 the US authorities themselves have not only stepped up their intervention in the foreign exchange markets but have also taken the financing of their payments deficit partly into their own hands — by using their gold and SDR reserves, drawing on the IMF, and (most importantly!) by issuing foreign-currency-denominated securities in other countries, up to now in West Germany and Switzerland.

But intervention and deficit financing deal only with the symptoms. To cure the weakness of the dollar at its roots, an attack on the 'fundamental' causes of this weakness is necessary. It is therefore of special importance that in their programme of 1 November 1978, the US authorities also tightened monetary policy. Nothing could demonstrate better that they have now recognized and acknowledged their responsibility for the dollar — a responsibility not only to their own nation, but also to the world. A country cannot escape the responsibilities arising out of its importance.

New trends in exchange rate policies

The vulnerable position of the dollar in the exchange markets since the autumn of 1977 has also had some influence on the US attitude towards floating. The Americans were originally the foremost supporters of pure floating. In November 1978, after the dramatic fall of the dollar and the equally dramatic introduction of a massive dollar support programme, a high US government official explained: 'The US still believes in floating exchange rates. What we have done on November 1st, is simply an extreme version of countering a disorderly market . . . because exchange rates became a victim of a doom and gloom psychology.' But a few days later he added: 'We have moved into a very activist definition of countering disorderly markets, and in fact, under present conditions, the phrase "disorderly markets" may be inappropriate because we are deter- mined to have stability in exchange markets.' And in the official American announcement of the recent dollar support programme it was said that the authorities would intervene 'to correct recent excessive exchange rate movements'. It is evident that, under the shock of last October's foreign exchange turbulence, US policy is at present more inclined to use the dollar exchange rate as a stabilizer for the domestic economy. But I would not exclude the possibility that sooner or later the minds of those responsible for the dollar will again be torn between wanting the dollar rate high and stable and at the same time wanting it sufficiently 'competitive'.

This recent interest in more exchange rate stability and in the correction of 'wrong' exchange rate levels should certainly not be interpreted as a move to a target rate for the dollar. But it is a significant shift towards a firmer management of the dollar exchange rate and above all it shows, together with other parts of the new dollar support programme, that the era of 'benign neglect' of the external value of the dollar is over.

While this development in the US attitude towards intervention is not unimportant for the world's exchange markets, other, perhaps more fundamental, lessons have been drawn from the experience of the last six years.

First, there has been the sobering experience that if there is a major external imbalance the adjustment cannot be left to the floating exchange rate alone. 'Adjustment' means always a shift in real resources from the domestic to the external sector (or vice versa) and a change in relative real wages. It cannot, therefore, be 'painless'. The change in exchange rates is a necessary, but not a sufficient condition of adjustment. Demand management is often more important. The IMF has tried to estimate in its 1978 *Annual Report* what the relative contributions to external adjustment of a change in real demand versus a change in the exchange rate were for various countries. In reality, a fundamental disequilibrium can be adjusted only by a combination of both demand and relative price (that is, exchange rate) measures. This realization has had some influence on the application of exchange rate changes. If domestic measures could not be dispensed with, why not put the emphasis mainly on the domestic stabilization programme and give the exchange rate only a minor supporting role? This one-sidedness can, however, also lead to illusions.

Second, it has been recognized that the exchange rate is a two-edged instrument. The effect of exchange rate variations on the balance of trade and on current account is often disappointingly slow, and during a transitional period often perverse (the J-curve effect). On the other hand, the impact on domestic prices has often been felt very quickly. Recently, a European central bank has claimed that a depreciation of its currency would rapidly raise domestic costs and prices not only to the same degree but possibly by even more than would correspond to the devaluation; thus the country would, after a short transitional period, be worse off as concerns price competitiveness than before the depreciation. Such reasoning has given rise to the theory of the *vicious circle*. In effect, it corresponds to the view of some monetarists that variations in the exchange rate will often have no appreciable effect on real trade flows at all but will in the end only determine relative inflation levels between the various countries. In reality, the vicious circle theory is an over-simplification. Everything depends on the combination of exchange rate policy with domestic policy. It has been shown, both in theory and in practice, that the vicious circle of depreciation, leading to more inflation and again to more depreciation, can be broken by an appropriate policy mix.

Third, as the inflation rates of the mid-1970s gave the fight against inflation a high priority, the emphasis in using the exchange rate shifted in a number of countries toward its stabilizing possibilities. Formerly, the main emphasis was on the role which exchange rates can play in improving central competitiveness and thereby adjusting payments imbalances. I would call this the period of 'competitive' exchange rate policy. Those were the times when international organizations like the IMF and the OECD feared 'competitive devaluations' on the model of the 1930s (although this is one of many myths in this field, as in the 1930s there were few competitive devaluations and many more cases of obstinate overvaluation of currencies).

Today, some countries give precedence to the direct effect of their exchange rate on domestic costs and prices. As they look at exchange rates as potential 'price stabilizers' they are more interested in relatively higher rather than lower exchange rates.

A good illustration of the change in emphasis from a competitive to a stabilizing exchange rate is the recent development in the UK. When the pound went over to floating in June 1972, the first reaction in the UK 'was one of almost jubilation'.[11]

The predominant view was that the UK had now a chance to get rid of the 'pseudo-problems artificially created by the attempt to freeze exchange rates' (Samuel Brittan). The balance of payments and the external value of the pound could — so it appeared — be safely left to the flexible exchange rate. This would at last provide more freedom of action in domestic demand management and relieve UK policy-makers from the nightmare of a stop-go policy. Some British experts went one step further and suggested deliberate manipulation to achieve a persistent undervaluation of the pound, in an attempt to change the structure of the UK economy towards greater export orientation.

Now compare this to the 'Conclusions' in the British government's Green Paper of 24 November 1978, on the European Monetary System, where we read:

The Government for its part has made it clear that *it does not regard exchange rate depreciation as a solution to the economic problems still facing the UK* . . . Only [an improvement in our industrial performance and victory in the battle against inflation] can provide a lasting basis for stability of the exchange rate.

Fourth, we can discern a new trend concerning exchange rate policy also in one or two surplus countries. Surplus countries have benefited from the *virtuous circle* — the balance of payments surplus leading to appreciation of the currency, and this again to greater domestic price stability with the consequence of further appreciation. If this circle is not broken, the appreciation may become so excessive that it ruins the external sector to the economy (export- and import-competing branches).

The Swiss case is a first-class example of the extremes to which a one-sided virtuous circle may lead. In 1973, when inflation was running high, exchange rate stability was sacrificed to allow control of the money supply in the interest of domestic price stability. A few years ago, the President of the Swiss National Bank explained his country's position as follows:

> We had to give up fixed rates because the volume of dollar purchases by the Swiss National Bank was just too big: we were creating billions of Swiss francs of additional liquidity and this was responsible for our high inflation in the early 1970s. Inflation was almost 12 per cent in 1973 . . . With the float we regained control of our domestic money supply.[12]

In October 1978, after the Swiss franc had been pushed up in the markets within twelve months by 51 per cent against the dollar and 27 per cent against the Deutschmark (end-September 1977 to 1978) — way above anything that could be justified by relative price trends or any other underlying factors — the Swiss National Bank announced a sort of ceiling rate for the Swiss franc, by defining the maximum appreciation of the Swiss franc *vis-à-vis* the Deutschmark which it would henceforth tolerate. It also announced that, in order to hold the Swiss franc below the ceiling, it would, if necessary, intervene on a massive scale in the foreign exchange markets, irrespective of the ensuing expansion of domestic liquidity. This was followed in January 1979 by the official suspension of a quantitative monetary target, after the Swiss M1 money supply had expanded in 1978 at a rate of about 16 per cent, more than three times the pre-announced target rate.

For the time being — as long as inflationary pressures do not re-emerge more visibly — control of the money supply has been sacrificed for the sake of better control of the exchange rate. Have the Swiss gone full circle? Not quite. First, they are not defending a fixed rate (as before 1973), but only a ceiling rate for the Swiss franc (which is high enough to be still very much on the side of overvaluation). Second, and more important, the Swiss central bank will not sacrifice domestic stability. The temporary suspension of the Swiss money supply target has expressly been justified by the fact that the deflationary effect of currency overvaluation offsets a possible inflationary effect of an excessive expansion of the money supply. The Swiss National Bank has made it clear that adequate control of the money supply will be reintroduced as soon as there are signs that the offsetting effect of the high exchange rate on prices is no longer assured.

The Swiss case presents an interesting example of a direct linkage — and trade-off — between exchange rate policy and money supply policy so as to achieve price stability in combination with some moderation of currency appreciation. In West Germany we have also had a touch of a virtuous circle and a similar linkage between money supply policy and exchange rate policy, but to a lesser degree than in Switzerland. Why? Because in West Germany we have pursued a very active policy of economic stimulation mainly by tax rebates and relatively high deficit spending by the public sector. We have allowed the money supply to overshoot our original target (although a much lesser degree than Switzerland); for the year 1978 the target was an average increase in the stock of 'central bank money' of 8 per cent, but the actual expansion was 11½ per cent. The main justification for this overshooting has been that the appreciation of the Deutschmark has up to now been acting as an offsetting counter-inflationary force. So much so, indeed, that the rate of price increase in 1978 (consumer prices rose 2.6 per cent) was slightly below our official forecast.

West German exchange rate policy has continued to adhere to the principle that the exchange rate of the Deutschmark — as far as it is not a fixed rate in relation to other EC currencies — should follow the underlying market trends, and that we should intervene in the dollar market only to counter disorderly conditions (in a broad sense) and try to smooth abrupt and excessive swings. Nevertheless, the appreciation of the Deutschmark, which from 1977 to the beginning of 1979 somewhat exceeded the average inflation differentials *vis-à-vis* major countries, gave us a welcome trade-off against the inflationary potential of an excessively expanding money supply.

There is, however, a difficult problem of timing involved. The dampening effect on prices of the high Deutschmark rate has made itself felt quickly. The simultaneous large expansion of the money supply may make itself felt much later when the offsetting price effect of currency appreciation may already have vanished. We have therefore to feel our way cautiously in future, especially as our economy has now entered a strong expansionary stage.

The experience of Germany is also of interest for future co-ordination of monetary policy in Europe. The Commission of the European Communities has for some time been trying to establish co-ordinated money supply targets of the EC member countries as a basis for stable exchange rate developments inside the Community. Experience has, however, shown that if a country like West Germany is committed to intervene heavily in support of other member currencies at fixed rates, this may make it difficult, or in the short run even impossible, to comply with a firm money supply target. There is here an as yet unresolved dilemma between intervention obligations in a fixed rate system and money supply targets.

The recent Swiss experience, which our experience in West Germany parallels — although not in such extreme terms — demonstrates that floating rates can exert strong pressures just as much on surplus as on deficit countries. In this sense it is a more symmetrical system.

Fifth, it has sometimes been said that, with a fixed exchange rate, a country has no longer any power over its inflation rate because it is forced to follow the level of international inflation. With a floating rate, it has no longer any power over its level of employment as the appreciating or depreciating exchange rate determines the rate of capacity utilization and profits.

The first thesis is borne out well by our own past experience. During the last stage of fixed rates from 1970 to 1973 West Germany was unable to dissociate itself from the average rate of price inflation in the major countries (the USA, UK, France and Italy). In the 1950s and 1960s, it had, however, significantly more price stability than its European neighbours — at the cost of an undervalued currency with a structural misallocation of resources and occasional crises followed by belated upvaluations. At the same time, however, it had some disinflationary influence on its trading partners — it exported stability and imported inflation.

The second thesis cannot so easily be proven by actual experience. Growth and employment are determined not only by the level of the exchange rate. They are affected as much, or even more, by domestic policies and developments. It is the combination of exchange rate developments and domestic policies that counts for the result.

This seems to me to be the most important general lesson to be learnt from the experience of the last six to ten years. Whether the exchange rate is used as a *competitive tool* for balance of payments adjustment, or as a *stabilizing influence* on domestic costs and prices, the result will always depend on the support that exchange rate policy is given by other economic and financial policies.

The new exchange rate system in Europe

'The exchange rate as an instrument of policy' has been my chosen subject. It would be tempting for me to enlarge upon the *political* importance of the exchange rate. By this, I mean its significance not only for economic and financial policy but also for politics in general. To illustrate the importance of this it suffices to point to the political and psychological fallout from the weakness of the dollar in 1977 and 1978.

It was probably partly in reaction to the 'dollar shock' — but, of course, also for other political and economic reasons — that the heads of state and government of the EC decided in the spring of 1978 to establish a 'wider zone of monetary stability' in Europe. The salient feature of this enterprise is no doubt the exchange rate system of fixed but adjustable parities. All the rest are 'flanking' measures to support and embellish this exchange rate system.

It is quite remarkable that exchange rate policy is the chosen instrument for a political demonstration of European unit and stability. For I consider the new EMS to be primarily a political event.

The Bundesbank welcomes more stable exchange rates in so far as they are symptoms and indicators of stable — and harmonious — underlying trends in the various member countries. Thus, I see in the attempt to stabilize mutual exchange rates in the EMS mainly a solemn declaration of intent that the member states will be trying to harmonize, on a stable basis, their economic and monetary performances. Membership of a 'stable rate club' with all its implied commitments may be a spur and help towards this goal.

We do not close our eyes to the difficulties and risks involved in such an enterprise. But the conditions for it are certainly better today than a few years back. Price stability, and monetary stability in general, now enjoy a higher priority everywhere in Europe than they used to; the will to fight inflation has increased. The foundations for the new scheme have also been strengthened by the impressive improvement in the balances of payments of the major European countries. I hope we will be able to add a third positive factor: that we have learnt how to adjust, in case of need, exchange rates in time and without disruptive foreign exchange crises. We know from experience that a system of fixed exchange rates where there are differences in the price and general economic performance of the member states cannot preclude occasional adjustments in exchange rates, if it is not to fall back into the old curse of over- and under-valued currencies with their attendant foreign exchange crises. I hope that we all have learnt to avoid making such adjustments the traumatic events that they were under the Bretton Woods system.

Notes

1. In the case of Germany and Switzerland against destabilizing inflows, in the case of the UK (1972) and Italy (January 1973) against destabilizing outflows.
2. West Germany's dollar holdings even declined by about $3.7 billion during these two-and-a-half years.

3. Measured by a comparison of relative unit labour costs, both the average 'real' depreciation of the dollar and the average 'real' appreciation of the Deutschmark were larger.

4. IMF, *Annual Report* (1976).

5. IMF, *Annual Report* (1977).

6. Samuel Brittan, *The Price of Economic Freedom: A Guide to Flexible Rates*, London, 1970.

7. IMF, *Annual Report* (1978), p. 41.

8. IMF, *Annual Report* (1978), p. 35.

9. IMF, *Annual Report* (1975), p. 33.

10. Cf. *The Economist*, 8 October 1977: 'The government wants to strengthen firms' resistance to wage claims. One way to do this is to dispel the notion of a permissive pound.'

11. *Euro-money*, July 1972.

12. *The European Monetary System*, 7405, London, 1978 (emphasis added).

13. In an interview with the *International Herald Tribune*, 10 May 1976.

7 The overvalued dollar

Rudiger Dornbusch

The strong dollar, large budget deficits, and high real interest rates are a major concern for US domestic macroeconomic policy. The recovery has been strong, but it has not been shared by the traded goods sector, which are suffering from the collapse in world trade and the continuing recession in Europe and the developing countries (LDCs), but even more importantly from a dramatic loss in external competitiveness. US business has naturally reacted by calling for exchange rate protection, with particular attention given to the yen. Unfortunately, the discussion is focussing excessively on what Japan may be doing wrong rather than on our own policies. I will argue that it is our own unbalanced fiscal policies, above all, that make for a high dollar, and a slow recovery of the world market for our goods.

Figure 7.1 shows an index of prices of US manufacturers compared with those of our trading partners. Since 1980 the prices of US manufactures have increased relative to those of other industrialized countries by about 25 per cent. The loss in competitiveness stems from three factors: lower US productivity growth than occurred abroad, significantly larger wage increases, and a large appreciation of the dollar relative to the yen and particularly the European currencies.

It is interesting to note from Table 7.1 that the nominal Deutschmark/dollar exchange rate did move very strongly, but this is clearly not the case for the nominal yen/dollar rate. Even looking at the 1978 to December 1983 period the yen has depreciated by only about 15 per cent. This underlines the fact that the loss in competitiveness relative to Japan comes not only from exchange rate movements but in good part from sharply divergent money wage and productivity performances. The superior Japanese cost performance has, of course, been perversely reinforced by the dollar appreciation. In the case of West Germany, the exchange rate movements have played a much more significant role, shown in Table 7.1.

The author is Professor of Economics at the Massachusetts Institute of Technology. This paper first appeared in *Lloyds Bank Review*, April 1984.

Figure 7.1 The Real Exchange Rate of the USA, effective exchange rate, quarterly averages, 1980–2 = 100

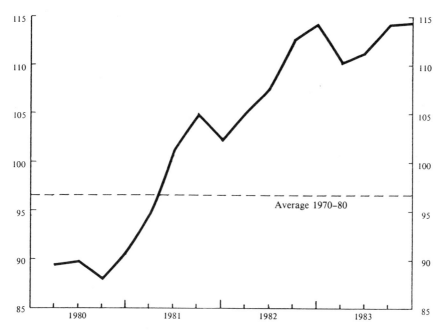

Source: World Financial Markets, Morgan Guaranty.

Table 7.1 Changes in Wages, Unit Labour Costs and Manufactured Export Prices, 1979–82 (cumulative percentage change)

	Wages	Unit labour costs	Depreciation	Export prices
	(in national currencies)		(relative to US$)	(in US dollars)
USA	30.0	28.4	–	31.3
Japan	20.9	8.3	13.6	0.8
Germany	22.7	15.5	31.9	– 12.9

Source: Bureau of Labor Statistics and UN *Monthly Bulletin of Statistics*, May 1983.

Table 7.2 shows the US loss in export competitiveness in more narrowly defined specific export products. The dollar prices of exports from West Germany and Japan have been declining for each of the product groups while the US export prices of the same goods increased sharply.

The data make an important point regarding the comparison between West Germany and Japan. It is clear that both countries

Table 7.2 Comparative Export Prices in the Fourth Quarter of 1982 (Export Price Indices in US dollars, 1979 = 100)

	West Germany	Japan	USA
Machinery other than electrical	86	96	133
Electrical machinery	83	90	126
Transport equipment	87	87	139

Source: UN *Monthly Bulletin of Statistics*, May 1983.

have gained vastly relative to the USA. But while Japan gained competitiveness relative to the USA, it lost by comparison with West Germany. Therefore it is no surprise that Japan's external competitiveness, as measured by the trade-weighted real effective exchange rate, moved by far less than that of the United States.

Reasons for dollar appreciation

Several reasons for the appreciation of the US dollar have emerged from public discussion. The first is that the strengthening of the dollar reflects an improved competitive condition of the USA in the world economy. The improvement is claimed to have made the USA more competitive in international trade other than in manufacturing, specifically in the area of services. In the same spirit it is recognized that political and economic instability, in Europe and in Latin America, has led to international portfolio shifts towards the USA and dollar assets, away from foreign capital markets. The resulting incipient improvement in both the current and capital account, in this view, has led to and justifies the real appreciation of the dollar.

There can be little doubt that international capital has moved towards the USA and that gains in competitiveness in the service sector are manifest. But it is equally hard to believe that the full extent of the sustained dollar appreciation can be explained this way. The major part of the explanation therefore must lie elsewhere, and in particular either in market irrationality or in the systematic effects of international differences in the monetary–fiscal policy mix.

Much of the exchange rate literature of the last ten years has focused on the short-run implications of monetary policy changes for exchange rate movements. The standard argument is that exchange rates are determined in asset markets, and share the flexibility and volatility of interest rates and security prices. Exchange rates share the volatility of asset prices and, therefore, often move very significantly relative to the much more sticky prices of goods. International investors, in choosing their portfolios, balance the gains from seeking high-interest currencies against the potential loss from adverse movements in exchange rates. In such a setting, markets are in equilibrium when interest differentials between countries are matched by expected rates of currency depreciation. Therefore, monetary policy changes that affect interest rates also immediately move exchange rates.

A tightening of monetary policy, for example, leads in the short run to an increase in interest rates relative to those prevailing abroad and therefore attracts capital flows. The resulting payments surplus brings about appreciation of the exchange rate. The interesting point is that the exchange rate appreciation will typically be extreme — there will be overshooting. The reason is that the exchange rate must appreciate enough so that assets markets expect that future losses from a reversal of the appreciation just match the increased earnings on domestic securities. Over time, as goods prices adjust to the changed monetary conditions, the exchange rate then returns to its long-run equilibrium value.

In the US context this theory of exchange rate overshooting is an obvious candidate to explain the strong dollar appreciation. Clearly the sharply contractionary monetary policy of the post-1979 period is exactly the setting where we would expect exchange rate overshooting in the direction of appreciation, with the dollar becoming expensive in world markets even though our inflation rate had not become lower than that abroad.

But the tight money story is not enough to explain the persistently high dollar. It explains why the dollar appreciated, but it cannot explain why the dollar remains high, unless one is willing to believe that the market continues to be surprised, month after month, by the persistence of tight money.

To have a complete explanation of the high dollar we must take into account not only monetary policy but also international differences in the stance of fiscal policy. Changes in full employment deficits change the full employment demand for goods and therefore affect both the real rate of interest *and* the real exchange rate. Crowding out in a closed-economy perspective has always singled out the impact of fiscal policy on real interest rates. But, in an open economy, crowding out (at full employment) also takes place via the exchange rate. An increase in aggregate demand, because of increased government spending or tax cuts, creates an excess demand for goods and therefore brings about a real appreciation. The real appreciation discourages demand for domestic goods. It shifts consumers to goods produced abroad, and reduces exports, making room for investment

Table 7.3 Cumulative Changes in High Employment Budgets (percentage of GNP)

	1976–79	1979–83
USA	+ 2.1	− 1.3
Japan	− 1.3	+ 2.6
West Germany	+ 1.3	+ 2.1

Source: OECD *Occasional Studies*, June 1983, *Economic Outlook*, July 1983

just as the higher interest rate induces firms not to invest or households to increase saving, thus making room for an increased budget deficit.

The fiscal explanation is highly relevant to the US situation because there has been an enormous shift in the relative fiscal position of the USA, on one side, and Europe and Japan, on the other side. This shift in fiscal policies is shown in Table 7.3. The table reports the changes in the high employment or cyclically adjusted budget surplus as a percentage of GNP. Clearly the USA has moved to a strongly expansionary stance while West Germany and Japan have moved in exactly the opposite direction. There is no surprise, therefore, that the dollar responded to the asynchronized fiscal policy by a sharp appreciation.

The fiscal interpretation of exchange rate movements does not suggest that US fiscal expansion leads to higher US real interest rates and lower real interest rates abroad.

The world capital market is integrated and securities are highly substitutable. Therefore, except for transitory anticipated real exchange rate movements, the real rate of interest is internationally approximately equal. Fiscal expansion in the world, given tight money, will raise the *world* real rate of interest in response to the current and anticipated stimulus to demand. In addition, the currency of the country that is relatively more expansionary will appreciate.

A second point to note is that not only present changes in high employment budget deficits but also anticipated future changes have an impact on the world rate of interest and on the exchange rate. This is a relevant consideration because also the medium-term fiscal stance in the USA is the opposite of that abroad. The anticipation of future increases in the full-employment deficit, and therefore in the full-employment demand for US goods, creates the expectation of future crowding out and currency appreciation. In forward-looking asset and exchange markets this crowding out is anticipated by an immediate appreciation.

It must be noted that the link between fiscal policy and exchange rates has three aspects: first, international differences in the direction or extent of fiscal expansion; second, the measurement of fiscal policy by changes in *full-employment* budgets, and finally the need to pay attention to anticipated future changes in fiscal policy. The failure to pay attention to these points explains why a recent US Treasury study arrived at the opposite, though inappropriate, conclusion:

> There is no reliable empirical evidence to support the contention that large government budget deficits cause appreciation of the country's currency, at least as far as the dollar is concerned. As a matter of record the opposite hypothesis, if anything, appears to be better supported by historical data.[1]

The discussion has made no room, so far, for current-account imbalances in the explanation of exchange rate movements. There are firm theoretical reasons for current-account deficits to lead to depreciation and surpluses to bring about appreciation. However, the channels through which these effects operate and their quantitative magnitude make it empirically implausible that the market's belief that the current account does matter could lead to a collapse of the dollar. The uncomfortable part in this view is that the deficits have been so clearly predictable and predicted that the collapse should already have occurred.

Effects of the appreciation

The appreciation of the dollar has played a major role in helping reduce inflation in the USA, but also in deepening the recession and perhaps slowing the recovery. By reducing the level or the rate of inflation of import prices, and in particular the prices of materials, the appreciation has slowed down inflation. In this process it is worth separating out three distinct channels. First, dollar appreciation lowers the dollar prices of primary commodities in world trade and therefore reduces US costs in producing manufactures, lowers producer prices and thus ultimately prices to consumers. Second, prices of manufactures produced abroad decline, or grow less, in dollar terms, as already seen in Table 7.2, which again lowers inflation.

The third channel emphasizes competitive effects. Dollar appreciation lowers import prices of manufactured goods relative to the prices of the same goods produced by domestic firms. This brings about pressure to cut domestic costs and prices in the affected industries. This effect is particularly significant because it was responsible for

Table 7.4 The Impact of Dollar Appreciation on the US Economy (Cumulative Effect in 1980–1983, first quarter)

Real GNP	Employment	Unemployment Rate
− 2.3%	− 1.1 million	− 0.9%

the break in wage patterns in the settlements in key industries exposed to severe competition by the persistently strong dollar. As a consequence, hourly earnings in manufacturing in 1983 have grown at a rate significantly smaller than in the economy at large, thus reflecting the wage discipline features of appreciation.

The price effects of appreciation are brought out by the large differences in the cumulative price increases in the traded goods sector compared with the entire economy. In the period 1980–3 (second quarter) the GNP deflator increased by 20.6 per cent, the export deflator by only 12.6 per cent, and the import deflator actually fell by 6.9 per cent. These price effects, of course, also reflect the behaviour of oil prices and of the world recession, but in good part must be attributed to the dollar. The overall effect of dollar appreciation on inflation in the USA has been estimated to be a reduction of about 1 to 1.5 percentage points per year over the past three years.

The counterpart of the disinflationary benefits is a sharp loss in international cost competitiveness and hence in output and employment. Table 7.4 reports estimates of the cumulative losses in output and employment in the US economy. It is worth emphasizing that the output and employment costs of dollar appreciation are concentrated on firms competing in world markets or competing in the US market with foreign producers. Moreover, the full adjustment to the overvaluation has, as yet, not been completed, and the growing losses in the international sector are exerting a drag on recovery elsewhere in the economy.

The gains from more rapid disinflation in the USA are offset abroad by increased inflationary pressure. The losses in output and employment here have as a counterpart export-led recovery in Europe and in Japan. Thus, for the rest of the world, dollar appreciation is a mixed blessing. Indeed, the inflationary impact has led many countries initially to tighten their policies to try and offset 'imported inflation', thus steeply reinforcing the collapse in world activity. Dollar appreciation and the world recession have severely reinforced in LDCs the consequences of their own policy mistakes. Low real prices of commodities, increases in the real value of dollar debts and high real interest rates due to our poor monetary–fiscal mix have precipitated payments crises and are forcing unprecedented economic and social distress, especially in Latin America. Advocating belt-tightening *abroad* by the US Treasury is an almost cynical misperception of the sources of the problem and the appropriate adjustments.

Overvaluation and exchange rate policy

The losses in output and employment which the US economy is suffering in industries that are competing with the rest of the world and the vast deterioration in the trade balance suggest an overvalued dollar. Indeed, the affected industries have left no doubt that they consider the dollar overvalued and have recommended that their competitiveness be restored, especially by Japanese policies to appreciate the yen.

I define as the equilibrium real exchange rate the rate which, in conjunction with real interest rates and fiscal policy, yields full employment. This definition takes as a bench-mark employment, not the current account or any other component of the external balance. It also emphasizes that exchange rates are only one of the key macroeconomic variables impinging on policy objectives.

With this definition in mind two points emerge. First, clearly the dollar is too high *and* real interest rates are too high because we do observe high unemployment. Second, high unemployment prevails not only in the USA but also abroad. In that sense all currencies are overvalued and, predictably, all countries seek competitive depreciation and might pursue such a policy aggressively were it not for the inflation costs following from currency depreciation.

The dollar appreciation and the increase in world real interest rates are part of the same anticipated adjustment to large high employment deficits and continuing tight money. If our fiscal policies persist then *ultimately* the current real exchange rates and real interest rates are warranted. The joint problem of dollar overvaluation and excess long-term real interest rates thus reflects primarily a premature adjustment of asset prices to future equilibrium values: asset markets are too much forward-looking and monetary policy (perhaps wisely) is too unaccommodating.

The dollar overvaluation has led to two kinds of proposal: exchange market intervention and exchange-rate orientated money policy, on one side; and measures to appreciate the yen, on the other.

The case for *sterilized* foreign exchange market intervention is well established: in the face of international shifts in portfolios, in a circumstance where no real adjustments in the economy are called for, the optimal policy is to intervene in financial markets to absorb the securities investors wish to sell off and to sell the securities investors wish to buy. Intervention in these conditions prevents any and all undesirable spillover effects to exchange rates, money supplies and interest rates, and therefore seals off the real economy from the purely financial disturbance. Suppose, for example, investors lose confidence in the political stability of West Germany and therefore attempt to shift out of Deutschmarks into dollar assets, in the process leading to a dollar appreciation. The correct response is to stabilize the exchange rate, buying German securities and selling dollar bonds. Note that the appropriate response is *sterilized* intervention. Printing money in response to an appreciation induced by portfolio shifts, however, is an entirely and totally unsound policy response. Exchange-rate-orientated monetary policy is appropriate only when, implausibly, international currency substitution is the dominant source of monetary disturbances.[2]

Of course, there are macro-economic disturbances that call for adjustments not only in the relative supplies of securities, but also in other macro-economic variables. It is hard to think of an empirically important disturbance where the only appropriate response is to sustain exchange rates by expanding money in one country and contracting it abroad. As a rule we would expect adjustments in interest rates, in exchange rates and in fiscal policy in both countries. Dealing with disturbances exclusively by unsterilized intervention as the cure-all may in fact aggravate the consequences of asynchronized policies.

The large, cumulative movements of real exchange rates of the past three years have once again brought up proposals for some international arrangement that limits cumulative exchange rate movements within a given time period, that is, some form of exchange rate target zone. The specifics of the proposals — crawling pegs with soft bumpers — are often reminiscent of Office of Safety and Health Administration regulations.

Limiting real exchange rate fluctuations by international understandings on target zones would be a good idea under some circumstances. But such agreements, without explicit and specific targets for real interest rates and the monetary–fiscal policy mix are a serious mistake.

Surely we have understood by now that implementing exchange rate targets requires changes in monetary and fiscal policy — the fundamentals. Even recognizing the potential for monetary policy to influence exchange rates, I believe it would be a mistake to leave fiscal policy out of an agreement on limits to the admissible range of key macro-economic variables. Specifically in the present context, I believe it is a serious error to expand the US money stock, and contract it in West Germany, to get the dollar down, leaving fiscal policy unchanged.

Exchange-rate-orientated monetary policy, in the current US conditions, would take a high dollar as a signal to expand money and would lead us to monetize fiscal deficits, rather than to correct the fiscal imbalance. Surely this must be considered extremely unwise policy advice, even on the part of those who believe money is tight. On the contrary, the appropriate adjustment for the USA is to cut future deficits and for Europe to engage in transitory fiscal expansion. Given the difficulties, however, of reconciling fiscal targets, I believe there is no practical room for exchange rate targets. On the contrary, the extreme exchange rate overvaluation is an almost desirable check against persistence of the fiscal imbalance.

Aside from exchange-rate-orientated monetary policy there have been specific proposals to reduce the competitive pressure on US business by causing a yen appreciation. The proposals involve various ways in which the world demand for yen securities would be increased — Japanese financial liberalization, the yen as a world currency, invoicing world trade in yen, and so on. The effectiveness of these proposals, unlike that of proposals in the area of trade and procurement liberalization, is vastly overrated and their merit is questionable. The experience with removal of exchange control in the UK or restrictions on US private gold holdings does not suggest that changes in controls in fact lead to major changes in asset prices.

More basically, the proposals involve the proposition that Japan should have higher unemployment and the USA less, unless Japan chooses to expand aggregate demand through fiscal policy. It is unreasonable that, faced with our own unbalanced fiscal policies, we should now recommend that Japan adjust. The more appropriate view is in the first place not to single out Japan, but to focus on the USA relative to other industrialized countries. This is appropriate because, as we saw above, the USA has got out of line. Any sensible cure of the dollar overvaluation requires restructuring world-wide fiscal policies to remove the extreme fiscal asynchronization already discussed above in Table 7.4.

It may be useful to add that fiscal co-ordination could take the form of a long-run cut in US deficits, matched in Europe by a transitory, cyclical increase in high employment deficits. The lower long-run US deficits would reduce long-run real interest rates and thus add to expansion, as would the European fiscal expansion. The world economy, and in particular the LDCs, would more certainly enjoy a sustained expansion without the risks of a slow down next year. A dollar depreciation that would be expected in such a policy package would prove inflationary for the USA, but it is certainly true that today we are in a much better position to accept some inflationary shock than another year into the recovery when commodities and labour markets will be much tighter.

Reform of the international monetary system

The world macro-economy is in the process of dramatic experiments with inflation stabilization and fiscal imbalance, superimposed on sharp changes in sectoral international competitiveness. This is a very poor time to think of moving towards an exchange rate regime that limits exchange rate fluctuations without, at the same time, achieving a believable co-ordination of monetary and fiscal policy. The initial conditions vary widely between countries — Europe and Japan are tightening while the USA is expanding; inflation rates diverge significantly, and the starting point is an overvalued dollar.

It is clear that the flexible exchange rate system is poorly suited to deal with asynchronized monetary and fiscal policy mixes: under these conditions flexible rates work poorly in the sense that they show large, cumulative movements away from levels justified by current levels of demand. But other exchange rate arrangements would cope as poorly. The problem is not the exchange rate system but the policy mix. Few would argue that bond markets need intervention just because real interest rates are unusually high. It is well understood, at least by those who understand, that this is a reflection of the policies that influence demand and supply conditions in the bond market. The same is true of the exchange market and the answer is more sensible policy mixes (monetary, fiscal and income policy), not schemes to fix interest rates or exchange rates.

Notes

1. See *Government Deficit Spending and Its Effects on Prices of Financial Assets*, Office of the Assistant Secretary for Economic Policy, Department of the Treasury, May 1983, p 15. The study not only fails to make the distinction between actual and full-employment budgets but also fails to understand the forward-looking nature of asset markets (see ibid., p. 7).
2. This point is well understood in the conduct of domestic monetary policy, but remains surprisingly controversial in a foreign exchange market context even today. See R. McKinnon, *Why Floating Exchange Rates Fail*, Stanford University, June 1983.

8 The international monetary system in the 1990s

Anthony Loehnis

Where we stand and prospects

As we stand on the threshold of a new decade, seeking to foresee what changes may befall the international monetary system in the years ahead, a useful starting point is to define where we currently are. The Heads of government meeting in Paris in July 1989 defined the status quo thus:

> Under the Plaza and Louvre Agreements, our countries agreed to pursue, in a mutually reinforcing way, policies of surveillance and co-ordination aimed at improving their economic fundamentals and at fostering stability of exchange rates consistent with these fundamentals . . .
>
> The co-ordination process has made a positive contribution to world economic development and it has also contributed greatly to improving the functioning of the International Monetary System. There has also been continued co-operation in exchange markets.
>
> It is important to continue, and where appropriate, to develop this cooperative and flexible approach to improve the functioning and stability of the International Monetary System in a manner consistent with economic fundamentals. We therefore ask the Finance Ministers to continue to keep under review possible steps that could be taken to improve the co-ordination process, exchange market co-operation, and the functioning of the International Monetary System.[1]

To some this will seem a complacent statement, masking the failure of G7 governments to pursue the logic of the Plaza and the Louvre agreements in order to move the international monetary system further along the spectrum from the freely floating exchange rate regime that prevailed in the early 1980s towards a more rule-based system of fixed but adjustable exchange rate relationships between the dollar, the yen and the Deutschmark. To others it will appear to be a realistic assertion that the process of international co-operation in economic policy-making with a view to ensuring greater exchange rate stability, begun at the Plaza meeting in September 1985

Anthony Loehnis is Vice Chairman, S.G. Warburg and was formerly an Executive Director at the Bank of England.

and refined at the Louvre meeting in February 1987 and subsequently, has not been unsuccessful and will be continued in a pragmatic rather than dramatic way into the period ahead. A third group, whose most forceful advocate is Martin Feldstein, might think such a statement meaningless rhetoric, on the grounds that 'foreign governments will inevitably pursue the policies they believe are in their own interests' and that 'the US should now in a clear but friendly way end the international co-ordination of macro-economic policy'.[2]

The experience of the 1980s suggests that the full-blooded cynicism expressed by Feldstein is hardly justified. It may be the case, as Feldstein argues, that 'it is frightening to the American public and upsetting to our financial markets to believe that the fate of our economy depends on the decisions made in Bonn and Tokyo'.[3] But complementary fears are felt by the public in West Germany, Japan or anywhere else at the prospect that the fate of *their* domestic economies depends on decisions about trade restrictions or budget deficits taken in the US Congress. It was surely this common perception of the interdependence of national economies in today's world which led to the sea-change in the conduct of international economic policy-making between the first and second halves of the 1980s, of which the Plaza agreement was the watershed. The evidence suggests that financial markets at least have been reassured by the change, notwithstanding the stock market crash of 1987.

Nevertheless, Feldstein's critique of international policy co-ordination contains a hard kernel of truth: expectations of what policy co-ordination may achieve should not be pitched too high, because domestic political considerations will constantly intervene in, if not overwhelm, the process. The difficulties of making progress with macro-economic policy co-ordination can almost be expressed as a paradoxical syllogism. What has been wrong with the post-Bretton Woods system has been the unwillingness or inability of governments to conduct their economic policies in a mutually compatible or consistent manner, resulting in sub-optimal performance nationally or internationally; therefore we need a rule-based system which will force them in the right policy direction and help them overcome the domestic political constraints against the adoption of appropriate policies; political will, however, is required to embrace a rule-based system, and if that political will existed the appropriate policies would be adopted without the need for a rule-based system. If this is so, it is unlikely that the 1990s will witness any quantum change in the shape of the international monetary system. This does not, of course, preclude that further useful and significant moves may be made along the spectrum from free floating to a rule-based system with effective policy co-ordination.

Such a priori scepticism that the international monetary system will be dramatically reformed, for instance along the lines advocated in January 1988 by the then Finance Minister Balladur of France,[4] is reinforced by a number of likely features of the landscape of the 1990s which will limit the scope (but not necessarily the need) for significant change. The economic hegemony of the United States is likely to continue to be eroded in the face of Japanese prosperity and the completion of the internal market in Europe (whether or not accompanied or followed by closer monetary and economic union). None the less, the US dollar will continue to be the dominant international currency, though ceding more of that dominance to the yen and the Deutschmark. Advances in the fields of telecommunications and information technology will push in the direction of more integrated and international financial and capital markets. Finally, there will continue to be a lack of coherent and agreed intellectual framework governing the way domestic economies work and interact, which has been a feature of the 1970s and 1980s.

It might be argued that a world in which economic leadership is shared, in which the communications revolution puts increasing power and resources at the disposal of markets as opposed to governments, and in which there is no consensus how the available instruments of economic adjustment operate or should appropriately be used, could turn out to be a very unstable world in which sufficiently serious mishaps or crises could occur to create a political will to provide a radical move towards a more rule-based system. Such a crisis might relate to strains in the exchange rate mechanism of the EMS should capital flows, following the implementation of the Directive on liberalization of capital movements in mid-1990, prove as large and disruptive as some European governments express themselves as fearing; or to a dramatic development in the trade protectionist spiral, provoked perhaps by some long-term shift in the Japanese political matrix resulting from the disarray experienced by the LDP in the course of 1989. Absent some systemic crisis of that nature, however, it is not easy to imagine the circumstances which would lead the existing G7 governments to accelerate the pace of change in the international monetary system, however persuasively the case may have been made for a voluntary commitment outside of a time of crisis to more effective policy co-ordination and a more structured mechanism for achieving currency stability.[5]

The Plaza and Louvre agreements assessed

The question must then be asked whether the continuation, or gradual evolution, of the present situation is as bad a prospect as is sometimes made out. Is the Louvre agreement dead or discredited? Has the world not become a financially safer place, and one in which it has become easier for businessmen to make rational investment judgements, than if the Plaza/Louvre process had not taken place?

It may seem strange to pose these questions when, within eight months of the Louvre agreement being signed, world stock markets were plunged into the greatest turmoil and price falls since 1929, and when the proximate cause of the crash was arguably the unco-ordinated raising of German interest rates earlier in October 1987, at a time when policy disagreements between two of the most important G7 countries were being publicly aired. It is important, however, to distinguish the proximate from the fundamental causes of the crash — indeed, what needs to be explained is not so much the causes of the crash as the causes of the persistent rise in stock market prices world-wide in the months that preceeded it. And the fact that 1988 proved to be not the year of world-wide recession which so many at the time of the crash had feared, but in many countries a year of unexpectedly strong, and largely unforecast, growth surely had much to do with the evidence of co-ordinated and controlled relaxation of monetary policy in G7 countries following the crash. The year 1988 began, therefore, with the reputation of international policy co-ordination rightly somewhat restored, and, following a conspicuously well-timed piece of concerted intervention by the G7 authorities early in the New Year, with the market's faith in the willingness of the authorities to co-operate to maintain currency stability intact.

It is certainly too early to reach a verdict on the efficacy or sustainability of what one may call the 'Plaza/Louvre process'. What can be said is that the verdict of some that the process is dead seems to be based on a misunderstanding of the essential nature of the agreements. The misunderstanding has arisen in part from frustration on the part of those who hanker after more structured and enforceable arrangements (whether they be outside commentators or some of the actual parties to the Agreements) at the gap between what they think desirable and what has proved achievable. It is a misunderstanding that has probably been fuelled by the well-researched but in parts misleading account of the 'inside story' of the agreements provided by Yoichi Funabashi.[6]

It is, of course, true that the dollar had already turned down from the peak achieved in February 1985, and that it should not be claimed for the Plaza agreement of September that it was responsible for stopping the rise of the dollar. The Plaza agreement was never-theless a turning point in the evolution of the international monetary system in three important respects: the US authorities accepted that the international dimension mattered and that virtue might consist of more than just putting one's own house in order and regarding the level of the exchange rate as a sort of international score-card measuring success in doing so; the G5 countries together openly acknowledged that the international marketplace's judgement on exchange rates could be wrong; and they also asserted that something could be done about it and committed themselves to doing it. It is unlikely that the fall of the effective rate of the dollar by 30 per cent from its peak of February 1985 to its level two years later when the Louvre agreement was signed would have been achievable without the Plaza declaration. Indeed, without the Plaza agreement it is inconceivable that such a decline in the dollar could have been accomplished without the 'hard landing' for the world economy that had looked so likely a prospect. Yet US interest rates declined over the same period by some 40 per cent.

So successful was the Plaza agreement in its aim of lowering the dollar exchange rate that one of the proximate motives for entering into the Louvre agreement, where the commitment was made 'to cooperate closely to foster stability of exchange rates around current levels', was to prevent an overshoot of the dollar on the downside. While the Plaza participants certainly had no specific target for the dollar other than lower, it is not the case that at the Louvre they felt that 'current levels' were in any special sense consistent with fundamentals. It was rather that they felt the markets needed to catch their breath and pause for adjustment after the dollar's precipitate decline since the Plaza.

It was noteworthy, moreover, that the reiteration of the commitment to foster exchange rate stability which was made in subsequent G7 statements of 8 April, 26 September and 22 December 1987, was in the first two cases at least still explained in terms of 'current levels', which perhaps gave the impression that the successive agreements were designed to fix exchange rates more rigidly than was in fact the intention. Indeed, the levels which were 'current' at the date of each statement were significantly different from those of the previous occasion. Nevertheless, particularly between April and October, markets believed the commitments sufficiently not to test them seriously. It is true that central bank intervention to support the dollar took place on a significant scale during 1987, but it often forgotten that a substantial amount of that support for the dollar was undertaken by two central banks (one of which was not even party to the G7 agreements) acting in accordance with their own domestic priorities.

The willing suspension of the market's disbelief that current exchange rates or current policies will deliver the desired current-account adjustment is an essential part of the whole process. But the suspension of disbelief depends not just on intervention, or fear of it, but on a very delicate balance between fear of intervention and confidence that policy commitments are appropriate and will be put into practice. The Plaza/Louvre process has a dual nature — policy co-ordination and joint action in the markets to stabilize exchange rates. One useful legacy of the limited international co-operation that took place in the first half of the 1980s was the January 1983 *Report of the Working Group on Exchange Market Intervention* commissioned at the 1981 summit,[7] (Chairman; Philippe Surgensen) which had as one of its main conclusions that concerted intervention could not be effective unless supported by appropriate policy measures. This lesson was taken on board in the Plaza agreement, nearly half of which was taken up by specific policy undertakings by each of the five participating governments. These undertakings were repeated and reinforced, in some cases in more quantified form, in the Louvre agreement, suggesting that their fulfilment had been less complete than desired or expected.

Undertakings regarding fiscal policy were more specific than those regarding monetary or structural policies, but certainly (and realistically) did not seek to establish a co-ordinated fiscal strategy. Shortcomings in the implementation of fiscal policy have been seen particularly in the United States, with the well-publicized differences of opinion between the administration and Congress on the implementation of deficit reduction measures, and in West Germany, where serious analytical differences have existed among G7 participants regarding the effects of expansionary measures. Over monetary policy, too, which has a more immediate impact on exchange rates, there have been differences, again reflecting differing judgements on where the relative risks between inflation or recession lie in individual countries.

Given that such policy judgements are rarely self-evident, it is not surprising that differences of opinion, or shortcomings in execution, exist. Inevitably, however, they weaken the credibility of the agreements, and the more so when they are publicly articulated. It is wholly understandable how the exigencies of the domestic political process lead responsible spokesmen from individual G7 countries to make statements about economic policy in a domestic context which may not be consistent with commitments made in the international context, or with statements made by spokesmen from other countries. But it must be realized that publicly expressed differences of opinion make more difficult the establishment of creditibility in both the policy undertakings and the commitment to exchange rate stability.

If the Plaza/Louvre process is to maintain, restore even, its credibility, what modifications need to be made? In a world where the *Zeitgeist* is in favour of deregulation, and where technology presses inexorably in the direction of integrated international markets, so that exchange rates are determined as much by asset movements as they are by trade imbalances, the balancing act between policy co-ordination and concerted action to indicate to markets the authorities' views of a broadly appropriate relationship between the main internationally traded currencies is one of great sensitivity: the crowd's belief that the performers will carry it off is far from robust. This being so, it would be unwise to seek to move prematurely towards agreement on more specific exchange rate targets. It is also moot whether the process would be more or less robust if the judgement of the G7 authorities on the appropriate exchange rate ranges at any particular time were to be publicly announced. This is a central plank of the proposals of Kenen and of Williamson and Miller,[8] but most practitioners believe that conditions are not yet ripe at the global level for any greater degree of specificity. It is enough for the moment to have reduced the scope and attraction of destabilizing market speculation by making markets wary of concerted intervention. A certain amount of obscurity and uncertainty about the timing and extent of such intervention is an important ingredient in its success.

Nevertheless, it would be impossible to maintain credibility if the market's understanding of the broad area of exchange rate relativities thought appropriate by the authorities was wrong, or if the authorities remained silent or indifferent when one or other currency moved clearly and permanently outside that range. Such a situation has been almost reached on two occasions: in the late summer and autumn of 1988, when the effective rate of the dollar rose by some 8 per cent, and in the early spring of 1989, when it rose by 12 per cent to a peak of DM 2.04. In each case the situation was eventually corrected, but the process suffered some damage to its creditability. The major piece of unfinished business at this stage of the move along the continuum towards managed floating is, as UK Chancellor of the Exchequer, Nigel Lawson, pointed out in his speech to the Annual Meeting of the IMF/IBRD in September 1987: 'to manage any changes [of key exchange rates] in an orderly way'. So far the shift from the 'current values' that seemed appropriate to defend in February 1987 to those which the authorities are now thought to consider acceptable has been accomplished by passive acquiescence to shifts brought about by the market rather than in response to an active steer from the authorities. Perhaps the G7 authorities should be prepared to be more explicit about whether or not they are satisfied with 'current values' of exchange rates when they meet together and issue a communiqué.

Two conclusions can be drawn from all this. First, the process of policy co-ordination and managing exchange rates begun in 1985 at the Plaza is still an infant industry, which needs careful nurturing and patient coaxing towards a more robust state. What has been achieved could all too easily be lost if the infant attempted to move too fast. Second, the minimalist nature of that conclusion does not mean that we are not palpably better off with what we have than if we were to return to the Hobbesian world of the early 1980s.

Lessons from the EMS?

Some of those who would dismiss these conclusions as altogether too unambitious might point to the European Monetary System (EMS) as a paradigm of what can be achieved through effective policy co-ordination and a clearly articulated, rule-based exchange rate mechanism. It is worth examining this proposition to see whether any lessons can be drawn from the EMS experience for management of the international monetary system and its possible evolution in the 1990s.

Prima facie, the experience of the EMS since its establishment in 1979 should give encouragement to the proponents of closer international monetary co-operation against the sceptics. At its outset scepticism abounded, not least among many of the central banks involved and other technical experts. The following is a typical example:

While some journalists have hailed the EMS as a step towards a common currency in Europe, there seems little in the experience since 1972, or the commitments now undertaken, to support bold claims or hopes. Until labour and capital have sufficient mobility among EEC countries that the countries experience excess demands or supplies in the labour market at about the same time and governments can justify common monetary and fiscal policies, it will be difficult for nations to relinquish their independence to deal with pressing domestic problems. As long as European governments engage in divergent monetary and fiscal policies, the goal of maintaining fixed ratios in the value of their currencies will remain unrealistic.[9]

Yet by its tenth anniversary its achievements were rightly being applauded. The aim of establishing a zone of monetary stability in Europe seemed well on the way to fulfilment. Rates of inflation in particular, but other measures of economic performance as well, had converged, reducing the need for realignments. Indeed, the last realignment took place in January 1987, and that, arguably, could have been avoided had the interest rate changes that then took place in France and West Germany been implemented voluntarily in the last quarter of 1986.

In the field of policy co-ordination also, significant advances had been made. The European Community has plenty of fora for the co-ordination of economic policy, but the rules of the exchange rate mechanism (ERM) have undoubtedly proved the most potent spur, with significant domestic policy changes being implemented in France, Italy and Belgium particularly, which might not have taken place had those countries had less commitment to the ideal of currency stability and the need to enhance the credibility of the ERM. The somewhat traumatic nature of the 1987 realignment was certainly an important factor in the enhancement of co-ordination of monetary policies provided for in the Basle/Nyborg agreements of September 1987. The persistence of significant trade imbalances between EC members suggests that the commitment to exchange rate stability — particularly in the context of pressures to move sooner rather than later to monetary union — may even result in the postponement of necessary and desirable parity adjustment. None the less, optimism that currency stability and economic policy co-ordination among twelve sovereign states is a practical possibility needs to be tempered by consideration both of the particular conditions which have made it possible, and of the differences between the reality and the theory of how the ERM works.

The particular conditions that underpin the success of the EMS amount basically to the prior political commitment in the Treaty of Rome and subsequent sacred texts not only to the establishment of a common market in goods, services and labour and capital movements, but also to 'an ever closer union'. As the next few years are bound to show, there are differences of opinion among member states as to what this involves, but there is little doubt that for the original signatories of the Rome Treaty it involves closer political integration somewhere down the road. And a layman (rather than a constitutional lawyer) reading the texts as a whole (including the Single European Act which came into force in 1987) could easily conclude that, taken together, they amount to a moral commitment to the establishment of monetary and economic union at some stage. All this has already involved sacrifices of national sovereignty in a number of areas, most notably, perhaps, that of trade policy, and has led to a significant increase in the percentage of member states' trade that is intra-Community rather than with non-Community countries. This has itself proved an added incentive to make the ERM work.

The ERM has worked, however, rather differently from the way its creators expected in at least three important respects. First, the ECU is in no sense central to the system. The commercial ECU has developed, parallel to the official ECU, and has had a fair degree of success as a hedging currency, particularly as a vehicle for borrowing. But it suffers from a relative lack of liquidity compared with national currencies, and remains an artefact of the banking system rather than a fully-fledged (let alone parallel) currency whose issue is controlled by a central authority ready to act as a lender of last resort. The official ECU remains a book-keeping concept, subject to quinquennial reweighting and little used to finance interventions within the ERM. Appetite for the commercial ECU may grow, particularly as its liquidity is improved by the development of a wider range of debt and money-market instruments so denominated, and as volatility between its constituent currencies reduces further. In this way it may become more attractive as a store of value both for official reserves and for the private sector, but it is still a long way from becoming a serious substitute for national currencies.

The second way in which the practice of the ERM has diverged from its blueprint is that it has obstinately remained an asymmetrical, Deutschmark-anchored system rather than a symmetrical one, in which adjustment obligations are shared between surplus and deficit countries. Given the different inflation performance of participants, and in some cases different stages of economic development, this has no doubt proved advantageous. But it is an area which produces persistent political if not economic friction within the system, which has been successfully overcome only because other political imperatives have been deemed more important. This underlines, however, the inherent tension in any system for exchange rate stabilization between those who see it as a discipline and those who see it as a mechanism for burden-sharing.

Finally, the intervention and financing mechanisms of the ERM have operated very differently from the way originally envisaged. Most of the intervention within the system has been intra-marginal rather than marginal. The automatic financing mechanism provided for in the central bank governors' agreement of 1979 related only to intervention at the margin. This again has caused difficulties from time to time, particularly where countries wishing to support their currencies intra-marginally by intervening in another member's currency have found the authorities of that counterparty unwilling to see its currency used in this way because of the implications for domestic monetary conditions. The situation was relieved somewhat by the technical adjustments to the original governors' agreement made under the Basle/Nyborg agreements, which provided for a degree of ECU settlement for intra-marginal intervention. But the whole experience suggests the importance of flexibility in any exchange rate stabilization system, both because of the essentially psychological battle that must be engaged with markets, and because of the occurrence from time to time of irreconcilable conflicts between the external constraint and intractable domestic political imperatives. It may be regrettable, but under almost any imaginable system it is almost inevitable, that such conflicts will be resolved in favour of the stronger party.

The EMS is now at an important crossroads. The path of gradual, pragmatic evolution implicit in the Basle/Nyborg agreements of 1987 along which it has been moving has now been intersected by the highway of the completion of the internal market by 1992 and the possible super-highway of accelerated moves towards economic and monetary union. These present two important tests for the existing EMS. Can it survive the liberalization of capital movements when that Directive comes into force in mid-1990? Could it survive the entry into the ERM of sterling, which is a necessary component of completing Stage 1 of the path towards economic and monetary union, the implementation of which is the one part of the Delors Report to have been already accepted by member governments?

On the effect of the EMS on the liberalization of capital movements opinions are sharply divided. There are those who argue that since free capital movements, fixed exchange rates and autonomous domestic monetary policies are incompatible, what has to give is the autonomy of domestic monetary policy. From this it is a short step to arguing that monetary union should be brought about sooner rather than later. This argument ignores, however, that the autonomy of domestic monetary policy has been progressively eroded over the life of the EMS, and not only for those members with higher inflation. Furthermore, the experience of the members of the EMS (in which the UK is included, despite not yet having adhered to the ERM) which have had no exchange controls for some time is that their abolition may lead to a gradual portfolio shift on the part of domestic investors, but this is likely to be balanced or exceeded by inflows from those encouraged to bring their funds in to take advantage of investment opportunities or interest rate differentials by the removal of the fear that they may not be able to remove such funds at will. Given that most restrictions on capital movements in France and Italy have already been removed, and that 'hot' or panic money has largely found its way abroad already, the complete removal of such controls in 1990 may well not lead to disequilibrating outflows. And there are, of course, transitional arrangements for countries where financial structures are still somewhat underdeveloped. There may be more justification for fears that some savings may shift to take advantage of different fiscal regimes, particularly in countries where fiscal discipline is not strong. But the solution in that case should lie in greater co-operation between the fiscal authorities in member countries and/or structural measures to alter attitudes to fiscal discipline in countries where it is weak.

As to the effect of the entry of sterling into the ERM, again opinions are sharply divided. There must be a risk that the introduction of another significant international trading currency such as sterling into a hitherto DM-based system would be destabilizing, particularly when the propensity to inflation in the UK and West Germany is so different, and when any further dramatic shift in oil prices, which cannot be ruled out for the future, would affect the two currencies in opposite directions. Certainly the recent divergence of the UK inflation rate from the much-reduced EC average provides a clearer justification for the unripe time argument than has often been the case. There may also be a strongish case for not trying to introduce sterling into the mechanism at the same time as the total liberalization of capital movements comes into effect, in case fears of the pessimists of subsequent strains are fulfilled. At the end of the day, however, and on both sides of the Channel, the strongest argument in favour of sterling's inclusion in the ERM is political. The likelihood therefore must be that sterling will join the ERM in the 1990s.

For the reasons indicated above, even if the time of sterling's entry was optimal in terms both of an improved inflation performance by the UK and an absence of currency turmoil more generally, the new, bipolar nature of the ERM would be likely sooner or later to provoke speculative movements which would test its robustness. Provided the enhanced moves towards closer intra-EC policy co-ordination envisaged for Stage 1 in the Delors Report are broadly and convincingly implemented, however, the experience and flexibility developed over the life of the EMS should enable the system to weather most storms. Some have suggested that in order to provide a margin for error or the unexpected sterling should enter with the wider 6 per cent margin rather than 2¼ per cent. Indeed, those most pessimistic about the ability of the system to survive the liberalization of capital movements have suggested widening the intervention margins for all. Such a move, if made *ex ante*, would hardly seem to be giving the right signals, either in respect of members' willingness to take the necessary policy measures to underpin exchange rate stability, or in terms of the readiness of the Community to move to monetary union. It would surely be better to maintain the narrow band, and for sterling to join that band, but to be ready to adjust central parities where necessary, until convergence of economic performance between members has advanced sufficiently for this no longer to be necessary.

A glance at Delors

Following the publication of the Delors Report and the European Council meeting in Madrid in June 1989, there is a possibility that the EMS will become transformed into a monetary union, with permanently locked parities if not a single currency and a single European monetary policy determined by some form of European central bank. It would be visionary to suppose that European monetary arrangements of that sort would have much relevance as a paradigm for the international monetary system, although obviously if and when European economic and monetary union comes about, the nature of international monetary arrangements will undergo significant change. In one sense the process of policy co-ordination should be simplified because there would only be three protagonists. In another sense it could become more complicated, because there must be some risk that the establishment of a Europe that was not only a common market, but also an economic and monetary union, would stimulate the division of the capitalist world into three major trading blocs based on the dollar, the yen and the common European currency. It is not obvious that such blocs would find it any easier to harmonize and co-ordinate economic policy than it is at present, particularly to the extent that the creation of the blocs might be associated with increased protectionism. Nor is it clear how the developing countries of the world or those with centrally planned economies endeavouring to become more market-orientated would fit into the picture.

In any event, this is not the place to analyse the Delors Report, or to prognosticate on the likelihood or timetable of its implementation. It may be worth recalling, however, that the Report is in essence descriptive rather than prescriptive. It describes first what economic and monetary union would involve, and then, if you like what you see, some concrete steps (the three stages) might be taken to achieve it. No specific timetable is envisaged, other than that Stage 1 should start no later than when the Directive for the full liberalization of capital movements comes into force; and the description of Stages 2 and 3 is a skimpy sketch rather than a detailed blueprint. These facts tend to be obscured by those who find it helpful to pray in aid a Report signed unanimously by all twelve central bank governors of the Community in order to accelerate institutional moves towards economic and monetary union. The second chapter of the report in fact spells out in some detail the political implications of economic and monetary union (in a way which has not received universal assent from economists, particularly in the area of fiscal policy). Since the Community has already embarked on a programme to complete the internal market by the end of 1992, which is itself fraught with political problems which will require much patience, skill and the spirit of compromise to overcome, it is hard not to be sympathetic to those who argue that it would be better to complete that 1992 programme as best we can before facing the even greater political challenges presented by institutional moves towards economic and monetary union. The completion of Stage 1 is likely to take some time, as the redefined policy co-ordination process is put in place and put through its paces, and the convergence of economic performance is achieved that is a necessary condition for embarking on Stage 2.

For much of the 1990s, therefore, we can expect that the EMS will continue as part of the scenery, as it has been in the 1980s. Because of the special political circumstances that brought it into being and which have enabled it to gain credibility as a rule-based system for establishing exchange rate stability, the lessons to be drawn for the international monetary system from the EMS experience are more general than particular. The first is that it takes time to build up credibility. The EMS has built that credibility, with the benefit of a specific political commitment towards union, over a decade or more. The rather traumatic realignments of the mid-1980s brought out many premature mourners. For the international monetary system, the Louvre agreement dates from barely three years ago. Patience and perseverance are needed. Second, the credibility of the commitment to exchange rate stability depends on the credibility of the underlying policies and of the commitment to carry them through. In that respect, the visibility of the French policy change in 1983 or of the Belgian adjustment programme in 1982 or latterly of timely and co-ordinated changes in monetary policy have been vital to the dampening of market speculation against EMS currencies. At the G7 level there is still room for improvement. Third, there is a natural tendency to rely too much on monetary policy. It can be changed instantaneously, without the need for the time-consuming parliamentary procedures which accompany budgetary change. But monetary policy is the natural focus for tension between domestic and external requirements. Credibility depends on perceptions that an appropriate overall policy mix is being pursued. Finally, while it is hardly to be expected that politicians or spokesmen for the authorities should always speak with the same voice within one country, let alone within the European or international economic communities, it is quite clear that credibility in the sustainability of agreed arrangements can very rapidly be destroyed through discordant statements made in public, particularly at moments when markets are putting exchange rate regimes to the test. The need to think before you speak is a lesson of universal application. If these lessons are remembered by those responsible for the international monetary system in the 1990s, some comfort can be drawn from the experience of the EMS in the 1980s.

Notes

1. Economic Declaration issued by the Paris summit, 15 July 1989, Paras 10 and 11.
2. Martin Feldstein 'The End of Policy Coordination', *The Wall Street Journal*, 9 November 1987.
3. Ibid.
4. See *Wall Street Journal*, 20 January 1988.
5. See, for example Peter B. Kenen, *Managing Exchange Rates* (RIIA, 1988); or *International Macroeconomic Policy Coordination*, the report of a study group of the Group of Thirty (Group of Thirty, 1988).
6. Yoichi Funabashi, *Managing the Dollar: From the Plaza to the Louvre* (Institute for International Economics, 1988).
7. Kenen, *Managing Exchange Rates*: John Williamson and Marcus H. Miller, *Targets and Indicators: a Blueprint for the International Coordination of Economic Policy*, Institute for International Economics, 1987.
8. J. Carter Murphy, *The International Monetary System: Beyond the First Stage of Reform*, American Enterprise Institute, 1979.

Part 3 European Monetary Union

9 European monetary union

Roy Jenkins

I would like to devote this first Jean Monnet Lecture, in this twentieth anniversary year of the Community, to a single major issue, but one which in its ramifications touches every aspect of European life. The hard, central core of the argument I shall develop turns around the case for monetary union. This, of course, is a familiar rather than a novel concept. Despite its familiarity, it is neither popular nor well understood. But even for those for whom it is part of the normal landscape of economic theory and policy, what is very different compared to the last time the Community discussed the subject in any basic way is the state of the European and world economy, and the state of international monetary affairs. We need also to take a fresh view as to how monetary union should be allied with associated Community policies and, more broadly, with the fundamental question as to how such an idea as monetary union fits with our view of the future division of functions between the Community and member states.

This choice of subject does not imply a narrow economic view of the Community's function. It derives from the obvious fact that the most important weakness of the Community today is its central economic mechanism. Of course, the Community has other primary functions. On the one hand, it stands for a certain type of democratic and political society within Europe; on the other hand, it stands as a viable political entity for dealing with a wide range of external relations.

On these two fronts, much remains to be done. But despite the shocks and difficulties of the recent past, the outlook is one of activity and promise. We are engaged in underpinning our democratic political values, not only in preparing the first direct elections to a new European Parliament, but at the same time confronting sympathetically but realistically the potential adhesion of three new

The author was formerly President of the Commission of the European Communities. This paper is the text of the Jean Monnet Lecture given at the European Institute, Florence, on 27 October 1977, and first appeared in *Lloyds Bank Review*, January 1978.

member states — three states which have recently made the historic shift from military dictatorship to parliamentary democracy. We have in the last fortnight seen a great European nation combat with resilience and skill a major terrorist threat to individual freedom and the rule of law — those fundamental values for the strengthening of which the applicants have turned to Europe for sustenance.

In the world beyond, the Community has a solid record: the Lomé Convention, the Mediterranean agreements, and our response to the North–South dialogue. During the past six months, the Community has continued to move forward at the centre of major world negotiations. Indeed, such has been the advance that we face the somewhat paradoxical spectacle of Europe being taken more seriously from outside than from within. It is a paradox which, in my view, we cannot indefinitely sustain. Our size as a trading *bloc* conceals, rather than heals, our divisions and inequalities in the realm of economic performance. This cannot persist. The central economic weaknesses of Europe, if they continue, will not allow our external cohesion to grow, or even perhaps be maintained. Moreover, the prospect of enlargement will face us with the clear choice either of a strengthening of the sinews of the Community or of tacit acceptance of a loose customs union, far removed from the hopes of its founders, and without much hope of recovering momentum.

The time is ripe

Some commentators believe the time is unpropitious for adventurous ideas. I do not agree. The concept and indeed the politics of monetary union stand immobilized in scepticism, following the demise of the Werner Plan, whose initial exchange rate mechanism was shattered by the turbulent monetary events of the past few years.

The consequence has been an understandable shift of emphasis. The concept of gradualism, which has been more imperceptible than inevitable, has come to supplant more ambitious schemes. Some people seem to believe that we can back our way into monetary union; others that better co-ordination is all that is required. I am afraid neither view is right. The last few years have seen a retreat rather than an advance. In any event, the idea of an antithesis between gradual evolution and dramatic advance is misconceived. Evolution is a process which, once begun, goes both gradually and in jumps. There is room for *tomorrow's* act of better co-ordination and for *today's* discussion of a more ambitious plan *for the day after tomorrow*. The process has to be seen as one. Examples are the Community's role in helping to restructure basic industries that are at present in deep economic difficulty, and measures to abolish the remaining effective frontiers to the free movement of goods and services.

We must now look afresh at the case for monetary union because there are new arguments, new needs and new approaches to be assessed, which go to the heart of our present apparently intractable problems of unemployment, inflation and international financing. There are no less than seven arguments that I would like to put forward. The first and the seventh are classical, but none the less valid for that. The remaining five, however, are all practical points that need to be formulated differently from the way in which they were presented in the early 1970s.

Basic to the case is the ineluctable internationalization of Western economic life. This has been a long and gradual process, but one which has been unmatched by a comparable evolution in the economic institutions of the Community. The past four years have shown the limitations in Europe even of good national economic policies. This has been superimposed on the revolutionary effect of the oil crisis — that sharp confirmation of the end of the old international monetary order which added the hazard of a massive overhang of maldistributed and largely uncontrolled international liquidity to an already vulnerable European economy.

No propositions as radical as monetary union in Europe can be achieved at a stroke. My belief is that we should use the period immediately prior to the first direct elections of the European Parliament to relaunch a major public debate on what monetary union has to offer. In doing so, we have to reckon with the problems of how to get from where we are to where we want to go and what must necessarily accompany monetary union if it is to appeal equally to strong and weak economies, to the richer and poorer parts of the Community.

I wish now to outline the major criteria by which the case has to be judged. I expect no easy consensus on the problems it raises, several of which are either at the heart of what is most controversial in modern economic theory, or the most debatable — in the best sense — in political terms. The debate must now be reopened and subsequently sustained. It will not be quickly foreclosed.

Rationalization

The first argument is that monetary union favours a more efficient and developed rationalization of industry and commerce than is possible under a customs union alone. This argument is as valid now as it has always been, and is reflected in the repeated attempts in European history to form monetary unions — for example the Austro-German monetary union of 1857, the Latin monetary union led by France in 1865, and the Scandinavian union of 1873. Somewhat later, sterling operated a different kind of imperial monetary union over large and disparate parts of the globe. But that is history, although relatively recent history. To return to the present day, discussion with businessmen across Europe produces a clear and consistent complaint that it is difficult, almost impossible, to plan a rational European dimension to their enterprises with the present exchange rate risks and inflation uncertainties as between member states. The same complaint is often heart from those outside who wish to increase their investment in and trade with Europe. This means that the potential benefits of the Community as a common market are far from fully achieved.

A new world currency

The second argument is based on the advantages of creating a major new international currency backed by the economic spread and strength of the Community, which would be comparable to that of the United States, were it not for our monetary divisions and differences. The benefits of a European currency, as a joint and alternative pillar of the world monetary system, would be great and made still more necessary by the current problems of the dollar, with its possible destabilizing effects. By such a development the Community would be relieved of many short-run balance of payments preoccupations. It could live through patches of unfavourable trading results with a few points' drop in the exchange rate and in relative equanimity. International capital would be more stable because there were fewer exchange risks to play on, and Europe would stand to gain through being the issuer of a world currency. National balance of payments problems, in the sense that are experienced today by the Community's member states, would be largely removed as an immediate constraint on economic management. There would still be major financial questions to be resolved, between regions, and between member states, and to these I will return in a moment; but the essential point is that economic welfare in Europe would be improved substantially if macro-economic policy was not subject to present exchange rate and external financial risks. They hang as a sword of Damocles over the heads of many of our countries in Europe today.

It will rightly be argued at this point that sound financial policies are in any case necessary for all countries and that we cannot escape from the need for certain universal disciplines by relocating the level of certain economic policy powers. I myself advocate prudent financial policies, and indeed was accused in the past as a British Chancellor of the Exchequer of that most terrible of sins — excessive prudence. But this is not an argument counter to my main thesis. The relevant question is what degree of reward will the public receive as a result of wise and even courageous policies on the part of its government; or, put another way, what will be the penalties inflicted on our people by a largely anonymous international monetary system which amplifies beyond all proportion any ill fortune of a political or economic nature.

My argument is that it is within our power to change, profoundly and to our advantage, the scale of rewards and retributions administered by the world monetary disorder. We should take it upon ourselves to redesign and restore a large part of that system. In the Community we have the political framework within which a workable alternative could be achieved if we so wish, and if we have the will. The Community is the right size of unit for monetary policy in the particular setting of our highly interdependent, closely packed, advanced industrialized societies. At the world or intercontinental level there is probably no real alternative to floating exchange rates; nor, indeed, is this system such a bad one in that very different context where the units of economic management are widely separated by distance, or society, or political system, or living standards, or several of these factors together.

Countering inflation

My third argument concerns inflation. It is fairly certain that monetary union would radically change the present landscape by leading to a common rate of price movement. But I would also like to argue, although I accept this to be more controversial, that monetary union could help establish a new era of price stability in Europe and achieve a decisive break with the present chronic inflationary disorder. Of course, the sources of contemporary inflation are diverse, and prominent among these are what may seem to be essentially domestic and highly political struggles over income distribution. But, let us suppose at some stage a currency reform: the issue of a new single currency by a European monetary authority; and adoption by this authority of a determined and relatively independent policy of controlling note issue and bank money creation. The authority would start by adopting target rates of growth of monetary expansion consistent with a new European standard of monetary stability, following the best tradition of our least inflationary member states. This would, of course, mean that national governments lost some considerable control over some aspects of macro-economic policy. But governments which do not discipline themselves already find themselves accepting very sharp surveillance from the International Monetary Fund, a body far further away from them and less susceptible to their individual views than is the Community. Furthermore, I must make it clear that my arguments are not addressed to those who would prefer to fail alone rather than succeed together. Attitudes such as theirs inevitably cause deaf ears. I am concerned with those who want to see a successful and strengthened Community, but who also expect to be convinced of the practical benefits of any move forward.

We have to remember what is new about the problem of inflation compared with that to which we were accustomed in the 1950s and 1960s. Floating exchange rates transmit violent and sudden inflationary impulses, which may strike a country at any moment, perhaps just at the time when employers, trade unions and government may be endeavouring to put or hold together a courageous and delicate stabilization programme.

Each new impulse ratchets up the inflationary process. The price rise effect on the devaluing country is much more than the price reduction effect on the revaluing currency because wages, and therefore a large part of costs, cannot be reduced in nominal terms.

Exchange rates may rise and fall, but the price level in all recent experience only goes up. The exchange rate problem feeds in turn the psychology of inflation — the high level of inflationary expectations now endemic in many of our own countries, leading to the danger, only recently averted in some member states, of hyperinflation — that condition in which, almost in the time it takes to walk from bank to shop, the product you planned to buy has become too expensive. Of course, there are conventional responses for trying to contain and reduce the pressures of inflation. But monetary union and reform stand available as the radical treatment for this disease. I do not pretend that the cure would be complete. For example, we would still have to reckon with the inflationary effects of reconciling competing claims on limited resources. The disciplines of monetary union will be more, not less, demanding. The change in inflationary behaviour would not have to be greater than that observed in some recent stabilization policies, but it would have to be permanent. The legitimate needs of the weaker regions would have to be met far more powerfully than is at present the case. I will return to this point in a moment. But the counterpart must be that wages across countries would remain in some kind of reasonable relationship to productivity: here the legitimate concern of the stronger regions and less inflationary states would also have to be met.

Employment

The fourth argument concerns employment: no medium-term recipe for reducing inflation which does not have a beneficial effect upon employment is now acceptable. Present levels of unemployment are the most damaging and dangerous social ill that confront us. At best they produce a self-defeating nationalistic caution and immobilism. At worst they threaten the stability of our social and political systems. We now have 6 million unemployed in the Community. Many have been surprised at the apparent tolerance of our populations to this level. Typically in our larger member states the level of 1 million unemployed long figured as some kind of post-war political barrier. The unthinkable has been surpassed without catastrophe — as yet. But no one should be so complacent as to suppose that this state of affairs can long persist without doing irreparable damage: to the well-being of the millions of families directly affected by unemployment, to the morale and motivation of a whole generation of young people, to stability and consensus in our societies.

In economic terms, I believe that our unemployment problem is essentially one of demand deficiency stemming from the constraints on our ability to cause a smooth, powerful, sustained groundswell of demand. I do not accept that Europe's capacity for creating new wealth, providing new employment and stimulating growth in the right direction is at an end. Environmental factors and the energy crisis mean that we have to look at the nature of our growth. In any event, we need increased output to pay for the present price of oil and for the replacement or adaptation of industrial processes that were designed for lower energy prices and lower environmental standards.

These structural and monetary problems combine to make present levels of unemployment highly intractable. But they should not be seen as justifying defeatist and misconceived policies which would permanently reduce the economic potential of the European economy: for example, excessive reduction in working hours or compulsory retirement at fifty-five.

We also need to view the present economic recession in a longer-term perspective. The extent and persistence of unemployment can no longer be seen as an exceptionally low and long bottom to the business cycle. To restore full employment requires a new impulse on a historic scale. We require a new driving force comparable with the major rejuvenations of the past two hundred years: the industrial revolution itself, the onset of the railway age, the impact of Keynes, the need for post-war reconstruction, the spread of what were previously regarded as middle-class standards to the mass of the population in the industrial countries. I believe that the needs of the Third World have a major part to play here. Two sources of new growth have in the past sometimes come together, the one world-wide, and the other regional.

Can we contemplate the prospect of European monetary union in this context? I believe that we can and should.

There is already broad agreement on what we need for a fundamental turn in the tide of Europe's employment prospects:

1. There has to be confidence in steady and more uniform policies favouring investment and expansion.
2. There has to be a strengthening of demand with a wide geographical base.
3. If inflation is to continue, it must be at a lower and more even rate than Europe has known in recent years.
4. We have to ensure that spasmodic, local economic difficulties will not be magnified by exchange rates and capital movements into general crises of confidence.

These four requirements may seem obvious enough. The challenge is how to change radically and for the better the institutional weaknesses that have been hindering our stability to restore high employment in conditions of price stability and a sound external payments position. I believe that monetary union can open perspectives of this kind.

My argument is not that the Community ought to make some new choice on the combination of these three objectives, still less that we should seek to impose a caricature of some country's traditional preference on the rest of the Community. Economists have now spent years tracking the deteriorating inflation–employment relationship and the deteriorating effectiveness of exchange rate changes in the balance of payments adjustment process. The decisions now required are political rather than simply economic; and I hope that these would in years ahead come to be recognized by economists as a break-out from their accepted systems and current models. In this process, we need also to discard political argument based on obsolete, inadequate, or irrelevant economic theory: that the objections to European integration are the differing preferences on inflation and unemployment as between member states, and that floating exchange rates within Europe allow each country to achieve on its own a happily optimal outcome of its own preference. This is not how the world really is, and we all know it.

Regional policies

The fifth argument to which I now turn concerns the regional distribution of employment and economic welfare in Europe. Monetary union will not of itself act as some invisible hand to ensure a smooth regional distribution of the gains from increased economic integration and union. Those who have criticized a purely liberal model of the Community economy, one that aims to establish perfect competition and do no more, have strong arguments on their side.

But the Community of today bears no relation to the laissez-faire caricature of some of its critics. Nor does it correspond to the model I suggest we should now contemplate for a monetary union. All our member states find themselves obliged to redistribute large sums of public money and to use less strong but more overt regional policy measures to secure a reasonable distribution of national wealth and employment.

In the Community of today, we have a battery of financial instruments, but all of them rather small guns: the Regional and Social Funds, the Coal and Steel Community's financial powers, the European Investment Bank and the Guidance Section of the Agricultural Fund. The Commission has recently made a number of decisions and proposals for the co-ordination and expansion of these operations. These are worthwhile developments in themselves, and they go in the right direction. But their scale is small in relation both to current needs and to the financial underpinning that would be required to support a full monetary union. This is an example of how short-term practical needs and the demands of a longer-term perspective march alongside each other. There is no contradiction in modern integrated economies.

The flow of public finance between regions performs several essential functions. First, it improves the infrastructure and promotes industrial investment in the poorer areas. Second, it evens out cyclical swings in the performance of individual regions. Third, it assures minimum standards in basic services. Fourth, it sustains a pattern of regional balance of payments surpluses and deficits which are of a different and larger order of magnitude than those which would cause crises if they existed between countries. This represents the principal offsetting factor compensating the region or state for its inability to conduct a distinct exchange or monetary policy.

Europe must think in terms of the same economic logic. If the Community is to take seriously its declared aim of monetary union — and there are great dangers in having declared aims which are not taken seriously — it is indispensable that an associated system of public finance should also be envisaged. The weak regions of the Community must have a convincing insurance against the fear that monetary union would aggravate their economic difficulties. The strong regions must for their part have a counterpart in terms of more stable, secure and prosperous markets. Their interest in the underpinning of the unity of the market is overwhelming. In the context of the enlarged Community, it should also be made clear that we are here talking of the means whereby we can avoid or reduce excessive movement of people from poorer to richer areas. This could all too easily lead to the further impoverishment of one and the intolerable congestion of the other.

The Community must also take a realistic view of the degree of convergence in economic performance which should be expected before and after the creation of a monetary union. On price performance, monetary union has uncompromising effects. Interregional differences in living standards cannot be dealt with so drastically. But we should not be too discouraged. The United States of fifty years ago had a greater degree of regional inequality than the Community has today. One hundred years ago it was almost certainly greater still. This analogy should not be pushed too far, nevertheless it is of considerable interest.

Decision-taking

The sixth argument concerns institutional questions, the level at which decisions have to be made, or the degree of decentralization that we should seek to maintain in the Community. Monetary union would imply a major new authority to manage the exchange rate, external reserves and the main lines of internal monetary policy.

The public finance underpinning of monetary union which I have just described would involve a substantial increase in the transfer of resources through the Community institutions. The question then is whether monetary union can be reconciled with the profound pressures that are manifest in almost all our member states in favour of more, rather than less, decentralized government? I believe the answer can and should be 'yes'. But this requires us to envisage a very special and original model for the future division of functions between levels of government. This is not a subject that has been considered at all systematically in the Community in the two decades which have passed since the Treaties of Paris and Rome laid down certain sectors of Community competence. Monetary policy can only be decentralized to a very limited degree. But for most policies requiring public expenditure, the reverse is the case. The vast growth of public expenditure in the post-war period, now approaching half of GNP, has emphasized the need for multi-tiered government with various levels according to country: local, regional, state, national, and so on. This is a natural and healthy development. It avoids a monolithic concentration of political and economic power and allows for more efficient specialization by level of government. It also associates people more closely with the decision-making process.

The federal model is clearly only one in a number of possibilities for multi-tiered government. Some support the federal model; others would prefer something confederal; others like neither. I, for my part, believe that the Community must devise its own arrangements and that these are unlikely to correspond to any existing prototype. We must build Europe upon the basis of our late twentieth-century nation states. We must only give to the Community functions which will, beyond reasonable doubt, deliver significantly better results because they are performed at a Community level. We must fashion a Community which gives to each member state the benefits of results which they cannot achieve alone. We must equally leave to them functions which they can do equally well or better on their own.

I would like to give an example of why Europe should not think in terms of copying existing models. The US federal government grew enormously in importance when it pushed the development of the social security system, because the states would not move forward quickly enough, and because some states were notable laggards. By contrast, our national social and welfare services, while neither perfect nor identical, are highly developed and not dissimilar. In most member states social and welfare expenditure amounts to around 25 per cent of GNP. This is a massive example of how the European model of government has no need to contemplate developing Community expenditure of a traditional federal scale.

I believe that we can identify those functions which make sense for Europe; those aspects of external relations where intercontinental bargaining power is called for; certain research and development functions which offer economies of scale at the level of 250 million people; policies relating to industrial sectors which have a natural European dimension either because they involve high-level economies of scale as in the case of aerospace or electronics; or because they are closely linked with trade policy, as is the case with industries in trouble with excess capacity like steel, textiles and shipbuilding; or because the areas involve strategic interests which are indivisible between member states, as in the case of energy policy. Last, we need financial policies that would help support the integration of the European economy, the maintenance of regional balance, and thus the viability of monetary union.

The community budget

The overall magnitude of budgetary spending at the European level for this type of Community has recently been estimated by a group of independent economists under the chairmanship of Sir Donald McDougall. As against present Community expenditure of the order of 1 per cent of GNP, they estimated that very substantial progress on economic integration could be achieved with the aid of expenditure of 2–2½ per cent of GNP; they believed that a definitive monetary union might be viable with expenditure of the order of 5–7 per cent of GNP. These are of course very large sums of money, which would have to be built up gradually by a transfer of some expenditure from national budgets and not by a superimposition, but they are quite small by the standards of the classic federations where the top tier of government takes 20–25 per cent of GNP.

There is, therefore, for the Community a new and realistic model for a highly decentralized type of monetary union in which the public procurement of goods and services is primarily in national, regional or other hands. The public finance function of such a Community would be stripped down to a few high-powered types of financial transfer, fulfilling specific tasks in sectors of particular Community concern, and assuring the flow of resources necessary to sustain monetary union. These characteristics also make for a quite small central bureaucracy, which I think we would all consider an advantage.

But the political implications would also be great. We must be frank about this. The relocation of monetary policy to the European level would be as big a political step for the present generation of European leaders as for the last generation in setting up the present Community. But we must face the fundamental question: Do we intend to create a European union or do we not? Do we, confronted with the inevitable and indeed desirable prospect of enlargement, intend to strengthen and deepen the Community, or do we not? There would be little point in asking the peoples and governments of Europe to contemplate union, were it not for the fact that real and efficient sovereignty over monetary issues already eludes them to a high and increasing degree. The prospect of monetary union should be seen as part of the process of recovering the substance of sovereign power. At present we tend to cling to its shadow. These arguments do not run against international co-operation, as for example in the OECD and the IMF. On the contrary, we need to improve the functioning of the international economy by a better shaping of its constituent parts. Monetary disunity in Europe is one of the major flaws in the international system as well as in the functioning of our small to medium-sized states.

Political integration

On the seventh and final argument, I can be quite brief since, like the first, it is a traditional one. It is the straight political argument that monetary union stands on offer as a vehicle for European political integration. Jacques Rueff said in 1949: '*L'Europe se fera par la monnaie ou ne se fera pas.*' I would not necessarily be quite so categorical. It should, however, be clear that the successful creation of a European monetary union would take Europe over a political threshold. It seems equally clear that Europe today is not prepared to pursue the objective of monetary union uniquely for ideological reasons. To move in this direction Europe also needs materially convincing arguments. I have tried to set out some of the economic arguments.

Conclusion

I summarize as follows. We must change the way we have been looking at monetary union. A few years ago we were looking at a mountain-top through powerful binoculars. The summit seemed quite close, and a relatively accessible smooth, gradual and short approach was marked out. But then an avalanche occurred and swept away this route. The shock was such that more recently it has even seemed as if we have been looking at the summit with the binoculars both the wrong way round and out of focus.

I believe that a new, more compelling and rewarding but still arduous approach is necessary. We must also change the metaphor. Let us think of a long-jumper. He starts with a rapid succession of steps, lengthens his stride, increases his momentum, and then makes his leap.

The creation of a monetary union would be a leap of this kind. Measures to improve the customs union and the free circulation of goods, services and persons are important steps. We look for bigger strides in working out external policies, establishing more democratic and thus accountable institutions, elaborating more coherent industrial and regional policies, and giving our financial instruments the means to keep the whole movement on a balanced course. We have to look before we leap, and know when we are to land. But leap we eventually must.

We must not only do what is best in the circumstances. We must give our people an aim beyond the immediately possible. Politics is not only the art of the possible, but also, as Jean Monnet said, it is the art of making possible tomorrow what may seem impossible today.

10 The path to European monetary union

Karl-Otto Pöhl

The Werner Report of 1970, which proposed the realisation of economic and monetary union in stages, has been experiencing a renaissance. The idea is that economic and monetary union is based on the parallelism of economic and monetary developments. Today, European economic and monetary union as described in the Werner Report is no longer a Utopia. We are in the middle of a dynamic process of merging markets.

A monetary union is based on three elements which were already broadly defined in the Werner Report: first, the irrevocable fixing of exchange rates, perhaps during a fairly long transitional period and with the option of exchange rate adjustments, but under more difficult conditions, similar to the old Bretton Woods system; second, the complete liberalization of money and capital transactions; and third, institutional changes going as far as the creation of a central bank or a central bank system, as was stated in the Delors Report, and, at the end, a common currency. Considerable progress has been made in all three areas in the last few years.

I

Substantial convergence of at least the hard core of the member countries in their economic development is the basic prerequisite for the EMS having functioned fairly smoothly since about 1984, after some severe teething troubles. The decisive moment came in March 1983, when the French government, in the middle of a deep crisis, decided to turn around its economic and fiscal policies and give defence of the fixed exchange rate *vis-à-vis* the Deutschmark priority in its own economic policy. Since then, there have only been a few relatively minor changes in exchange rates. At the time, it was

The author is President of the Deutsche Bundesbank. This article is an abridged version of an address given at the 40th Annual General Meeting of the Ifo Institute for Economic Research, Munich, in June 1989.

accepted that the Deutschmark had an anchor function. The usefulness of the Deutschmark as a standard of stability has been expressly recognized by all central bank governors in the Delors Report.

Thus, the criticism that the Bundesbank is forcing its EMS partners into a deflationary policy stance has been finally refuted. As long as no better alternative is available, the Deutschmark is probably going to have to play this leading role in the EMS in future, too. Being the reserve and intervention currency of the system is, however, by no means an unmixed blessing. It sometimes poses considerable problems for our monetary policy.

The EMS has developed into a zone of stability. Exchange rate fluctuations remain within the limits set under the agreed margins of fluctuation, and the pressure for realignments has almost completely disappeared. Cost and price trends cannot easily be used as arguments in favour of correcting central rates, either. In terms of inflation, the EMS states have turned in a better performance than most comparable industrial countries. Whether this will always be the case naturally still remains to be seen.

At any rate, as a matter of principle, we cannot dispense with the option of adjusting exchange rates in the EMS. This would only shift the adjustment pressure to other areas, such as wages policy and fiscal policy. At the same time we have to acknowledge that the readiness to make exchange rate changes in the EMS has been decreasing steadily, because member countries have found that depreciation leads to only a temporary improvement in their competitiveness on the one hand, and to more inflation, on the other. As I understand it, this can only mean that countries with significant inflation and foreign trade problems, which after all always exhibit a macro-economic disequilibrium, are going to have to make additional efforts to prevent their economies from overheating and conduct an effective fight against inflation. It can by no means imply that a country with less strongly rising prices is forced into inflationary adjustment.

II

The second element of a monetary union which I have mentioned is the liberalization of money and capital transactions. We have made considerable progress here, too, in the last few years. Most countries for example, the Federal Republic of Germany and the Benelux countries, the United Kingdom and Denmark — completely liberalized their capital transactions a long time ago. France and Italy have partly lifted their controls. One of the major decisions of the last few years, in my opinion, was the passing of the so-called Liberalization Directive under German EC chairmanship in 1988.

The abolition of foreign exchange restrictions and capital controls is not a concession for which one can demand something in return, for example harmonization of taxes on investment income. There is no room here for give and take: on the contrary, for a long time now there has been a clear commitment, to which all member states have subscribed, in the Treaties of Rome.

The Liberalization Directive was thus overdue. I think the liberalization of capital transactions will proceed rapidly and be irreversible. The markets will enforce this state of affairs, as we have in the EC a competition of financial systems. If, for instance, Paris wants to turn into an important financial centre, then this is inconsistent with a policy which did not even allow citizens to hold a foreign currency account. Today this is not possible in either France or Italy. So I think that, when harmonizing regulations, one should confine oneself to the absolutely necessary minimum and have more faith in competition and in the market.

Countries which hitherto have only been hesitant in reducing capital controls, fear again and again that this could lead to capital outflows, and that the stability of the exchange rate system could be adversely affected. The final test of this is in fact not yet in sight but I think that experience hitherto has tended to show the contrary. Experience in Spain, Italy and in France, too, has indicated that a reduction in capital controls tends to lead more to capital inflows, i.e. more to a strengthening than to a weakening of the currency, and to interest rate reductions rather than interest rate rises.

III

The third aspect concerns the question of institutional changes. The Delors Report made some suggestions here, but it is necessary to mention that it was not the Commission's mandate to assess the desirability of an economic and monetary union. This aim has been accepted unanimously by all European heads of state and government and was reiterated in the communiqué of the Madrid summit at the end of June 1989.

Seen from the German point of view, the Delors Report has a great number of positive features. But the report is obviously a compromise and for that reason it has certain weaknesses. This goes particularly for the section describing the second stage, namely the transition from the current situation to the final stage of an economic and monetary union. This is in fact the weakest part of the report, but we were fully aware of that. All the controversial questions as to what this transitional stage should actually look like have ultimately been excluded. It says in the report, and I would like to repeat the sentence, in order to emphasize it:

At this juncture, the Committee does not consider it possible to propose a detailed blueprint for accomplishing this transition, as this would depend on the effectiveness of the policy co-ordination achieved during the first stage, on the provisions of the Treaty, and on decisions to be taken by the new institutions.

That is to say, we were well aware of the problems and there were some very different concepts of this second stage.

As we did not want to go our separate ways in complete discord, we had to avoid this question, just as we avoid many other questions which will have to be discussed in more detail and decided on in future. This is also a major reason why negotiations on a new treaty on economic and monetary union should not be set in motion too hastily. They should start when preparations have proceeded far enough, i.e. particularly when there is clarity on the approach to be adopted in the second stage.

So the Delors Report has not laid down anything in hard and fast terms. The decisions which will have to be taken in the first stage, too, are still ahead of us.

IV

In line with our suggestions, the European Council decided in Madrid at the end of June to begin the first stage of the realization of economic and monetary union on 1 July, 1990. This stage comprises measures which can all be taken on the basis of current legislation or which have already been decided on but are yet to be implemented. Primarily, this includes the full realization of the internal market, the harmonization of indirect taxes, the strengthening of the Directive on the convergence of economic and fiscal policies which was adopted as early as 1974, and, last but not least, the complete liberalization of capital movements. So far, not much use has been made of this.

Of particular relevance is the proposal to strengthen the role of the Committee of EC Central Bank Governors in Basle, that is to give it a higher profile, and to enable it to make public comments, and — not least — to influence exchange rate policies within the EMS more strongly. The Committee is to enable closer co-operation to take place in preparing monetary policy decision-making. It has been expressly said that such preparations are not binding and that the Committee's comments cannot be binding either under the prevailing conditions. But naturally they would have some weight if they came from the Committee of EC Central Bank Governors. We think that the Committee of EC Central Bank Governors should become something like a nucleus of and a training ground for a future European central bank system.

The Delors Report reaffirmed what had already been established by the Single European Act, namely that institutional changes and the transfer of monetary policy powers to supranational institutions are possible only on the basis of a treaty approved by governments and ratified by parliaments. Such a treaty — and we must be fully aware of this — would strongly affect national laws, in Germany for instance the Bundesbank Act. It would thus be a very important change, with far-reaching consequences. In our opinion it cannot be said from the outset when the time will come for such a far-reaching waiver of sovereignty as the transfer of monetary policy powers to a supranational institution. This should be decided in the light of the experience gained in a first stage, with further progress in economic and monetary policy co-operation, in the implementation of capital movements free of any restrictions and an integrated financial market, in the establishment of a common internal market, in the full participation of all partners in the EMS and in other major elements. Neither a single currency nor a European central bank is required from the beginning for the functioning of economic and monetary union. They may ultimately be desirable, for both economic and political reasons as well. It is more important, however, for the member countries to pursue a consistent policy, and thus make economic and monetary union a promising prospect. Once exchange rates have been fixed irrevocably, currencies become perfect substitutes. Then one can give these currencies a common designation, that is, replace them by a single currency. But that is still a long way off.

I think the Bundesbank's monetary policy-making powers can be surrendered — in the framework of a European treaty on monetary union — only when it is certain that something equally good, or even better, will take their place. There seems to be no guarantee of this at present.

The Delors Report lists the most important principles of a future European central bank constitution as: price stability as the top priority of monetary policy, independence from government, the instruments of a free-market economy; and no financing of government deficits. All this constitutes a stable foundation on which to build a European monetary house.

11 Regional problems and common currencies

E. Victor Morgan

Two of the many issues now being debated in relation to Britain's entry into the European Economic Community are regional policy and monetary union. In general, these two debates have been kept separate, though the economic theory relevant to both is very similar, and it may be that part of the reason why certain regions remain depressed is that they share a common currency with their more prosperous neighbours. If this were so, it would clearly have an important bearing on the monetary union issue — an international currency union could help perpetuate depression among some member nations analogous to the depression suffered, in most nations, by some of their regions.

The first part of this paper discusses, with particular reference to the United Kingdom, why regions become depressed. The second part examines why they remain depressed, that is, it considers various adjustment processes that might be expected to correct depression and asks why they have not done so. The third and fourth sections make brief comments on the findings of the first two in relation to domestic regional policies and to monetary union.

How regions become depressed

Before 1914 the present problem regions of the UK were among the most prosperous parts of the country. That prosperity returned very briefly in the post-war boom but vanished in the ensuing depression. Since then, they have followed the ups and downs of national economic activity, but always with an unemployment rate well above the national average. The names have changed: 'depressed', 'special', 'development', 'special development' or just 'the regions'. But the geographical areas where most of the affected people live — the

The author was formerly Professor of Economics in the University of Manchester. This paper first appeared in *Lloyds Bank Review*, October 1973.

North East, the North West, South Wales, the South West, Scotland and Northern Ireland — have not changed very much.

The differences between nations and regions are political rather than economic. Economically, a region is a community trading with the rest of the world, including other regions of its own country. Like other trading communities, it will have a balance of payments and that balance may run into deficit. If a nation runs a payments deficit, it can take monetary or fiscal measures to reduce its costs and prices relatively to those of other countries; or it can allow the value of its currency to fall on the foreign-exchange market. If it does neither, the payments deficit tends to depress domestic demand and create stagnation and unemployment. It is generally recognized that this has happened in the UK as a country (for example, in 1964–7) and it can also happen between regions within a country.

This way of looking at the matter suggests that there are three ways in which a region might run into balance of payments problems: by a fall in the 'foreign' demand for its exports; by a rise in regional demand for 'imports' (including those from other regions); and by exporting too much capital.

The first is much the most obvious, and is the only one that has received much consideration in relation to the UK's problem regions. In the days of their prosperity these were highly specialized in a few industries: coal, iron and steel, shipbuilding, cotton, and (in Northern Ireland) linen. All of these, except iron and steel, have been in secular decline in the UK over the past fifty years because of either the development of substitutes or foreign competition or both. In the case of iron and steel, the long-term trend has been upward, but there have been severe cyclical fluctuations and big technological changes that have affected some of the regions adversely.

It is much more difficult to get evidence of changes in regional demands for 'imports', both from other regions and from other countries. There have, however, been changes in the structure of the economy and also in the pattern of spending that seem likely to have raised regional spending (out of any given income) on goods and, especially, on services from outside. Consider, for example, the great increase in the civil service, still largely based on London, during the past fifty years; the growth of financial, insurance, legal and advertising services, again largely based on London; the increasing frequency of shopping trips to London; and the habit of taking holidays abroad. All these are 'invisible imports' to regions such as South Wales, the North West or the North East.

A more subtle, and even less discussed, effect may arise from the centralization of the capital market in London. In certain circumstances, this may cause a region to become virtually an enforced exporter of capital, and so it raises the kind of question posed by economic historians in relation to the operations of the early nineteenth-century banking system within the UK and the late nineteenth-century international capital market centred on London. Can capital exports be detrimental to the growth of an exporting country or region?

The nature of the process can be illustrated by reference to three sections of the capital market: banks; life insurance and pension funds; and the stock exchange.

Consider a particular region, which we will call South Wales, though the argument applies generally, and assume that its inhabitants have roughly similar per capita incomes, a similar propensity to save, and similar propensities to hold their wealth in bank deposits and in other assets to those of the rest of the country. On these assumptions, South Wales would hold about its share, in relation to population, of bank deposits. Whether it would also do its share of bank borrowing depends partly on local demand and partly on the banks' lending rules. If the banks follow the kind of rule that they have done in the past, of charging fairly uniform interest rates and lending according to some internally-established standards of creditworthiness, South Wales would have more or less than its share of bank loans according to whether it had more or less than its share of creditworthy borrowers.

Insurance premiums and pension contributions originating in South Wales are nearly all paid to funds administered outside the region so, again, the question is how much comes back, either directly in lending to Welsh firms or acquisition of Welsh securities, or indirectly through the operations of other borrowers in Wales. A glance at the portfolio structure of the institutions concerned suggests a strong possibility of net capital exports through this channel.

Although there is a local capital market in South Wales (and in most of the other problem regions), a high proportion of the stock exchange securities held locally are those either of the central government or of companies based outside the region. Again, therefore, there will be a net capital export, unless there is a sufficient indirect reflux through the activities of the borrowing institutions.

Many other sections of the market could be considered in the same way, but these three illustrations should suffice. If all markets were perfect, and the opportunities for profitable investment were the same in South Wales as elsewhere, there is no reason why the region should not get its share of loans from institutions either directly or indirectly through investment in the region by firms based outside. Three circumstances can prevent this from happening. First, ignorance or prejudice of a kind that leads investors to overestimate the risks or underestimate the opportunities of investment in South Wales. This would lead both to a net export of capital and to difficulties in borrowing by local firms. There is certainly a feeling among some businessmen in the problem regions that they are the victims of such discrimination, though it is very difficult to get any real evidence. In so far as it does exist, discrimination of this kind damages the local economy and also impedes the most economic allocation of resources in the country as a whole. Second, South Wales may contribute its share to government borrowing, but receive less than its share of the resulting expenditure. However, this is purely an academic point since, in practice, the balance is almost certainly the other way. Third, and far more important, is the possibility that our problem region may have less than its share of profitable investment opportunities. In that case, it seems right that it should be a net lender to other regions where capital can be more productively employed. But a lending region, like a lending country, must have a surplus on its current-account payments in order to finance its lending. If outside demand for a region's exports is weak, while internal demand for imports is strong, how can a surplus be generated? The generation of a surplus is essentially the same as the curing of a deficit and the same conclusions follow. If it cannot be done either by cost and price adjustments or by exchange devaluation, there will be a depressing effect on demand that is likely to inhibit growth and accentuate unemployment.

On the international scene, this kind of situation has arisen in many guises, from the payment of reparations by Germany after the First World War to the finance of overseas investment by American companies in the past few years. In the theory of international trade, it has received a great deal of discussion under the name of the transfer problem'; in regional economics it has been largely ignored.

Why regions stay depressed

In a world where both demand and technology are constantly changing, and where new industrial communities are emerging, it is not surprising that particular regions should suffer setbacks. What is surprising is that the resulting depression should last for so long, and in spite of many attempts by governments to put matters right. It could be that our diagnosis of the problem, as suggested above, is imperfect and hence that our prescriptions are faulty. It could be that policies have not been applied with sufficient vigour or consistency. But this is by no means the whole story. There are also important rigidities that impede the normal ways in which a market economy adjusts to changes in supply and demand.

This adjustment process is very complex and only the most sketchy account of it can be given here. To illustrate, suppose that we have a region, again called South Wales, that was enjoying prosperity until it suffered a severe decline in the demand for one of its major products, coal. 'South Wales' and 'coal' are chosen purely for convenience; the argument would apply to any major product of any region.

The fall in sales of coal would cause South Wales to run a balance of payments deficit with the rest of the country, but it would also upset the balance of supply and demand in the market for all the 'inputs' to the coal industry; in the markets for all the goods on which people earning incomes in the coal industry spent their money; and in all the financial markets into which these people put their savings or through which they borrowed. In the world of perfect flexibility beloved of the economic theorists, there would be a great number of changes in prices and interest rates, many of them very small, but each doing its bit in the process of adjustment. If this process is checked by rigidities in one particular market, adjustment can still take place in other ways, but the greater and more numerous the rigidities, the greater the strain and the greater the risk that the whole process will break down. The following paragraphs look at this problem in relation to a few of the more important markets.

First, the decline in the demand for coal should lead to a fall in its price but, unless there are also reductions in the prices of inputs used by the industry, the extent of the price reduction will be limited by the rigidity of costs. Moreover, it may also be checked by monopolistic arrangements among producers, as happened, with the encouragement of the state, during the inter-war period.

There will also be excess supply in the markets for mining labour, pit props, and so on, and a reduction in their prices would permit a further fall in the price of coal. Here, however, we come to the question of relative earnings. Relative position in the pay scale seems to be an important element in union bargaining, and is likely to be more important within a national community than outside (British miners consider the relationship between earnings and those of British motor workers, but not those of American miners).

In any case, those concerned in the coal industry will suffer a loss of earnings from either lower prices or less work or both, and this will reduce their spending power and lead to a generalized fall in demand both for domestic products of the region and for imports from outside. The fall in the demand for imports will help to redress the regional payments balance, but it will not in itself be enough. Extensive analysis of this problem at the international level has shown that it is also necessary for prices in the deficit country to fall relatively to prices elsewhere, and the same principle applies between regions.

Again, there is only limited scope for price adjustments in final product markets without similar movements in factor markets, but there appear to be some constraints on price flexibility between regions that do not operate between nations. Many of the firms operating in the depressed areas are branches of multi-plant organizations. Sometimes, the different plants produce similar products and, in that case, firms normally charge a uniform price regardless of where the product is made (a firm does not charge lower prices for, say, Welsh potato crisps than for English ones). Sometimes, the plant in the depressed area produces components for products assembled elsewhere, and then only a 'transfer price' is involved.

A general fall in demand for goods implies general unemployment and raises the question of rigidities in relative wages, not between one industry and another but between one region and another. Again, there can be no doubt that the prevalence of national bargaining imposes rigidities between regions that do not exist between nations. This does not mean that no differences can arise; national agreements are not universal, and the various kinds of 'wage drift' that raise actual earnings above basic rates may occur less strongly in regions of high unemployment. However, the extent of differences in earnings due to these influences is quite small, at least with the amount of unemployment that we have experienced in recent years.

This can be illustrated by reference to the October 1972 earnings' survey of the Department of Employment. The Table 11.1 shows the national average and the figures for the North, the North West, Wales and Scotland for eight industries that are widely distributed within the regions and outside. In ten of the thirty-two cases, the regional earnings are actually higher than the national average. Of the remaining twenty-two, there are only seven where the gap is more than 5 per cent below the national average and only four where it is more than 10 per cent below.

In so far as interregional differences in earnings do arise, in spite of national agreements, we come to the question of how firms react to the resulting cost differences. To the extent that they switch production, even though they do not alter their prices, adjustment is greatly facilitated. Indeed, if prices were completely rigid but production completely mobile, a region would be in a position equivalent to that of selling its output in a perfectly elastic world market. Unfortunately, this is likely to be very far from the real situation. When a factory is making components, its output is geared to that of the final products and, if the component is a small part of the whole cost, the demand for it must be inelastic. To extend the range of

Table 11.1 Average hourly earnings of adult male manual workers, October 1972 (pence; index in italics)

	National average	North West	North	Scotland	Wales
Food, drink and tobacco	77.05	75.80	71.89	76.79	69.22
	100.0	98.4	93.3	99.7	89.8
Chemicals	83.19	86.50	89.23	81.70	81.71
	100.0	104.0	107.3	98.2	98.2
Metal manufacture	85.13	80.71	83.55	85.36	92.92
	100.0	94.8	98.1	100.3	109.2
Mechanical engineering	79.84	77.19	83.49	85.07	78.38
	100.0	96.7	104.6	106.6	98.2
Electrical engineering	79.45	81.05	81.64	78.31	82.32
	100.0	102.0	102.8	98.6	103.6
Vehicles	98.42	94.60	84.98	94.95	91.85
	100.0	96.1	86.3	96.5	93.3
Clothing and footwear	71.13	68.50	73.41	69.42	69.64
	100.0	96.3	103.2	97.6	97.9
Paper and printing	92.19	91.31	91.72	82.28	80.42
	100.0	99.0	99.5	89.3	87.2

components produced would normally require heavy capital investment and quite possibly cause trouble with trade unions, so that this kind of change would seem likely only in response to substantial cost differences persisting over a considerable time.

The situation where a firm has plants inside and outside a region producing the same product appears more hopeful. If English crisps and Welsh crisps are to be sold at the same price, surely one could expect more crisps to be made in Wales if Welsh wages fall. Again, however, capacity limitations and transport costs limit the response to moderate cost differences.

If the inhabitants of a region as a group spend outside it more than they receive in payments from outsiders, this implies that some individuals or firms are living above their income. This excess expenditure must be financed by running down their bank balances, selling financial assets or borrowing. In an international setting, these transactions tend to raise interest rates in the deficit country. Again, the fact that the regions all have access to a centralized capital market prevents this from happening; banks do not vary their lending rates from one region to another, and yields on any given type of security are the same whether its owner lives in Cardiff or London. Finally, the combination of a common currency and a centralized banking system rules out any possibility of exchange rate fluctuations between regions.

To sum up the argument so far, problems for regions can arise not only because of a decline in the outside demand for their products, but because of an increase in their own demand for the goods and services of the rest of the country and the world. It is also possible that the centralized national financial system may help to create regional difficulties by inducing capital exports from some regions. The solution to these problems has been inhibited by a number of cost and price rigidities that prevent the regions from making the kind of adjustments that would tend to occur between nations in similar circumstances; and, given these rigidities, the regions have probably been handicapped by sharing a common currency with the rest of the country.

Regional policies

Traditional policies towards depressed regions are of six kinds: charity; improvement of 'infrastructure' (services such as transport, power, housing); capital subsidies; labour subsidies; aids to intraregional mobility; and aids to interregional migration.

The new policies introduced in Britain in 1972 are the latest of a long line and, to a large extent, they are 'the mixture as before', though there are a few important differences. The new policies are less closely linked to new or incoming businesses; and less closely linked to the direct creation of employment, and more closely linked to profitability; relate more to capital investment and (with the phasing out of the regional employment premium) less to labour; and involve less discrimination between different forms of economic activity, though they are not wholly free from this taint.

Measures to promote interregional migration can be quickly dismissed in any discussion of British official policy; there has been a fair amount of 'private enterprise' migration but the amount of state aid has been trivial. Aids to intraregional mobility are simply ways of overcoming market imperfections, and are desirable in prosperous as well as depressed regions, provided that the cost does not exceed the benefit.

'Charity' takes the form mainly of social security payments, though it also includes various grants to local authorities. Such payments can be viewed as similar to the remittances from abroad that play a significant part in the balance of payments of some national economies. They contribute to the relief of poverty and they enhance the general level of income (or prices or exchange rate) at which the economy can maintain a balance between total external receipts and payments. However, they do nothing to cure the real trouble; in fact, large social security payments may even hinder the cure by delaying wage reduction and labour redeployment.

Improvements to infrastructure are helpful if and only if they reduce a region's costs relatively to costs elsewhere. From this point of view, the popular grants for clearing tips, for example, are little more than charity, however much they may improve the quality of life for local residents. Motorways and other improvements to inter-regional communications carry a double edge. They may reduce the cost of transporting regional exports to their markets, but they also reduce the cost to local inhabitants of going outside for shopping and services. For example, the opening of the Severn Bridge led a large Bristol store to advertise in South Wales's newspapers under the slogan 'Bridgeway to Bristol'!

Capital subsidies are often attacked by those who think of regional difficulties primarily in terms of unemployment, but they may have more merit than is generally allowed for. They help to correct financial flows that may otherwise impede investment, as well as to reduce the cost of one of the factors of production. They need, however, to be balanced by similar reductions in the cost of labour in order to avoid distortion between capital-intensive and labour-intensive industries.

From the point of view from which the case for regional policies has been generally argued, there is a strong case for measures to reduce the cost of labour, provided that they are general (for example, a differential pay-roll tax or social security contribution) rather than discriminating in favour of particular activities.

The discrimination against services in the selective employment tax had two disadvantages, which also attach to the regional employment premium payable to manufacturers. It discouraged regional 'invisible exports', and it discouraged local industries from providing 'import substitutes'. London and a few other major cities enjoy a big 'pull' in respect of many forms of service — shopping facilities, entertainment, legal and financial services — and this is enhanced by improvements in interregional communications. Very often this operates to the disadvantage of local service industries. Action to encourage rather than discourage the development of local financial, shopping and service centres could be among the most fruitful of regional policies.

Measures to reduce the cost of capital and labour in the depressed regions enhance their competitive position *vis-à-vis* the rest of the world in the same way as a country's competitive position is improved by currency devaluation, but with two important differences. First, devaluation normally turns the terms of trade against the deficit country and so reduces the real incomes of its inhabitants, whereas regional policies protect the real income of the inhabitants of depressed regions by a subsidy from more prosperous ones. Second, if carried to the point at which a new equilibrium rate is established, devaluation provides a permanent cure, whereas the benefits of subsidies last only as long as the subsidies themselves. There is very little case, on grounds of social justice, for a permanent subsidy to people living in a particular place that is independent of national policies for the relief of poverty.

The original argument for such policies was based largely on the concept of 'footloose' industries and cumulative forces of expansion and contraction. An initial decline in the demand for coal and thus in the income of its producers was supposed to make South Wales unattractive for other investment and so to set up cumulative forces of decline. Once, however, enough assistance had been given to bring in investment and start a rise in income, cumulative forces of expansion would take over, and the region could regain and sustain health on its own. Assistance was thus seen as a temporary 'pump-priming' operation.

British experience certainly does not support this hypothesis. Regional policies have largely protected depressed regions from a decline in their standard of living, but they have not cured unemployment and they have not brought the regions back to a state where they could 'stand on their own feet'. The analysis of earlier sections suggests three reasons for this. Regional policies have not checked the 'pull' of London and the South East in service industries; they have not significantly reduced the centralization of the capital market; and, most important of all, they have not induced flexibility in costs and prices between regions.

Common currencies

Finally, let us consider whether our depressed region, South Wales, would have done better if it had enjoyed its own currency — say the 'leek' — that could have fluctuated in value against the sterling. The question is an academic one so far as regions in the UK are concerned but the answer may have very practical applications to whether, for example, Britain should join a European monetary union.

It has been argued that the difficulty experienced by regions in adjusting to adverse economic shocks arises partly from the operation of centralized institutions and partly from the interregional cost and price rigidities. Given this situation, has South Wales been better off with the combination of relatively high income for those in employment, relatively heavy unemployment and external aid, than it would have been if it could have devalued the 'leek', dispensing with aid, reducing the real earnings of those in work, but also reducing unemployment and probably accelerating growth?

The answer clearly depends partly on the amount of aid. Aid not only helps to keep up the real incomes of those in employment, but also raises the level of employment that is consistent with the payments constraint. It may well be that South Wales and other regions have done better (in terms of aggregate real income) as the recipients of aid, but it is highly unlikely that Britain would get much in the way of aid from other members of a European monetary union. In this broader context, the question has to be put in a different form.

Given that aid is not available, a decline in the demand for exports has to be met by a great number of individual price adjustments in individual markets for goods and factors; or by a general adjustment operating through the exchange rate; or by an adjustment of the level of income and employment that would be likely, on present assumptions, to involve fairly heavy and prolonged unemployment. Let us assume that the third possibility is unacceptable and concentrate on the other two. Which is better depends on the frictions that operate in each of a great many different markets, but three general points may be made.

First, devaluation has a kind of 'summer-time' effect. Just as it is easier to put the clocks on an hour than to arrange for everyone to get up and all activities to take place an hour earlier by the clock, so devaluation may reduce or avoid many of the frictions that impede price changes in individual markets for goods and services. Second, though devaluation does not avoid the need for internal price changes altogether, many of the secondary changes required are small and most of them are in an upward direction, which minimizes the effect of rigidities. Third, and perhaps most important, there is the question of incentives and choice in relation to new and expanding activities. Depressed regions need to develop new industries to replace declining ones and, with appropriate wage and price adjustments, the need would be reflected in opportunities for profit. But in the initial stages of the fall in demand for the old goods it is very difficult to see where the new needs and opportunities will lie, and there is not even much incentive to look for them. If excess demand for labour produced a general fall in money wages, the incentive would be provided and entrepreneurs could explore the opportunities, expanding most in those where comparative advantages were greatest. In the absence of wage flexibility, devaluation is the only way in which such a generalized incentive to exploit new opportunities can be created.

It has been suggested earlier that part of the regional problem stems from the fact that there are rigidities within countries that do not exist between them. The development of the Common Market must make its member states more like regions and less like 'old-fashioned' countries. The abolition of trade restrictions and the 'harmonization' of fiscal policies, social security, hours and conditions of work, and legal systems will all reduce the number of instruments available to national governments for the regulation of their own economies. Already, international companies are extending their activities over Europe in the same way as national companies were extending over the regions two generations ago; already trade unions are paying increasing attention to wages and conditions in Europe; and already financial institutions are making the first moves in a process that is likely to culminate in a European capital market. In these circumstances, the retention of national currencies with some flexibility in exchange rates could help to prevent temporary setbacks, at the national level, from turning into chronic depression.

12 The EMS and UK membership: five years on

Geoffrey Dennis and Joseph Nellis

On the 13 March 1984, the European Monetary System (EMS) celebrated its fifth birthday. Contrary to the gloomy predictions made by
many of its early critics, who feared that it would quickly collapse
under both internal and external pressures, the system has survived
intact. Given the turbulence in the international monetary system
since 1979, this in itself is a considerable achievement.

Once the debate over the ability of the EMS to survive for any
length of time had been silenced by events, much attention was
focused on the possibility that the UK might, at some point in time,
become a full member of the system. Since the EMS's inception,
successive UK governments have staunchly rejected the possibility of
any greater involvement than membership of the European Monetary
Co-operation Fund (EMCF) and the inclusion of sterling in the European Currency Unit (ECU). No decision has yet been taken for sterling to become a member of the exchange rate mechanism (ERM) of
the system, which is, clearly, the most public element of the EMS.

The successes of the EMS

That the EMS has been able to overcome certain 'crisis' periods in
the past five years is testament to the flexibility inherent in the
system's design and arrangements. This flexibility has had two main
elements. First, the value of each member currency has been allowed
to fluctuate within a 2¼ per cent range on either side of its bilateral
central rate against all other currencies (with Italy availing itself, as
a non-member of the previous snake arrangements, of fluctuation
bands of 6 per cent). These fluctuation bands have reduced the
amount of intervention needed in comparison to a system of

Geoffrey Dennis is Director of the MBA Programme, Cranfield School of Management and
Joseph G. Nellis is Chief International Economist, James Capel Inc., New York. This
paper first appeared in *Lloyds Bank Review*, October 1984.

Table 12.1 Realignments of Exchange Rates within the EMS, 1979–84*

				Realignments dates**			
	24 September 1979	30 November 1979	23 March 1981	5 October 1981	22 February 1982	14 June 1982	21 March 1983
Belgian franc/Luxembourg franc	0	0	0	0	−8.5	0	+1.5
Danish krone	−2.9	−4.8	0	0	−3.0	0	+2.5
Deutschmark	+2.0	0	0	+5.5	0	+4.25	+5.5
French franc	0	0	0	−3.0	0	−5.75	−2.5
Irish punt	0	0	0	0	0	0	−3.5
Italian lira	0	0	−6.0	−3.0	0	−2.75	−2.5
Dutch guilder	0	0	0	+5.5	0	+4.25	+3.5

*Source: Commission of the European Communities.

**Calculated as the percentage change against the group of currencies whose bilateral parities remained unchanged in the realignment, except for the most recent alignment (21 March 1983) in which the bilateral central rates of all currencies were adjusted as shown — for details see *Bulletin of the European Communities*, vol. 16, no. 3, 1983.

immutably fixed parities. Second, as an arrangement of 'adjustable' parities, necessary realignments of central rates were always envisaged if the divergence pressure between two or more currencies became too persistent to be accommodated at the existing central rates.

One notable success of the EMS has been the way in which the realignments of central rates have been carried out. Seven realignments have occurred to date and their details are set out in Table 12.1. One trend has been the increasing complexity of these realignments as time has passed, culminating in the general reorganization of parities in March 1983. With the exception, perhaps, of the Belgian franc devaluation in February 1982, the realignments have, however, been fairly modest in scale. The result has been a considerably lower volatility of member currencies than that generally experienced by other major currencies outside the EMS.

Table 12.2 illustrates this argument,[1] by demonstrating that the monthly changes in the effective exchange rates of EMS currencies have been significantly lower than those of the three major outside currencies in all years since 1979 except, perhaps, 1982. In 1979, 1980 and again between 1983 and mid-1984, the limited volatility of EMS currencies was remarkable, with the average absolute monthly change being under 1 per cent except for the Danish krone and Irish punt. Such a comparison of the volatility of exchange rates inside the EMS with outside currencies is a much more reliable guide to the success of the EMS in stabilizing currency values than is any comparison with a period, such as prior to 1979, when the EMS was not in existence.

The timing of EMS realignments has frequently been linked to the performance of the US dollar. Dollar weakness generally causes strains in the system as flows of money move out of the US currency and into the two major 'hard' currency alternatives, namely the yen and, with implications for the EMS, the Deutschmark. Given that these flows do not go into the other EMS currencies in similar quantities, upward pressure on the Deutschmark in the system is inevitable. This experience illustrates that the desire of the founders of the EMS to achieve a situation where all EMS currencies would be considered as equal alternatives to the dollar has not yet materialized. Moreover, it is unlikely to do so given the existing institutional framework of the EMS. In contrast, it is widely agreed that the relative calm within the system since March 1983 has been due above all to the *strength* of the US dollar relative to the Deutschmark and also at times to a *weak* Deutschmark within the EMS. This stresses the point that the EMS is crucially linked to the fortunes of an external currency.

Table 12.2 Variablity* of EMS and other major currencies

	April–Dec 1979	1980	1981	1982	Jan 1983–June 1984	Apr 1979–June 1984
DM	0.823	0.906	1.471	0.665	0.923	0.962
NFl	0.656	0.644	1.375	0.540	0.733	0.793
FFr	0.704	0.770	1.373	1.290	0.999	1.041
Lira	0.526	0.851	1.326	0.649	0.684	0.813
BFr	0.538	0.683	0.712	1.783	0.701	0.934
DKr	1.183	1.031	1.493	1.220	0.966	1.164
I£	0.836	1.137	1.365	1.513	1.270	1.246
£	1.962	1.161	1.698	1.110	1.478	1.458
US$	1.063	1.619	1.875	1.993	1.306	1.595
Yen	2.120	2.331	1.621	2.253	1.259	1.864

*Calculated as the average of monthly percentage changes in the effective index for each currency.
Source: Bank of England.

A common criticism made of the EMS is that it has failed to bring about greater convergence of economic policies and performances. This is a complicated issue in many respects, not least concerning the definition of convergence and the debate over the standard against which EMS performance in this respect should be compared. Although, since 1980–1, virtually all EEC governments (apart from France and Italy who followed this trend somewhat later) have pursued restrictive monetary policies, at times supported by similar tightness in public finance, with the overriding objective of reducing inflation, there has been limited convergence of macro-economic policy *design* arising from the EMS itself. Certainly the recent moves to achieve the deindexation of wage increases in Belgium, France and Italy and the reversal of the policies of the Mitterrand administration may be in part attributable to the constraints of the EMS. However, the overall similarity of policy in this period was much more a reaction to the fear of high inflation in the aftermath of the second round of oil-price increases and latterly to cope with the increasing strength of the US dollar than to any planned harmonization of policy to further the objectives of the EMS.

Convergence itself may be measured in an 'internal' or 'external' sense. In the latter sense of exchange rate stability, the EMS has, as already argued, been relatively successful. Internally, there is still a wide disparity between the *real* economic performances of EMS nations, in terms of the level of economic development and regional disparities. However, convergence within the *domestic* economy is typically taken to mean a narrowing of monetary policy differentials in terms of either the intermediate objectives (monetary growth and rates of interest) or the goals of economic policy, notably inflation rates. As shown in the following section, the EMS was relatively unsuccessful on these terms of reference early in its life; however, since early 1982 a notable convergence of performances has been achieved.

A crucial point is that any judgement on convergence must be made in the light of the prevailing economic environment. The true comparison is between the EMS period and that same period had the EMS *not been* in existence. This requires a genuine counterfactual exercise[2] which in the field of political economy is difficult if not impossible to undertake. In particular, any comparison of economic performance between the EMS era and the more tranquil 1975–8 period, as was the case when looking at exchange rate volatility, is biased against the EMS. What is clear, however, is that the EMS, by its very existence and the constraints built into it, has helped to prevent a *greater* divergence of economic developments in the member countries.

UK government attitudes to the EMS

Although a member of the other institutional elements of the EMS, sterling has remained outside the ERM throughout its existence. Despite this consistency of action (or inaction), official justification for the refusal to link sterling to the EMS has changed significantly more than once since the system was first mooted.[3] These, at times very subtle, changes of position may be easily identified from the study of official documents, speeches, and the like, since 1978.

At the time of the main EMS discussions in November 1978, a Green Paper[4] was issued, setting out a number of characteristics that the EMS should possess, presumably before full membership by the UK would be contemplated by the then Labour government. Without listing all of these, the major requirements were that the EMS should be durable; should involve symmetrical adjustment obligations on both strong and weak members; should be truly European by aiding economic convergence in the Community; and should reinforce efforts to improve world-wide currency stability. The UK government hoped that the new arrangement would be sufficiently different from the old snake scheme in the sense that it would be flexible enough to cope with any initial differences of economic situation. Linked to this, and perhaps of even more immediate relevance, the authorities were clearly afraid that sterling would be unable to hold its position in the EMS once a decision to join had been taken. It was hoped that the flexibility of the EMS would help the system's overall cohesion and durability, in comparison with the snake, and increase the likelihood that sterling would not be faced with an early and embarrassing exist. In practice, the UK government considered that the EMS was insufficiently innovative to provide this durability.

It is widely accepted that, like the Bretton Woods system of fixed exchange rates prior to December 1971, the snake arrangement had imposed greater adjustment responsibilities on countries with balance of payments deficits than on surplus nations. The UK government wished to see a system established that would involve equal obligations on all divergent member states to intervene and make domestic policy adjustments. Such symmetrical adjustment would be best facilitated by what became known as the 'basket' system of intervention rules, whereby intervention obligations would be determined by an exchange rate's position *vis-à-vis* the weighted average of other Community currencies (the ECU). In this situation, one currency *alone* could be considered 'divergent'. In contrast, many other Community member governments proposed the introduction of a 'parity grid' arrangement in which the crucial trigger would be a currency's position against any one or more other currencies, on an individual cross-rate basis. Under this alternative system, if one currency is too strong, the mirror image is that at least one other is too weak. In this situation, the burden of adjustment is unclear, but likely to fall primarily on the deficit country. The final compromise of parity grid with a 'divergence indicator' based on the ECU basket[5] was seen as sufficiently unsatisfactory for sterling not to join the ERM. The anticipated deflationary bias of such a system, with West Germany widely expected to be the dominant country, was considered unacceptable to the government.

The third official concern was the ability of the EMS to achieve genuine convergence, which 'cannot be imposed by a particular exchange rate mechanism; it must develop from adequate co-ordination of economic policies.[6]

This argument was a throwback to the debate in the context of European monetary union at the end of the 1960s between those economists who favoured convergence before exchange rates were fixed and those who held the view that this chain of events should be reversed. Although, like Ireland and Italy, the UK was offered special credit arrangements to facilitate sterling's transition to the EMS, these, along with certain regional policy initiatives, were considered inadequate. Accordingly, they were used as a widely publicised reason for the failure of sterling to join the ERM.

Finally, the absence of any attempt to design a co-ordinated strategy for outside currencies was seen as a considerable drawback. In particular, the weakness of the dollar was one of the factors behind the initial moves towards the EMS and yet no formal decision on a common dollar policy was reached.[7]

A further argument that forcibly entered the discussion was advanced by the Trades Union Congress, in particular, and fully supported by the government. This was that full membership of the EMS would restrict the scope of policy-making in the UK and specifically would remove the freedom to devalue the currency to create jobs in the face of declining industrial competitiveness.

These arguments, then, constituted the official UK case for sterling remaining outside the ERM at the outset. There was little or no discussion of the now familiar arguments of the correct exchange rate for sterling's entry to the EMS or of its emerging petro-currency status. Perhaps most surprisingly, given the introduction of money supply targets in 1976, there was little discussion of the issue of the independence of monetary policy. On the contrary, the authorities argued against the ability of a floating exchange rate to insulate an economy from overseas disturbances and stated that some stability of sterling's external value was important. Almost as an afterthought towards the end of the Green Paper, it was stated that 'there is the possibility of a conflict between a fixed exchange rate policy and a policy for control of the money supply'.[8] However, the perceived limits to this conflict were clear from the statement that 'the claim that joining the EMS would involve a loss of economic independence is only partially true'.[9]

The proponents of the EMS hoped in May 1979 that the new Conservative government, with its more pro-EEC views than the outgoing administration, would allow sterling, albeit a little belatedly, to join the EMS in full. That this did not happen was the result of a completely different set of arguments than those officially advanced only a few months previously.

One of the leading aims of the new government was the reduction of inflation through firm control of the money supply. This objective was enshrined in the Medium-Term Financial Strategy (MTFS), first announced in the March 1980 budget, which established a four-year path for monetary growth, public spending and taxation. Despite a variety of other economic objectives, including the strengthening of economic incentives and other moves to improve the 'supply side' of the economy, there was to be no wavering from the path of monetary discipline, even in the event of unanticipated exogenous shocks (of which one, a substantial rise in the price of oil, had already occurred during 1979 and was still affecting the performance of the economy when the MTFS was first announced): 'There would be no question of relaxing the money supply policy, which is essential to the success of any anti-inflationary strategy'.[10]

These early police strictures amounted to the new world of rigid monetarism.[11] The implication for all prices – including interest rates and exchange rates — of such extreme monetarism is that they are market-determined. Such crucial variables must be allowed to adjust fully in the unrelenting pursuit of money supply control. Given these views, membership of any fixed exchange rate scheme, even the EMS, with its inbuilt flexibility of fluctuation bands and the possibility of realignments, became unthinkable. Despite statements that membership may be contemplated 'when the time is right', such a move would have been a theoretical *non sequitur*, given the policy approach of the new Conservative government.

One argument against membership of the EMS was the effect of higher oil prices on the performance of sterling. Accompanying the most recent oil crisis in 1979 and its aftermath, sterling rose sharply in value, aided by the tough anti-inflationary stance of the new government. Many argued that sterling had become a petro-currency and, as such, would be buffeted by the vagaries of the oil market. This would make close links with the EMS currencies, none of which had this petro-status to any significant degree, very difficult.[12]

Furthermore, if sterling were to join the EMS at its inflated 1980–1 value, the loss of competitiveness in UK industry would be severe. The logical conclusion was to continue to allow sterling to float outside the EMS.

The first signs that some modification of this rigid approach to economic policy might be underway came early. They may be traced initially to the aberrant behaviour of the authorities' chosen target aggregate, sterling M3, in 1980–1. With excessive growth of this aggregate being accompanied by declining inflation, higher rates of interest and more modest growth of the other monetary aggregates, it was clear that sterling M3 was an unreliable indicator of the degree of monetary stringency at that time. Although the March 1981 budget retained sterling M3 as the only specified monetary target, a more flexible approach was ushered in with other monetary and financial indicators also being considered in the operation of interest rate policy.

A radical adjustment to the MTFS followed in the March 1982 budget. The target growth rate for sterling M3 planned for 1982–3 in the original MTFS was raised significantly and other aggregates, namely M1 and PSL2, were identified as target aggregates. Further, there was the first explicit mention of the exchange rate in the operation of monetary policy: 'The exchange rate will also normally give useful information on monetary conditions. For, while the Government have no target for the exchange rate, its effect on the economy and, therefore, its behaviour cannot be ignored'.[13] Such statements, plus subsequent experience, suggest that, while the exchange rate has not actually become a target variable, significant variation from a certain (unspecified) level, particularly if accompanied by deviant money supply trends in the same direction, would trigger a policy reaction.

Therefore, the overall approach set out in the 1982 Budget constituted a movement away from the uncompromising type of monetarism of the first months of the Conservative government. As such, it became feasible once more to consider the possibility of the UK joining the EMS in full.[14] A commitment to some exchange rate stability was no longer unacceptable. Despite this, the Chancellor chose to reiterate in that budget speech that he did not intend sterling to join the EMS.

Theoretical background

It is important to stress the reasons for, first, the significant loss of enthusiasm for rigid money supply targeting in 1981–2 (which was not restricted to the UK) and, second, the consequent greater attention paid to exchange rate targets, at least by economic commentators.

The increased flexibility towards money supply targets in the UK was closely linked to evidence of greater instability of the demand for money. This involved much greater variation in recent years in the relationship between the money stock and nominal income (the velocity of circulation) and the apparent need to raise nominal interest rates ever higher to achieve money supply control. Many of these problems may be traced to the process of financial innovation[15] and ultimately to the whole strategy of money supply targeting itself.

In turn, certain other arguments were advanced in favour of treating the exchange rate as a target variable.[16] First, an exchange rate target may be both more understandable and more credible than a money supply target. Second, it is widely accepted that short-term fluctuations in money supply growth away from the target (even up to six months) have little, if any, lasting effect on an economy. Therefore, any short-term intervention in foreign exchange markets, if reversed in time, will not compromise any long-term monetary objectives, while helping to stabilize exchange rates.

Third, given the huge external payments disequilibria, despite floating exchange rates since 1973, there is increasing doubt over the ability of floating exchange rates to achieve adjustment of a country's external payments position and therefore to affect real economic variables. Allied to the widespread recent experience of overshooting, the attractions of greater exchange rate stability are considerable.

Fourth, it is now widely agreed that the relative amount of autonomy over monetary policy given up in a fixed exchange rate arrangement is limited. Even under completely floating exchange rates, total insulation from real economic disturbances is unlikely to be achieved, particularly for a small, open economy in the EMS. On the other side of the argument, some monetary autonomy is likely to be retained under fixed rates due to the ability of monetary authorities to undertake short-term sterilization operations and the fact that capital is unlikely to be infinitely mobile internationally. The thrust of this argument is that this discussion is not, therefore, a comparison of two extremes.[17] The adoption of an exchange rate target will only involve moving along a spectrum of policy choices.

This point is given further weight by the institutional details of the EMS. Despite the limitation on cross-rate variations of ± 2¼ per cent around central rates and the constraints of the divergence indicator, the system has twice the flexibility of the defunct snake, while Italy makes use of even wider bands. Further, the operation of the EMS has been very flexible given the number of realignments and the tendency for the system to operate as a sophisticated form of 'crawling peg'. Combining these arguments it is notable that West Germany, in particular, has successfully reconciled monetary targets with EMS membership as it has both been pursued with a degree of flexibility.

The current position

Despite the perceptible shift in the discussion of money supply targets since the beginning of 1982, official pronouncements are little different in substance from those made at that time and UK entry into the EMS is clearly not imminent. In the Mais Lecture in June, the Chancellor reiterated that while 'the role of other measures of money was made explicit both in 1982 and again in this year's Budget, when targets were set for both narrow and broad monetary aggregate . . . we continue to pay attention to other relevant indicators of financial conditions, such as the exchange rate'.[18] One of the Chancellor's worries is that exchange rate movements may not be a good indicator of monetary conditions if policy adjustment and shocks come from abroad. For example, sterling would be likely to increase in value if the continued pursuit of tight monetary policy in the UK were accompanied by excessive monetary growth or other expansionary measures in major foreign countries. In addition, the official view now held is that the overall effective rate of sterling, which includes non-EMS currencies, is a better external guide than sterling's rate against the ECU.

In at least one other sense, however, the conditions for UK entry into the EMS are better than at any time in the system's lifetime. Figures 12.1 and 12.2 show rates of inflation and monetary growth in EMS member countries and the UK since 1979. These show that after some divergence of economic performance immediately after the system was established, there has been an impressive degree of convergence within the EMS since the end of 1981. Moreover, the performance of the UK in these two respects is, after the excesses of 1980, now well in line with the least inflationary member countries.

There are, however, two warning signals even within this impressive convergence of performance. First, as argued earlier, convergence has only in part been the result of the EMS *per se* and generally reflects a common reaction by European governments to the second oil shock and its aftermath. It is possible, therefore, that less unanimity of policy purpose in the future will encourage new economic divergence despite the presence of the EMS. Second,

Figure 12.1 Inflation rates in the EEC (per cent)

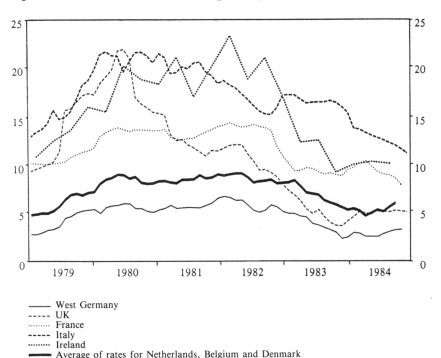

——— West Germany
- - - - - UK
········· France
- - - - - Italy
········· Ireland
▬▬▬ Average of rates for Netherlands, Belgium and Denmark

looking at the EMS members as a whole, despite increased convergence, significant differences of performance remain. This is particularly relevant in the case of the pivotal German–French relationship[19] where, although the inflation differential has declined from 8.8 per cent in April 1982, it still stood as high as 4.6 per cent two years later. The performance of the UK as an average member of the low-inflation group in the EMS is, however, both encouraging and wholly compatible with sterling's entry into the ERM.

Several remaining doubts, in addition to the issues discussed above, still persist in the minds of some UK observers; these may be discussed in turn. First, the tendency for sterling to follow the fortunes of the dollar, particularly since the mid-1970s, such that its value has tended to rise and fall in tandem with the US currency, had led to fears that this relationship could pose a serious problem for the UK authorities if sterling was to join the EMS.[20] A solution to such a problem may exist in the form of a common European strategy towards the dollar and US interest rate policy. There is growing sympathy for such an approach within Europe, though positive steps in that direction have been slow to emerge.

Figure 12.2 Monetary growth rates in the EEC (per cent)

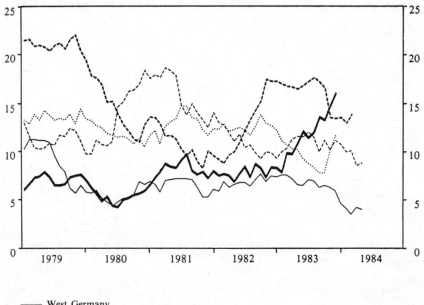

——— West Germany
----- UK
········ France
----- Italy
▬▬ Average of rates for Netherlands, Belgium and Denmark

Second, it is argued that Britain's North Sea oil and petro-currency status make sterling fundamentally unstable. Sterling is the only leading petro-currency of the Community; consequently, movements in the price of oil tend to have opposite effects on the current accounts of the UK and of the other member states, which could increase disruptive pressures within the EMS if the UK were to become a fully-fledged member. However, in answer to this point, it should be realized that any argument centred around sterling's petro-currency status would seem to rule out UK membership of the system for rather longer than most governments plan ahead, since the UK's oil resources are expected to last until well into the twenty-first century. Further, signs are emerging which indicate that the world may be facing a relatively weak oil market in the medium term, although the immediate course of events will ultimately be directly related to the development of the present Middle East and Persian Gulf crises. It could also be argued that membership of the EMS is a way of stabilizing petro-currency fluctuations, especially as North Sea oil declines. Finally, and of great importance, the UK government's willingness to take up full membership of the EMS may well depend on certain psychological and political factors. In essence, these can be reduced to two key issues, namely that the UK seems to possess an in-built aversion to being bracketed in the same monetary category as the rest of Europe, and that the UK authorities seem to have an innate reluctance to consider formal devaluations of sterling. Some commentators go so far as to argue that the EMS survives only as a 'Deutschmark bloc', such that the addition of sterling would add to any disruptive pressures already present in the system. UK membership would result in the system embracing three of the world's major currencies — the Deutschmark, the French franc, and sterling. The sheer mechanics of keeping these currencies aligned *could* prove to be much more difficult than maintaining stability between just two.[21]

Institutional development of the EMS

While the history of the EMS has seen considerable success in the operation of its ERM, the institutional development in the system has been disappointing, with the notable exception of the increasing private role of the ECU.

Full membership by sterling, and ultimately the Greek drachma, of the EMS will significantly aid the process of financial integration in the EEC. In particular, it is likely to facilitate the move to Stage 2 of the institutional development of the EMS. At the outset of the system, it was planned that within two years, the second stage, involving the translation of the EMCF into the European Monetary Fund (EMF) and the full use of the ECU as a reserve asset and means of settlement, would be achieved. In practice, the delay in completing this stage of the integration process was confirmed at the December 1980 summit meeting. There were two main difficulties. First, the worsening economic situation exposed the hollowness of such institutional moves and the West German authorities, in particular, were reluctant to consider such steps when economic performances were actually diverging. Second, disagreement surfaced over how the powers and responsibilities of the newly created EMF would be discharged and over the actual route by which greater institutional integration would be achieved. The result was an *impasse* which full UK membership might just have helped to avoid.

In a wider sense, too, the cohesion of the EC would be aided by all member countries being full partners in the EMS. The design of the Common Agricultural Policy (CAP) was always such that its optimum performance would occur in a system of fixed exchange rates. The system of Monetary Compensation Amounts (MCAs) would be much simpler to operate with no divergent currencies. It is often argued that the UK would only agree to full EMS membership if a less wasteful CAP were in operation and, closer to home, in the event of a satisfactory resolution of the wrangle over the UK's budget contributions. If correct, the long-term budget agreement reached at the Fontainebleau summit meeting in June 1984 is one further reason why UK membership of the EMS is more likely in the current situation than at any other time in its five-year history.

A further point is that if the UK does not intend to become a member of the EMS, whatever the circumstances, sterling should logically cease to be a constituent of the ECU. It is claimed that one of the reasons for the, at times, unsatisfactory performance of the divergence indicator is the anomalous position of sterling being in the ECU but outside the ERM.[22]

Future evolution of the EMS is planned to take place along the lines of some proposals presented to the Council of Ministers by the Commission in early 1982. Alongside some general comments on convergence and policy towards third currencies, these proposals considered the further enhancement of the role of the ECU.

Apart from its central role as the numeraire of the exchange rate system and the basis of the divergence indicator, the ECU was provided with a potentially significant function as a reserve asset for EC monetary authorities. This was achieved through the depositing by each member country of 20 per cent of the value of its gold and foreign currency reserves at the EMCF in return for a corresponding amount of ECUs. However, these were three-month revolving 'swaps' which would only be transformed into permanent transactions when the EMF was formed.

The actual use of ECUs in this role as a means of settlement has been limited. This was mainly because of the reluctance of debtor central banks to adopt them (arising from the transitional nature of the EMS, which could eventually require such banks to clear negative ECU positions by acquiring ECUs from other members) and because creditor central banks viewed them as having limited attractiveness (largely due to the lack of convertibility and the constraints on their usage within the EMS).

The rapidly increasing use of the ECU in private-sector transactions stands in marked contrast to this official slowness. Table 12.3 shows the rapid expansion of international bond issues denominated in ECUs since 1981. In 1983 the ECU was the third most important currency, after the dominant dollar and the Deutschmark, in the international bond markets. In particular, it is clearly the most important of the available currency baskets, with Special Drawing Rights (SDRs) having played no role at all in these markets since 1981.

Table 12.3 International bond issues by currency ($ millions)

	1981	1982	1983	First half 1984
Dollars	25 761.2	42 228.2	39 230.4	27 272.5
Deutschmarks	1 396.3	3 252.7	4 042.1	2 120.5
Sterling	535.0	845.6	2 152.5	1 801.4
ECUs	152.9	823.4	2 191.4	1 482.1
SDRs	429.6	—	—	—
Total Issues	31 294.1	50 328.6	50 123.2	34 513.3
Shares (%) in total of				
ECUs	0.5	1.6	4.4	4.3
SDRs	1.4	—	—	—

Source: OCED.

The reason for the ECU's increasing private use is that, as with other currency baskets, it provides greater exchange rate stability than the strongest and weakest currencies in the basket. It has, also, generally provided a relatively cheap form of finance in terms of both interest costs and exchange rate risk.[23]

Conclusion

Over five years after its formal establishment, the EMS is still very much in operation. The system has demonstrated an ability to overcome certain difficulties, not least through the agreement of major exchange rate realignments. However, the EMS can, in no sense, be considered complete while the UK is not a full member. As we have set out in this paper, the ability of successive UK governments to advance arguments against EMS membership has been remarkable. Notwithstanding this, the present configuration of relevant factors including the current design of macro-economic policy, the level of sterling against EMS currencies and the gradual, but inevitable, decline of the petro-status of the pound makes full membership of the EMS particularly appropriate. Now is the time for the UK government to give this commitment to a united Europe.

Notes

1. For more detailed results of this sort, including evidence that the volatility of the real (i.e. inflation adjusted) exchange rates has also been lower in the EMS than outside, see also H. Ungerer with P. Evans and P. Nyberg, 'The

European Monetary System: The Experience, 1979–82', *International Monetary Fund* Occasional Paper no 19, May 1983.

2. See T. Padoa-Schioppa, 'What the EMS has achieved', *The Banker*, August 1983; D, Cobham, 'Comments on Peeters and Emerson' in M.T. Sumner and G. Zis (eds), *European Monetary Union: Progress and Prospects* (Macmillan, 1982).

3. For further discussion see J.G. Nellis, 'Britain and the EMS — to be or not to be?', SUERF S no 45A (1984).

4. *The European Monetary System*, Cmnd 7405 (HMSO, 1978).

5. For the technical details of this system, see 'Intervention arrangements in the EMS', *Bank of England Quarterly Bulletin*, June 1979, or 'A Guide to the Arithmetic of the EMS Exchange Rate Mechanism', *Central Bank of Ireland Quarterly Bulletin*, Autumn 1979.

6. *The European Monetary System*, p. 7.

7. For a discussion of some of the theoretical issues for members of a fixed exchange rate union in their approach to a third currency and specifically on the role of the dollar in the EMS, see G.D. Baer, 'Some Reflections on a Co-ordinated Dollar Policy: The Pivotal Role of Germany in the EMS', *Aussenwirtschaft*, 1982.

8. *The European Monetary System*, p. 10.

9. Ibid, p. 9.

10. *Economic Progress Report*, April 1980, p. 4.

11. The determination of the authorities' views on monetary policy are clear from 'Monetary Policy and the Economy', *Economic Progress Report*, July 1980, pp. 1–4.

12. These arguments focused, therefore, on the possibility that sterling's petro-currency status may encourage de-industrialisation. They were similar to those faced somewhat earlier by the Netherlands (the so-called 'Dutch disease') as a result of that country's natural gas resources.

13. *Economic Progress Report*, March 1982, p. 2.

14. See, for example, M. Crawford 'No EMS for Britain', *The Banker*, April 1982.

15. For a survey of recent financial innovations in various countries and a discussion of their effects on monetary policy, see M.A. Akhtar, 'Financial Innovations and their Implications for Monetary Policy: An International Perspective', *BIS Economic Paper*, no 9, December 1983.

16. For much fuller discussions of the points in the remainder of this section, see D.T. Llewellyn, 'EC Monetary Arrangements: Britain's Strategy' in A.M. El-Agraa (ed), *Britain within the European Community* (Macmillan, 1983) and G.E.J. Dennis, 'The European Monetary System' in A.M. El-Agraa (ed), *The Economics of the EC* (Philip Allan, 1980).

17. See A.K. Swoboda, 'Exchange Rate Regimes and European-US Policy Interdependence', *International Monetary Fund Staff Papers*, March 1983, for a full discussion of this issue.

18. 'The British Experiment', the fifth Mais Lecture at the City University, 18 June 1984.

19. See P. Stephens, 'The blessing of the quiet life should not be devalued', *Financial Times*, 10 May 1984.

20. Furthermore, sterling tends to fluctuate against the dollar more than the EMS currencies and this creates additional problems for the EMS.

21. Some commentators have suggested that the crux of this problem lies in Mrs Thatcher's unwillingness to sacrifice financial sovereignty. The problem is

not insuperable, however, since sterling/Deutschmark swaps, for example, could be employed.

22. See G. Zis, 'The EMS 1979-84: An Assessment', paper presented to the International Economics Study Group, June 1984.

23. See 'Private Sector Use of the ECU', *European Economy*, November 1983; 'Composite Currency Units in Private Markets', *Financial Market Trends* (OECD), June 1983.

13 An approach to European currency unification

Charles Goodhart

Introduction

With the establishment of the Delors Committee of central bank governors and monetary experts, charged with the task of exploring the possibilities of moving towards enhanced European currency harmonization, and of examining whether a role exists for a European central bank, the whole question of the fundamental monetary structure of the European Community has become immediately relevant. In the meantime, however, well in advance of the timetable for the Delors Committee to report to the Council of Ministers in 1990, the Prime Minister, Mrs Thatcher, has made her own views quite clear. Indeed, she has expressed her undying opposition to the adoption of a single currency union, or to the institution of a European central bank, first in more gentle form — though that is perhaps not *le mot juste* — in her September 1988 Bruges speech, and then in more forthright and brusque mode in her Press Conference on the occasion of her October 1988 visit to the Italian Prime Minister, Mr de Mita. And I use the words 'undying opposition' advisedly, since she stated that she hoped that no such European central bank would be established, not only in her own lifetime, but subsequently while she was 'twanging her harp'.

In view of the dominant political position in the UK of the Prime Minister, any further consideration of moves towards currency unification and/or to a European central bank from a UK viewpoint may be considered academic. Yet I do not think that it would be entirely correct in this instance to conclude that, since the PM has spoken, the matter is effectively closed, as far as this country is concerned, for the foreseeable future.

In the first place, the political reaction elsewhere in Europe,

Charles Goodhart is Norman Sosnow Professor of Banking and Finance at the London School of Economics and was formerly Adviser on Monetary Affairs to the Governor of the Bank of England.

especially among the other non-socialist, political leaders indicates that there is a groundswell of enthusiasm towards moving on from our *Europe des patries*, a loosely knit customs union confederation of nation states, towards a more harmonized quasi-federal Europe.

It may well be that Mrs Thatcher's refusal to join with the other member states in attempting to move towards closer harmonization, and even unification in some economic aspects, would leave the UK in an isolated position. Not only would this be politically uncomfortable, but it would — for example, within the monetary field — have a number of potentially adverse economic consequences, notably, but not only, for the City of London, a subject to which I shall revert later. This means that there will be continuing pressures and incentives to reopen and reconsider the issue. The question of currency unification is too large even for Mrs Thatcher to foreclose it.

Why is this subject so important?

These monetary matters have become major issues at this juncture precisely because they are intimately connected with the establishment of a single European market, notably in financial services. It was not just by chance that the prospect of having a single market in 1992 led on to consideration of fundamental changes in the monetary framework. There are several interconnections. First, the abolition of all barriers to free capital and monetary flows across borders would greatly increase the potential extent of speculative attack on a currency seen as a subject to a potential one-way revaluation. It would no longer be possible to defer exchange rate adjustments until a time-consuming political process of discussion, compromise and agreement had been reached; nor in the meantime to hold domestic interest rates at a reasonably stable level, protected through the operation of exchange controls from the full free-market effect of speculative expectations operating in free Euro-markets. Thus the establishment of a unified, fluid European market in money and capital will make it progressively harder to run the pegged, but adjustable, exchange rate mechanism (ERM) in the same way as it has been conducted since 1979. It will probably be necessary either to resile towards a much softer, more flexible form of ERM, with wider bands and more frequent realignments, which would reduce the discipline and counter-inflationary thrust of the present system, or else to move on towards a truly fixed exchange rate system, effectively being, or approximating to, a single currency union, in which discretionary revaluations were eschewed, and in which speculation would then become stabilizing.

There are, perhaps, some who would like to see the EMS revert towards a more flexible format, perhaps including the use of crawling pegs and target zones, as are also now advocated more broadly on the global scene. A drawback with that approach is that the uncertainty, complexities and transactions costs involved in having fluctuating exchange rates greatly impede the unification of the market that many other EC measures, supported by everyone, including the UK government, are meant to enhance.

The calculations, included in the Cecchini Report, of the likely gains from having a single market for financial services, are, at best, broad brush estimates. The authors of this section of the report followed the standard trade theory approach applied to other industrial sectors. They estimated the divergence between prices of certain products/services charged by financial intermediaries in the different countries, and then assumed that greater competition would lead to a reduction in prices in the high-cost countries, towards the average charged in the better countries. Then, together with certain assumptions about the elasticities of demand and supply, it is possible to estimate the resulting consumer benefit, the loss of producer profits, and the net overall gain. There is nothing wrong with this, but, given the limited range of services analysed, the small sample of intermediaries, the uncertainties of the various assumptions involved, the results can hardly do more than provide an order of magnitude at best.

Furthermore, this approach leaves out, to my mind, the *much* larger-scale potential benefits that would arise from currency unification, and the countervailing costs if currencies in parts of a supposedly single market should continue to vary considerably and unpredictably. I am not referring so much to the extra transactions costs of actual currency exchanges, hedging operations in the forward market, and so on, but more to the utilization of time, effort and brain-power that has to be expended in order to cope with this considerable, and ultimately unnecessary, source of market disturbance.

Let me take a simile. Let us assume that the weather, instead of being uncertain, was fixed, but with the same mean temperature, sunlight and rainfall as now. Rain every Thursday and sun every Saturday. Would that not remove an enormous amount of unnecessary complexity and expense of time and effort from life? Or, *per contra*, think what it would be like if the timing of sunrise and dusk, instead of being fixed, was stochastic and subject to some dimly understood influences. Now you may say that such similes are far-fetched and extreme, since the weather and daylight affect everyone all the time, while exchange rate uncertainty is only faced on occasions. Maybe; but from the point of view of most businesses, most industries, some stochastic fluctuation around a given mean for daylight and weather has relatively little impact, while the fluctuations in exchange rates in an economy where almost a third of production goes in exports, or comes in as imports, is a continuing major concern.

Indeed, I would reckon that a significant proportion of the general economies of scale and scope expected to arise from the unification of the European market, and the enhancement of competition and efficiency within that market, especially within the financial services section, would depend on the concurrent achievement of effective currency unification, and would by the same token be lost, or dissipated, if the exchange rates were to prove as, or even more, volatile between European trading partners compared with the past.

The disadvantages of currency unification

I would, therefore, contend that there is a prima-facie case that the welfare benefits of currency unification are potentially large, perhaps very large. If that case is even partially accepted, what are the arguments, whereby the opponents of such unification, naming no names, seem to deny the people such welfare benefits?

There *are* a number of such arguments. Remember that the UK Chancellor of the Exchequer, on several recent occasions, not least at the Mansion House, stated that variations in nominal interest rates were his, and *the*, main instrument of economic control. If interest rates in the UK have to be set to maintain a fixed exchange rate, even more so if with complete currency unification there is a single European interest rate, over which we have at most only partial influence, have we not then lost control over our own economic destiny, lost our ability to direct and protect our own national interest?

But how much *real* control do the authorities have anyhow, and how well can they generally use it? It has been generally accepted, since a famous article by Sargent and Wallace in 1975,[1] that if markets adjust and clear perfectly, and economic agents are rational, then monetary policy cannot systematically affect real output and real economic allocative decisions, but can only affect the rate of inflation and nominal magnitudes. Now that line of analysis should put the present UK government in difficulties in arguing against currency unification, since it tends normally to be an ideological believer in the perfection of free markets and the rationality of economic agents.

If, then, the free market system does work so efficiently, all you lose from currency unification is the choice of the rate of inflation,

1. *Journal of Political Economy*, Volume 83, April 1975.

nothing more. There are some economists who believe that governments hang on to their ability to control national monetary policies, because the ability to run the note printing presses faster, and to depreciate existing nominal debt via inflation, effectively provides an additional source of revenue, the inflation tax. Indeed, some countries in southern Europe will face a problem in replacing revenue obtained form seignorage (and from the comparatively high tax burdens placed on their national financial intermediaries by large required reserve ratios), within a unified low-inflation fixed exchange rate system. But that is not the case in the UK, where the extent of government revenue from seignorage is minute. Given the present UK government's strong commitment to controlling inflation and to sound finance, it can hardly object to currency unification on the grounds that it removes its option to obtain a fiscal benefit from some temporary, unanticipated inflation. Nor is the contrary position, that we in the UK could maintain a significantly lower rate of monetary expansion and lower inflation independently than would a federal European central bank, a plausible one given our past history and the likely insistence of the West Germans that any such bank not only have the independence, but also be imbued with much of the spirit, and possibly the personnel, of the Deutsche Bundesbank.

Moreover, the ability of UK governments to use monetary policy, interest rate variations, as an independent autonomous policy instrument is relatively recent. Until 1914 at least, not only was the Bank of England largely, though not entirely, independent of Whitehall, but also, more important, interest rates were varied primarily to maintain unquestioned convertibility of sterling into gold at the established parity. Does not — should not — the gold standard, which provided a considerable degree of global currency unification, count as one of the pillars of the Victorian system of self-discipline and rectitude, to which the Mrs Thatcher so often refers admiringly? Even thereafter, in those calmer and generally prosperous decades of the 1950s and 1960s during which the Bretton Woods system held sway, interest rates were generally adjusted in order to maintain external balance, not as a general domestic instrument of autonomous control.

One conclusion might then be that the loss of national autonomy, and the ability to control one's own destiny, occasioned by adopting first permanently fixed exchange rates, and then currency unification, is much more symbolic than real. There is, I believe, some considerable truth in this; *but* one should not then make the mistake of going on to treat 'symbolic' as being synonymous with lack of importance or as unlikely to stir deep passions. After all, the national flag is but a symbol. Yet replacing it by some more fetching arrangement of colours would generate considerable emotion. Indeed, I am inclined to the view that it would be, and indeed is, so easy to mount a political attack on any steps which might endanger the major symbols of nationalism, that considerable attention will have to be given to the preservation of key national symbols in this field, for example the individual national currencies and even probably the national central banks, during the period of effective transition to greater European unification.

But monetary policy is only unable to affect real variables systematically when markets work perfectly. The experience of continuing massive unemployment in the 1980s, itself partly occasioned by a massive overvaluation of sterling early in the decade, indicates that labour markets, and quite possibly other markets as well, do not demonstrate the degree of perfection that would make money act only as a nominal veil, without real effect. If wage rates, say, in Birmingham remain too high relative to those in Essen or in Lyons to maintain competitiveness, then one faces the choice of accepting depression and unemployment in Birmingham, or depreciating sterling, so as artificially to restore a competitiveness that labour markets seem incapable of achieving by themselves. Note, however, that exactly the same problem of labour-market stickiness causing competitive failure and depressed regions as between countries within Europe also has the same effect within each country between, say, London, Coventry and Newcastle; and yet we do not hear of calls for a West Midlands currency and a Birmingham central bank. The fact that we did once hear calls for a Scottish central bank and separate currency, and the choice of the Irish to revoke their fixed currency link with sterling in order to join the ERM, once again points to the overriding importance of political considerations, and of national symbolism, rather than of economic logic in this area.

There are, however, some further economic reasons why it is easier to maintain currency unification within a nation state (indeed it is jolly hard to think of a nation state which does not maintain such unification) than between them. First, the common institutions within such a state should make internal labour migration easier than cross-border migration, thereby allowing regional labour market disparities to be more easily resolved. Second, much, though not all, of the tax receipts and government expenditure decisions are centralized in the nation state. Moreover, decision-makers and opinion formers tend to weight the welfare of all inhabitants within the nation state on a broadly equal basis, an approach that demonstrably shifts when we compare the welfare of foreigners to ourselves. Accordingly, the government expenditure/tax regime will quasi-automatically provide large-scale fiscal transfers within each country to a (temporarily) depressed region. Newcastle may lose on the competitiveness swings, because it cannot devalue *vis-à-vis* London, but it gains handsomely on the fiscal roundabouts.

These same fiscal conditions — for example, tax centralization — do not, as yet, hold within the EC, so there is far less transnational, and certainly less quasi-automatic, fiscal offset in response to comparative regional labour market failures. It is arguable that the success of a system of fixed exchange rates, leading to currency unification, would depend on the rapid development of just such quasi-automatic fiscal transfers. It is also possible that this provides another reason for Mrs Thatcher's dislike of moves towards a single currency, because she can see clearly enough that this in turn will generate pressure for transfers of fiscal, as well as monetary, powers from the individual nation states to the federal centre.

One important, but difficult, question is just how much fiscal redistribution might be necessary to reconcile temporarily depressed, uncompetitive regions to being unable to apply exchange rate adjustments to improve their condition. It is clearly not necessary to have complete fiscal centralization. Quite a sizeable proportion of total taxation is levied at the state and local level in the USA. Again, the more that tax revenues obtained at the federal centre are specifically earmarked for such redistributive purposes, the less is the need for more general centralization; on the other hand, it may well be harder to define the criteria for, and obtain general political agreement on, such specifically redistributional transfers, than when such net fiscal transfers take place quasi-automatically within a more generally centralized fiscal system. There is, indeed a dilemma here. Fiscal redistribution specifically targeted at benefiting depressed regions may be hard to agree politically, and, like the UK's own regional policy, go too often towards propping up senile industries. On the other hand, the alleviation of regional depression through the quasi-automatic operation on centralized federal fiscal stabilizers would require far more fiscal centralization than is likely to prove acceptable. A formula that would achieve this objective via alterations in a country's net contribution to the Community budget is discussed by King.[1]

Anyhow, this view that the pressures arising from labour-market imperfections within a fixed exchange rate system need to be ameliorated by fiscal transfers — or else unbearable economic and political pressures may build up — runs up against a counter-example, in the case of the gold standard once again. This was certainly a quasi-permanent fixed exchange rate system, and it worked well, but there were no cross-country fiscal transfers. Were labour-market imperfections less before 1914 than since, or is the argument about needing to soften economic pressures on depressed regions by offsetting fiscal transfers overstated?

A gold standard approach

I do not know the answer to that. But what these comparative, historical analogies may suggest, also taking into account the widespread concern lest national symbols become submerged in an, as yet, unformed and thinly supported federalism, is that the way forward to a fixed exchange rate system and ultimately to currency unification may be rather by analogy with a return to the gold standard than, as yet, to a move to a United States of Europe. Indeed, a return to a monetary discipline such as the gold standard has been advocated by many on the radical right whom Mrs Thatcher tends to admire. President Reagan even set up a Gold Standard Commission some years ago; this proved ineffectual, not because any of its members approved of the discretionary basis of current US monetary policy, but because they could not agree among themselves on which alternative regime would be preferable.

The essence of the gold standard, of course, was that central banks bought, or sold, gold within quite narrow limits in order to maintain the convertibility of their currencies into gold (though transport and insurance costs of shipping gold widened the effective gold points). We cannot, and should not, I believe, go back to making gold itself the centrepiece of our current monetary system, but there is no reason why we should not require each central bank to operate in the foreign exchange market to maintain bilateral, or multilateral, exchange rates against all the other members of the EMS within very narrow margins indeed, effectively to ensure that they are rigidly fixed against each other.

What one needs for this would be a simple set of operational adjustments. First, each central bank would lend massive sums denominated in its own currency to the other central banks, and equivalently borrow huge sums in foreign currency, a massive multilateral expansion of reserves. The advantage of this is that it would both provide the *masse de manoeuvre* for deterring any remaining speculative attack, and also represent a further deterrent to unilateral devaluation, owing to the resulting loss on the borrowed foreign currency. Second, and more important, as a general principle each central bank would undertake its open market operations only and entirely in the foreign exchange market, and only and entirely to stabilize its exchange rate. Each central bank would refrain entirely, and totally, from monetizing, or operating in the markets for, the debt instruments of its own central government. Mrs Thatcher ought to like that. One reason why she approved of index-linked bonds was that they might deter some future more inflationary government. A constitutional shift of practice whereby no European central bank would contemplate ever monetizing the debt of its own government would be a far stronger safeguard.

On the other hand, central banks would still need the ability to lend to private sector financial intermediaries directly as part of their operations as lenders of last resort. I see no reason why they should not do so, so long as any consequential effects on the exchange rate are vigorously sterilized.

This would leave national central banks and national currencies at centre stage. The main difference would be that the focus of such central bank operations would be the foreign-exchange market, not domestic money markets, and the aim would be to peg exchange rates, rather than national interest rates. Disturbances to the demand for money in the individual countries, say as a result of differing day-of-the-week or seasonal pressures, would be ironed out by commercial bank arbitrage. Indeed, one of the advantages of a wider area of effective currency unification is that particular disturbances in one part, such as strikes, mergers, new issues, become ironed out in the wider community. Thus if Thursdays saw a rise in the demand for money in the UK, any rise in UK interest rates would set in motion a flow of money, out of, say, Deutschmarks into sterling. Both the Bank of England and the Bundesbank would sell sterling for Deutschmarks, thereby stabilizing exchange rates and equalizing interest rates in both countries.

This exercise would be, I assume, symmetrical in that central bank operations would, through their foreign-exchange operations, be exchanging one national money for another at fixed exchange rates, thereby leaving the overall European stock of outstanding base money unchanged. While some might advocate a constant nominal stock of base money, it would seem to impart an excessively deflationist bias to economies with real growth potential. Thus, in addition to their primary focus of foreign-exchange operations, to stabilize exchange rates by swapping one currency for another, central banks would have to have a co-ordinated way of expanding the monetary base. So long as we are maintaining our national symbols, as I believe we should, this would have to be done by simultaneous, co-ordinated open-market purchases, preferably of private, rather than public, sector paper, leading to exactly equivalent proportional percentage increases in the monetary base in each centre. But the decision on how much this increase should be, would have to be a common, binding, central, European decision. Those who took that decision would in effect be European central bankers, and the format, and support staff, if any, would represent a prototype European central bank.

This leaves, of course, the question on what principles to vary the common rate of expansion of the European monetary base, whether by some simple rule, by discretion in the light of movements in nominal incomes, inflation and interest rates, or whatever. The existence of a European dimension does not affect the main outlines of the general argumentation on rules versus discretion.

Again, all this may seem rather far-fetched, but I do not think that it is. Any move to a truly fixed exchange rate system implies that continuing national central banks must concentrate exclusively on this as their primary task, and that they abstain either from pegging local national interest rates at a level inconsistent with exchange rate stabilization, or from providing support to the paper of their own governments. Moreover the overall rate of monetary expansion would have to be determined in one European forum and accepted by all.

Once this was done, subsequent moves towards full currency unification, for example by making a common European monetary numeraire, with a fixed exchange rate with respect to each local currency, legal tender in each country would be simple to envisage.

The transition

The technical changes to the operational procedures of central banks that would be necessary to run a truly fixed exchange rate system are relatively simple. But they would represent a major change in priorities, giving exchange rate stabilization absolute precedence above domestic considerations, whether the latter relate to nominal interest rates or to local labour-market conditions, in the conduct of monetary operations.

In my view such a change of priorities has to be a conscious, and major, act of political will. It must be a decisive quantum step, for it will, and must, determine how central banks respond to changing market conditions. So long as each central bank may react in recurring 'dilemma' situations (where there is some conflict between the objectives of maintaining internal as contrasted with external stability) by operating so as to maintain internal macro-economic stability, then this will simply not be consistent with fixed exchange rates. This in turn would be appreciated in free markets, and speculative attacks would be made on the currency.

I do not believe that the frequency, or likely occurrence, of such dilemma situations is likely to be eliminated, or even greatly lessened, by an asymptotic process of converging gradually towards unification, nor that a move towards real fixity of exchange rates can be undertaken as a consequence of market forces operating from below. With each country maintaining its independent government, with its separate national programmes of expenditure and taxes, and so long as labour markets in each country have some separate identity — which would seem to cover the indefinite future — dilemma conditions in which the pursuit of national internal stability would seem to conflict with the objective of external stability are *bound* to recur. The only way to achieve truly fixed exchange rates is to take the political decision from above to order each central bank to operate so as always to give absolute priority to external stability.

It is at this point that I fear that the great and good will burke the issue. There is all too likely to be talk about a process of gradual policy convergence, and harmonization of objectives, allowing a steady move towards increasing exchange rate stability, ultimately leading almost imperceptibly to complete fixity. One can easily envisage the Delors Committee of central bankers asserting that while currency unification is the long-run objective, the path to it must be through some gradual process of convergence. But what exactly is meant by policy convergence in this respect? Suppose that unit labour costs rise faster in the UK than in West Germany, then convergence to a common inflation rate, and to equal competitiveness, imply that domestic interest rates should be higher in the UK than in West Germany, but such interest differentials, as we saw in the spring of 1989, might well, indeed often will, be inconsistent with external exchange rate stability. Again, given differing national propensities to save and invest, and uncertain and unpredictable shifts in such propensities, and differing needs for expenditures — occasioned, for example, by differing demographic profiles — just how should one seek to measure policy convergence between EC members in the field of fiscal policy? Can anyone say whether the fiscal policies of France, West Germany and the UK are currently convergent? How could the conduct of national fiscal policies either be assessed for, or encouraged to be, more convergent?

There *may* be a problem in that the existence of a common pool of European savings tempts those governments which are more impatient for quick results to try to scoop the pool, but I wonder just how serious that problem would be. With the option of monetizing national public sector debt removed, the markets' ranking of the relative riskiness of each country's debt should prove a more effective market constraint on excessive government borrowing than currently exists.

This appeal to some gradual convergence of economic policies as the route towards eventual currency unification runs as a constant theme, for example, through Anthony Loehnis's speech to the European Parliament in Strasbourg in June this year on 'European currency and European central bank — a British view'. When this was reprinted in the Bank's Quarterly Bulletin this August, the summary records that Loehnis

argues that monetary union will be the culmination of a gradual progression towards greater convergence in economic policy and performance, in which completion of the internal market will be an important step, and that premature moves towards monetary union could jeopardize the progress being made towards the internal market.

It remains a seductive line for central bankers, in the Delors Committee, for example, to record that, whereas currency unification is a desirable ultimate objective, the path to it must lie in a gradual move to greater policy convergence, which is, of course, the responsibility of governments rather than of central bankers.

Having registered my disagreement with one major theme of Anthony Loehnis's paper, I am glad to be able to record my complete agreement with another facet of his analysis: 'As far as union is concerned it seems to me that development of the ECU as a currency is a distraction.' That phrase may, indeed, represent a slight embarrassment to its author now that the UK has given so much play to this distraction in the hopes of refurbishing its European credentials by establishing an ECU Treasury Bill market. Useful and valuable though the development of a market in a financial instrument with the particular characteristics of the ECU will be, not least in allowing central banks to adjust their reserve positions without having to get involved in potentially difficult bilateral negotiations with colleagues in central banks elsewhere, the fundamental requirement for a move towards currency unification, via a fixed exchange rate system, is for changes in central banks' operating priorities and procedures, not for the development of novel, alternative financial instruments.

I believe that this line of argument, whereby currency unification is the ultimate achievement of a gradual process of policy convergence, is fundamentally misleading, a snare and a delusion. There are, to be sure, a lot of steps that could be taken, for example to improve the working of labour markets, to ease cross-border labour migration and to facilitate fiscal transfers to depressed regions — say, by making unemployment benefits payable out of the European budget — that would greatly help to smooth the transition to a fixed exchange rate system. But, so long as fiscal decisions are taken, and wage bargains are struck, primarily at the national level

— which will remain so for a very long time — the concept of policy convergence leading painlessly and steadily to truly fixed exchange rates, let alone to full unification of currencies, is in my view chimerical. But that does not debar us from moving to a fixed rate system. What is needed for that is a major political act of will, to bring about a major change of priorities for the conduct of national monetary policies.

What will happen?

Are we likely to experience such a quantum jump, such a major political act of will, in the next few years. I doubt whether Mrs Thatcher will be prepared to do so; she has already declared her implacable opposition, and she does not easily bend once her mind is made up on major issues.

There used to be a time in the Victorian era, when young ladies at a delicate stage in their life cycle were admonished to close their eyes, lie still and think of the Empire. One might suggest to the Prime Minister that, when faced with talk of currency unification, she closes her eyes and thinks of the gold standard. Seen in those terms, the progress towards a fixed exchange rate system, ultimately to currency unification, could be seen as providing an opportunity to establish a monetary regime on an impeccable counter-inflationary, sound finance basis. But whether or not she can see the potential advantages of removing the opportunity for monetary management, or mismanagement, in future from some succeeding government, I fear that her attention will instead be focused on the immediate loss of autonomy and power in her own hands.

I doubt whether the prospects of investing the Prime Minister with slightly less power than she presently wields would wring the withers of the general public. But one public's opposition to any such structural changes will be more easily provoked by an apparent trespass on national symbols, the national currency, the national central bank. This is why, I believe, the route to eventual currency unification must lie in the establishment of a truly fixed exchange rate system, in which national currencies and central banks remain in place, but are firmly linked together by requiring the central banks to conduct monetary policy with somewhat altered operational techniques and with decisively altered priorities.

Whether or not others agree with my own arguments and proposals — and I expect that many may not — my own reading of the tealeaves is that the incentive provided by the advent of the single European market to move on towards greater exchange rate fixity, towards perhaps some form of currency unification, will prove to be powerful enough for a central core of the members of the EMS to move in that direction. If that should be successfully undertaken, leaving the UK and probably some other southern European countries outside the new monetary system, would that matter greatly, either for UK industry or for the City of London?

I do not know — and I do not think that anyone else knows — the answer to that. As earlier stated, I believe that fluctuating exchange rates do represent a serious barrier to the establishment of a truly unified market, so that the UK would then benefit far less than the others from the wider, more competitive market which is intended to be achieved by 1992, under such circumstances. As regards financial services, the influence of sterling would obviously decline considerably *vis-à-vis* the fixed, possibly unified, currency system on the Continent. Does that matter for the City? The historical example of the growth of the Euro-markets in London is often brought up to suggest that it would not do so, because the City is adept at offshore intermediation. Perhaps so, but we then had the advantage of many fewer unnecessary burdens — for example, in the form of no required reserve ratios and a more relaxed regulatory system — than the Americans imposed upon themselves. If the Americans had not so handicapped themselves, would it not have been more immediately sensible to intermediate dollars in New York than in London? And if regulation and controls are harmonized throughout Europe, and just as tight, or tighter, in London compared with Paris or Frankfurt, will it not seem more sensible to intermediate the common European currency in Frankfurt, Brussels, or Paris, rather than in London?

I doubt whether we can stand aside from the evolution of a European common monetary regime without some damage both to our political and economic position.

Notes

1. Mervyn King, 'Reforming the EEC Budget', LSE Financial Markets Group Special Paper no.5 (1988).

Index